To the Ends of the Earth

A History of the Canadian Bible Society

by
Gerald E. Benson
with
Kenneth G. McMillan

CANADIAN BIBLE SOCIETY

Toronto 1998

10 Carnforth Road, Toronto, Ontario, Canada M4A 2S4

Canadian Cataloguing in Publication Data:
Benson, Gerald E.
To the Ends of the Earth: A History of the Canadian Bible Society.
Includes index. ISBN 0-88834-094-X
1. Canadian Bible Society – History.
2. Bible – Publication and distribution – Canada – History.
I. McMillan, Kenneth G. II. Canadian Bible Society. III. Title.
BV2370.C3B45 1998 220'.06'0971 C97-931905-6

Publishing Consultant: John W. Irwin
Liaison: Michèle Owens, Connie Stamp
Editor: Elma Schemenauer
With the help of the Design and Production Department
of the Canadian Bible Society

91902 Printed and bound in Canada CBS-1998-7.5M

THE SOWER

Luke 8.11

For many decades the British and Foreign Bible Society
had as its logo the Sower with the words
"The seed is the Word."

The Rev. Howard G. Zurbrigg designed
a new and distinctive Sower for the Canadian Bible Society,
and the above logo is now the Society's official emblem.

"To the Ends of the Earth"

". . . You will be my witnesses in Jerusalem, and in all Judea and Samaria, and to the ends of the earth."

Acts 1.8

The motto on the Coat of Arms of Canada, taken from Psalm 72, reads as follows: "He shall have dominion also from sea to sea, and from the river unto the ends of the earth."

Contents

Acknowledgements

No history of the Society could adequately recognize the contributions that so many people have made to the work – both supporters and those on staff. One golden thread that runs through the Bible Society is the sacrificial service of staff members. Only a few are mentioned here as examples. When Lenore McCracken retired as bookkeeper in 1963, she had served under five General Secretaries, over a period of 43 years. Nellie Bradley joined the staff in Regina in 1942 and for the next 37 years, while District Secretaries came and went, she was the key person in Bible Society work in South Saskatchewan.

Bernice Harris of the Accounting department, who joined the Society in 1970, is the longest serving member on staff today. The Rev. Martyn C. Thomas served first in Montreal and then in Ottawa, and is now District Director in Calgary. He has provided outstanding service since 1971. Derek R. Patton ably managed the Central Stock Depot from 1978 to 1998 and Barbara Walkden, Director of Ministry Funding, served on staff from 1979 to 1998. The Rev. Dr. Russell T. Hall was trained as a business administrator. When he was a missionary in Africa, he was moderator of the Presbyterian Church of Nigeria. Upon his return to Canada in 1976, he became the Bible Society's chief financial officer – a position he held for 11 years.

Madeleine Dovlet, BA, who speaks five languages, served the American Board of Commissioners for Foreign Missions in Istanbul and then the Canadian Council of Churches in Toronto. She was a key person in the Finance department from 1966 until 1985. When she retired she began studies at the University of Toronto, receiving her Bachelor of Arts degree at the age of 80. The work of Velma Cross in BC for 35 years, of the Rev. E. J. Heuer for 30 years, and the Rev. Howard G. Zurbrigg for 15 years is described elsewhere in this book. A great number of other staff members and officers of the

Districts and of the National Society deserve recognition, which is not given in this book.

This history is not the work of only two people. The Society staff have helped with the research, and have reviewed some of the manuscript. The Rev. Dr. Floyd C. Babcock, General Secretary 1989-1997, has provided constant support. Ruth Benson participated in the research. Isobel McMillan assisted with the writing and has made innumerable corrections and additions. John W. Irwin, with his long experience in publishing, has contributed most helpful guidance. Michèle Owens and Connie Stamp have provided valuable liaison services among various people working on the project. Lastly, the book would not have been possible without the work of the editor, Elma Schemenauer, who has refined our work and made it ready for publication. Sincere appreciation is expressed to all who have provided assistance.

Gerald E. Benson
Kenneth G. McMillan
September 1998

Foreword

The road to tomorrow leads through yesterday.
John A. Mackay

When Samuel Horwood of Brampton, Ontario died in 1990, his will provided $50,000 to publish an up-to-date history of the Canadian Bible Society. Mr. Horwood was a member of the Salvation Army all his life, and an ardent supporter of the Canadian Bible Society. He specified that his nephew, the Rev. Dr. Gerald E. Benson, who already had books to his credit, should be involved in writing the history.

Since 1990, Dr. Benson and his wife Ruth have travelled extensively, examining records and visiting Bible Society offices and archives. They have interviewed former and present Bible Society staff, and also officers of many Bible Society Branches and Districts, as well as officers of the National Society. The Bensons have not only travelled from coast to coast in Canada, but have also visited the United Kingdom, where they spent many hours in the library of the British and Foreign Bible Society and in the archives of Cambridge University.

Dr. Benson planned to write the history after his retirement, when he could give the project the time and attention it required. On May 9, 1996, however, the history of the first 50 years of the United Bible Societies, written by the Rev. Edwin H. Robertson, became available. The Canadian Bible Society asked that its own up-to-date history be completed as soon as possible. In order to have the history ready at the earliest possible date, the Canadian Bible Society's General Board asked the Rev. Dr. Kenneth G. McMillan to write the history, using material gathered by Dr. Benson and his wife, as well as additional information as appropriate.

The writing of the history took longer than expected since, owing to his other responsibilities, Dr. McMillan could attend to this project only in his spare time. He has been able to draw on the firsthand knowledge he gained from his 26 years as Canadian Bible Society General Secretary, and to provide important insights into the Society's history.

We at the Canadian Bible Society hope that this history will provide some recognition of the life and work of the men and women who have served on its staff, and to all who have given their time, talent and resources to make it a major Canadian Christian enterprise. This history will also be an inspiration to all who today carry on the work of translating, publishing and distributing the Word of God. The context in which the Bible Society works today is vastly different from what it was in the past, but the enduring Word has not changed, and the need for it is now greater than ever.

May God continue to bless and prosper the spread of His Word.

The Reverend Father Greg Bailey
National Director
August 1998

About the Authors

The Rev. Dr. Gerald E. Benson, DD

Dr. Gerald E. Benson was born in St. John's, Newfoundland, September 4, 1936. He received his early education at Dawson Elementary, Booth Memorial High and the Salvation Army College in St. John's. He did his theological studies at Ontario Bible College and at Trinity College in the United States, where he was awarded a Doctor of Divinity degree.

An ordained minister of the Pentecostal Assemblies of Newfoundland, he was appointed Canadian Bible Society District Secretary in 1979. He retired February 28, 1997 as Chief Executive Officer of the District.

A member of the Association of Canadian Television and Radio Artists (ACTRA), Dr. Benson is a well-known musician and writer. An avid student of hymnology, he has researched the history and authorship of hundreds of hymns for the Canadian Broadcasting Corporation (CBC) and other organizations. His monthly column "Hymns We Sing" appeared in *Good Tidings* magazine for more than 15 years. In 1987 he published a collection of favourite hymns of Newfoundland and Labrador, complete with their histories and pictures of the hymn-writers. It became an immediate bestseller, and raised more than $30,000 for Bibles in Russia.

A keen student of church history, Dr. Benson has spent time both in England and Rome studying the development of the English Bible. His recent publication *Churches of Newfoundland and Labrador* has sold 5,000 copies, with proceeds to Amity Press, Nanjing, China.

Dr. Benson has travelled around the world on behalf of the Church and the United Bible Societies. He engaged in a fact-finding mission within the People's Republic of China, returning to London, England to write reports. He has also undertaken similar missions within the former Soviet Union and the Amazon region of South America.

A missionary statesman and frequent speaker, he has addressed numerous missionary conventions and retreats, not only in North America but also in Great Britain, Scandinavia, Korea, Taiwan, Hong Kong, Malaysia, Indonesia, Singapore and India. In his travels he has met personally with many key church leaders including Pope John Paul II and two Archbishops of Canterbury.

Dr. Benson is married to the former Ruth Bishop of St. John's. They have one daughter, Gillian, and two sons, Scott and Todd, who are all active in their local church. The Bensons also have two grandchildren, Rachel and Zachary.

The Rev. Dr. Kenneth G. McMillan, CM, BA, MDiv, DD

Dr. McMillan was born at Mount Forest, Ontario and attended schools in Palmerston and Listowel. A minister of the Presbyterian Church in Canada, he is a graduate of the University of Toronto and of Knox College (Presbyterian), University of Toronto. In recognition of his service to all Canadian churches, three honorary Doctor of Divinity degrees have been conferred upon him: one by Knox College; another by Wycliffe College (Anglican), University of Toronto; and a third by Acadia University (Baptist), Wolfville, Nova Scotia.

In 1957, after having served pastorates in Bruce County, Niagara Falls and Guelph, Ontario, Dr. McMillan was appointed General Secretary of the Canadian Bible Society – an office he was to hold for over 26 years. For four years he chaired the General Committee of the United Bible Societies. He has travelled extensively on all continents, and has served on a multitude of inter-church committees and advisory councils.

In 1974, when the Bible Society in Australia inaugurated the Olivier Béguin Lectures, Dr. McMillan was selected to be the first lecturer. This annual lectureship on "The Authority and Relevance of the Bible in the Modern World" has since 1974 been given by such distinguished people as Malcolm Muggeridge; Francis B. Sayre, when he was Dean of the Washington Cathedral; Dr. John R. Stott; Dr. Donald Coggan, former Archbishop of Canterbury; and Dr. Oswald C. J. Hoffmann.

In June 1979, Dr. McMillan was elected moderator of the Presbyterian Church in Canada. Previously he had served as moderator of the Presbyterian Synod of Toronto and Kingston.

In October 1983, upon leaving the Canadian Bible Society, Dr. McMillan joined the staff of the Christian humanitarian organization World Vision, Canada, which undertakes major relief and development projects in some 80 countries around the globe. He served first as director of church relations, and is now minister-at-large for World Vision.

Dr. McMillan is recognized as one of Canada's outstanding church leaders and as a missionary statesman. His influence is widely felt in the religious life of the nation and in the social concerns of all the churches. He is in demand as a conference speaker in Canada and internationally. In 1984 the Governor General made him a Member of the Order of Canada in recognition of his outstanding services and achievements. In 1992 he was awarded the Commemorative Medal for the 125th anniversary of Canadian Confederation.

His most recent book, *Against the Tide,* was published by Image Publishing in 1984. It went into a second printing in 1985. He is a frequent contributor to various periodicals.

Dr. McMillan is married to the former Isobel McCannel of Burgoyne, Ontario and has two daughters, Catherine and Barbara. Catherine is Mrs. Andrew D. McGee of Toronto and Barbara is Mrs. Peter C. Donaldson of Barrie, Ontario. The McMillans also have two granddaughters and two grandsons.

Preface

The judgement of history depends on who writes it.
Richard Nixon

These things have I spoken unto you, being yet present with you. But the Comforter, which is the Holy Ghost, whom the Father will send in my name, he shall teach you all things, and bring all things to your remembrance, whatsoever I have said unto you.
John 14.25, 26

The year 1953 saw the publication of the book *The Bible in Canada*, a history of the Bible Society in Canada by E. C. Woodley, MA. Mr. Woodley, a historian and seasoned author, produced a valuable and interesting account of how the Bible Society spread from England all across Canada. *The Bible in Canada* gives facts and figures about the Bible Society, and tells of the role distinguished Canadians played in the work.

Since 1953, however, the world has changed. Canada has changed. The place of the churches in Canadian society has changed, and the Bible Society is working in an entirely new context. It is no exaggeration to say that the world of 1953 has passed away, and we are living in a brand new era of history. The Christian worldview that once prevailed in Canada has been replaced by a secular worldview. Until recently the Church played a dominant role in the development of Canadian society. In few countries of the western world did religion exert as great an influence as in Canada.

From the 16th century, when Jacques Cartier set up a great wooden cross on the Gaspé Peninsula, until World War II, the quality of Canadian life was profoundly affected by the Bible. The Bible, to a large extent, constituted the basis for the values and attitudes of

Canadians. Persistent interaction between Church and State fostered the creation of a largely non-violent Canada. Canada achieved independence from Britain gradually, through constitutional negotiations, not through violent rebellion as in the United States.

Many forces have been at work to change the context in which the Bible Society now functions. One of these has been the advent of television and the whole field of electronic communication. Some people declare that the Gutenberg Era – the era of books and literature – has ended. TV and the Internet have become the new authorities which, for many, are primary sources of information. Too often these sources present non-Biblical values.

When television first became widely accessible, Reinhold Niebuhr said it would "complete the vulgarization of American life." That prophecy appears to be in the process of fulfilment. The Bible teaches that to be carnally minded is death. Much of TV and computerized entertainment, and also many of the ads, communicate the concept that to be carnally minded is life. Too often the electronic media promote the belief that acquiring possessions is the ideal. The Bible, on the other hand, warns that life does not consist in the abundance of possessions. The Bible proclaims that service to God and others is the way to happiness. This is a view not widely proclaimed today.

The most profound effect of TV and other modern electronic media is the manner in which the human brain receives their messages. The printed page, and also radio, communicate with the side of the brain that is rational and evaluates information. Television, video games and other electronic messages, on the other hand, are often received by the side of the brain that deals with emotions, feelings, intuition and images. Those who have forsaken the printed page for electronic communication often find it difficult to distinguish between reality and illusion, between fact and fiction.

When the 25th anniversary of the coronation of Queen Elizabeth II was televised at length, some viewers asked, "Who played the part of the Queen?" They did not know it was real. The "new people" created by the electronic age are a challenge to the Bible Society, since it communicates largely through the printed page and deals with historical facts, not myths.

As recently as when Woodley's *The Bible in Canada* appeared, a supreme virtue for most Canadians was truth, and the Bible was considered a solid guide for ethics and morals. Now tolerance is trumpeted as the supreme virtue. Surveys of Canadian life clearly indicate that right and wrong are considered by most (and even by those who attend church) to be a matter of personal opinion. Many do not believe that the Bible presents absolutes for human behaviour. The academics who comprise "The Jesus Seminar," and the writings of influential church leaders who do not regard the Bible as revealed truth, have further eroded the authority of the Scriptures.

As the Bible Society seeks to communicate the message of the Scriptures, it faces an enormous challenge. The barrier of language has to be overcome, and this means publishing in languages that modern people can understand. The Word of God needs to be in a form that will entice people to read and use it. It has to be easy to obtain and, in many parts of the world, this means providing the Bible below cost or free. But when everything humanly possible has been done, the reader may still not really grasp the Word of God. Only as the Holy Spirit breathes upon the Scriptures do they come alive. The Bible Society, made up of human beings, has many weaknesses; its failures are many. However, it has one asset that cannot be minimized. That is the nature of the book the Society offers. It is the inspired Word of the Almighty God.

Like no other book in history, the Bible has been criticized and scrutinized by foes as well as friends. Higher criticism, lower criticism, textual criticism, the book "Quest for the Historic Jesus" and studies coming out of "The Jesus Seminar" have questioned its reliability. Sceptics have dismissed the Bible as just another book of ancient superstitions and myths. It is amazing that, with all its detractors, the Bible continues to be the world's best-selling book, and is regarded by millions as God's Holy Word. It has proven to be an anvil that wears out many hammers. This reality is what sustains the Bible Society and enables it to continue.

It is significant that archaeological findings and the discovery of documents such as the Dead Sea Scrolls have enhanced the credibility of the Biblical text. The greater our understanding of the era in which Biblical events took place, the more authentic the records appear. Some have argued that since Jesus wrote no Gospels, since He died about 30 AD, and since the earliest Gospel (probably that of Mark) dates from about 65 AD, there can be no definite proof that the events of the intervening 35 years are accurate. It is important to note, however, that one reason nothing was written for three decades is that society at the time was accustomed to communicating by means of the spoken word. There is a growing conviction among Biblical scholars that the Gospels are eye-witness accounts.

Certainly many books, including Old Testament writings, existed in early Christian times. On the other hand, many people could not read or, if they could, had little access to books. Passing down stories by means of the spoken word was a common way of conveying information. The educational system of the times was characterized by rote learning and memorization. We today have largely lost the art of repeating even short stories from memory. In the "period of oral tradition," however, the birth, life, teaching, death and resurrection of Jesus were passed down with remarkable accuracy from one generation to another.

Such arguments may not convince sceptics of the reliability of the Scriptures. Nevertheless, millions today attest to the fact that the Bible is a veritable letter from God to them, and that they have met Christ in its pages. It is because the Bible speaks to the human heart today, and has, as J. B. Phillips said, "the ring of truth," that it continues to hold the place it does in the world. Readers have found that it gives a reasonable account of the plight of the human race, and also presents a way of deliverance from the human predicament. The Canadian Bible Society pursues its task with the conviction that the Bible is "the most valuable thing this world affords."[1]

---

[1] At the coronation service of a British Monarch, the new King or Queen is handed a copy of the Bible and these words are spoken:

> Your Majesty, I present you with this Book, the most valuable thing this world affords. Here is wisdom, this is the royal law, these are the Lively Oracles of God.

This use of the Bible at the coronation dates back to 1547, when Edward VI was crowned in Westminster Abbey. On that occasion there were presented to him swords symbolic of his sovereignty over England and Ireland. But the king, to the general astonishment, asked for another sword, "the sword of the Spirit, the Bible, which is to be preferred to all other swords." He then commanded that a Bible be brought and carried before him. So began a custom which has grown in significance with the passing years.

Part I

A Work Well Begun

CHAPTER 1

God's Word in Human Language: Pre-Christian Times to the 1800s

The Israelites seem to have been a rather unhandy people, not distinguished for architecture or sculpture or even pottery. . . . In general it was the heathen kingdoms that produced the really impressive temples and palaces, while the Israelites produced a book. This doubtless seemed at best only a consolation prize to people who thought of buildings as more substantial than words, but history has long since reversed such a perspective.

Northrop Frye, one of Canada's most renowned academics

The Christian hope is beautifully expressed by the inscription regarding one who has been called the Patron Saint of Bible Translators. Near the tomb of the Venerable Bede in the Galilee Chapel of Durham Cathedral, England is this inscription:

Christ is the morning star who, when the night of this world is past, brings to His saints the promise of the light of life and opens everlasting day.

If a bugle call isn't clear, how would you know to get ready for battle?

1 Corinthians 14.8

The Bible first appeared in Hebrew, Aramaic and Greek. Since these languages are understood by only a small percentage of the world's population, the Scriptures would speak to few people today without translation. The need for the Old Testament to be available in a language other than Hebrew was already recognized in pre-Christian times. Among some Jews, Greek was better understood than Hebrew and translators worked from about the 3rd to the 1st century BC to produce the version of the Old Testament called the Septuagint. In this translation a number of "additional" books appeared, and these became known as the Deuterocanon, or Apocrypha. The translation known as the Septuagint was produced by various scholars in Alexandria. In the time of the Early Church, it was the version of the Bible in common use.

In the 2nd century AD, when Latin was widely used, the "Old Latin" translation of the Bible was completed. Other early translations included one for Syrian churches and one in Coptic for those in Egypt. The Bible in Armenian was another early translation. Towards the end of the 4th century AD, the Latin Vulgate translation was produced by Jerome, the scholarly Church Father. It is interesting that this new translation was resisted by those who loved the "Old Latin." Nevertheless, the Latin Vulgate became the commonly accepted Bible of the West through the Middle Ages. It was in such wide use that it still exists today in some 8,000 manuscripts.

Over the centuries, translation of the Old and New Testaments continued. The first translation of the complete Bible into English was the work of the reformer John Wycliffe. The early version appeared in 1382 with a revision in 1388. The drawback of this version was that it originated with the Latin Vulgate, rather than with the original Hebrew, Aramaic and Greek. Unlike some later translations, Wycliffe's version included 12 of the books of the Apocrypha.

With Johann Gutenberg's invention of printing by moveable type, about 1450, the Bible became available to many more people and a new era began. It is significant that the first book printed by Gutenberg, about 1455 at Mainz, was the Bible in Latin. One of the most significant translations in the following years was Martin Luther's, into German. Luther began his translation while in exile in Wartburg Castle in 1521. Over the next 20 years, Scripture translation was a very important part of his ministry.

During the years 1525 through 1535, English reformer William Tyndale produced his translation of the New Testament and part of the Old Testament. This was the first time a translation into English from the original languages had appeared. Miles Coverdale, Bishop of Exeter, assisted Tyndale in translating the first five books of the Old Testament. Coverdale then went on to translate the whole Bible. His translation, which appeared in 1535, was the first printed English Bible.

The year 1611 saw the publication of the King James Version, a direct descendant of Coverdale's translation. The King James Bible was to be as important for the English language as Martin Luther's translation was for the German. Since the time of Luther, Coverdale, Tyndale, Wycliffe and other early Bible translators, there have been dozens of English and other translations. Some parts of the Scriptures are now available in over 2,000 languages.

In the early years, however, channels of distribution for the Scriptures were not very efficient. By 1567, for example, the New Testament had been published in the Welsh language, as had the liturgy of the Church of Wales. In December 1588 the first complete Welsh Bible, known as Bishop Morgan's Bible, was issued. In spite of the existence of such translations, Bibles were always scarce and expensive.

Across the Atlantic Ocean in the New World, translation of the Scriptures into the Native languages was underway relatively early. By 1715, for example, missionaries of the Society for the Propagation of the Gospel had translated the Gospel of Matthew and parts of both the Old and New Testaments into the Mohawk language. Unfortunately, the book of Matthew was never published but Scripture selections were printed by William Bradford at New York. In 1787 a Mohawk translation of the Gospel of Mark was produced by Mohawk Chief Joseph Brant, after whom the city of Brantford, Ontario is named. He was helped by the Rev. John Stuart, an Anglican missionary of the Society for the Propagation of the Gospel. A zealous Christian and lay preacher, Brant also translated the Book of Common Prayer.

Despite encouraging translation stories such as these, many people in North America had only limited access to the Scriptures – like many on the world's other continents. The limited nature of that access is illustrated by the often repeated story of Mary Jones of Wales. The story exists in several versions, but the following account was written by Doris W. Street. It was published by the Canadian Bible Society, a "daughter" of the British and Foreign Bible Society, whose founding was partly inspired by Mary Jones' experience.

In a little cottage home in Wales (in the late 1700s) lived a father, a mother and a little girl called Mary. Mary's father was a weaver and made soft cloth from the wool off the backs of the Welsh sheep. Her mother kept the house clean and then she helped Mary's father, and they both worked hard making cloth. When she was quite a tiny girl, Mary would help in the house, too, dusting and getting meals ready so that her mother had more time to make cloth. When work was over and darkness came, her father would tell stories to Mary – stories about when he was a boy or tales of great people. Sometimes he told stories from the Bible – about David, Samuel or Peter, and especially about Jesus. He always spoke them, for there was not a Bible in the house, so he could not read them to Mary. Anyway, no one there had learned to read.

"I wish I had a Bible and could read the stories for myself," said Mary when she listened to the stories of Jesus.

"I have heard you say that a hundred times, my little girl," said her father, "but the stories from the Bible are read every Sunday in chapel. If you listen carefully you will be able to learn them for yourself. The only Bibles in Wales belong to people with a lot of money like Farmer Evans. Even if you had one, we could none of us read it." But Mary wanted a Bible of her very own so much, and she made up her mind to try and get one.

Quite often she went to the home of Farmer Evans. Sometimes she saw the precious Bible and Mrs. Evans let her touch it and sometimes read it to her. "If you ever learn to read, Mary," she said, "I will let you come here and read our Bible."

When she went to bed at night, Mary asked God to help her to learn to read. Every night for two years, Mary never forgot that part of her prayer, but there were no schools near where she lived and nobody to teach her to read.

One day her father came home with some special news. "There is to be a school two miles away across the hills," he said. "If you want to go, Mary, and learn to read, you may." Of course 10-year-old Mary wanted to go and did not mind a bit walking two miles every day to school. That night she said a special "thank you" to God for giving her the chance to learn. Very soon she was able to read and then she went to see Mrs. Evans. "Please may I read your Bible? I can read stories now." "Come in," said Mrs. Evans, "I am so glad you can read the lovely stories in our Bible.

Come whenever you want to read them." So Mary was often able to read those stories for herself and sometimes she read to Mrs. Evans.

Mary loved reading from Mrs. Evans' beautiful Bible, but she wanted one in her own home so that she could read to her father and mother whenever she liked. So she began to save every penny she could. This was not easy for there were very few pennies to spare in Mary's home: her father and mother were poor. But in holiday time, when Mary had helped her mother, she began to earn some pennies by helping the neighbours with their work. Sometimes she earned a penny, another day a halfpenny, sometimes only a farthing. Her father made her a little wooden money-box and every coin that Mary could earn went into it so that some day she might buy her own Bible.

One day when Mary went to see Mrs. Evans, she told her all about it. Mrs. Evans smiled and said, "I am going to give you a cock and two hens for your very own. The eggs the hens will lay will be yours. You can sell them and the money can go to help to buy your Bible."

"Thank you, oh, thank you, Mrs. Evans," said Mary. So the money-box grew gradually heavier, but it was a very long time before there was enough money to buy a Bible – six whole years. Mary was 16 years old then, and she had learned to read when she was 10.

"Mr. Charles, the Minister at Bala over the hills, has some Bibles for sale," she was told, and she made up her mind to walk there and try and buy a Bible in her own language, Welsh. It was 25 miles (40 km) across the hills, but she was so happy that at last she had enough money. She never thought what a long way it was.

Very early one morning she set off, walking barefoot and carrying her only pair of shoes so that she could put them on when she reached the town of Bala. It was a long, long walk, but at last she reached Bala and the house of Mr. Charles.

Mr. Charles listened while Mary told him about the way she had learned to read and how she had saved her pennies to buy a Bible. Then he shook his head. "I have only three Bibles left," he said, "and they have all been promised to other people. I don't know when I shall get any more Welsh Bibles to sell."

Mary was so disappointed. She couldn't help crying a little. Mr. Charles looked at her and wondered what he could do to help. "I will find you a Bible somehow," he said. "Perhaps one of the other people will wait a little longer and share with someone else living near." Then he went out of the room and came back with a Bible in his hand. It made Mary feel very glad. "Thank you, Mr. Charles," she said, "I am so happy to have a Bible of my very own."

Over the hills again went Mary on that journey of 25 miles (40 km). She walked all day carrying the precious Bible and it was quite dark when she reached her own home. Her mother came out to meet her. "I have my Bible here," Mary called out proudly and soon she was in her warm home with the precious Book on her knees reading to her mother and father.

She read to them the stories she loved most. I wonder which they were and which she read first! How happy Mary was, and when she went to bed she remembered to tell God how glad she felt. "Thank you, God, for letting me have a Bible of my own," she whispered. "I shall read about Jesus every day and try to be like Him."

Source: Account written by Doris W. Street, published by the Canadian Bible Society.

A treasure in the archives of the British and Foreign Bible Society in England is the Bible that Mary Jones received in Bala, Wales in the year 1800.

CHAPTER 2

The Parent Society 1804 to 1904

Look unto the rock, whence ye are hewn.

Isaiah 51.11

During the 1700s, there had been a growing awareness of the need for a society to improve the accessibility of Bibles. But it was the Rev. Thomas Charles of Bala, Wales whose zeal at last launched the movement. He had been deeply moved by Mary Jones' experience (recounted in Chapter 1). Charles was greatly concerned about the shortage of Welsh Bibles at a time when more and more people were learning to read.

At a meeting of the Committee of the Religious Tract Society, held in London on December 7, 1802, he presented the need of the Welsh people for the Scriptures with such eloquence that the Rev. Thomas Hughes, minister of the Baptist Church in Battersea, cried out, "Surely a society might be formed for the purpose. But if for Wales, why not for the Kingdom? Why not for the world?"

There was an excellent response to an appeal letter with the title "The Excellency of the Holy Scriptures: An argument for their general dispersion." Over the next two years, interest in meeting the need for Scriptures further increased. At last, on March 7, 1804, at a public meeting held at the London Tavern in Bishopsgate, the British and Foreign Bible Society (BFBS) was launched. The historic inaugural meeting was attended by 300 people.

It is remarkable that, to this day, in Bible Society circles all over the world, the "Parent Society" means the British and Foreign Bible Society, England. While there had been Bible Societies prior to the founding of BFBS, it was this Society that inspired the worldwide Bible Society movement. At the beginning of the 19th century, the modern missionary movement was in its infancy, and the sun never set on the British Empire. These two factors motivated the distribution of the Bible. As pioneer missionaries engaged in evangelism and humanitarian work, the Bible in the language of the people was an essential tool. BFBS responded to that need, and was recognized early on as an "arm of the churches." The Bible had shaped the life of England, and there was a strong desire on the part of Empire-minded Britishers to have this book in the hands of their subjects in the colonies. The Bible was seen as a civilizing influence, and this motivated even people not interested in evangelism to distribute the Scriptures.

The British and Foreign Bible Society was founded by Christians from different denominations and from all walks of life. For example, the great British statesman and humanitarian William Wilberforce was among those interested. One of the treasures in the Society's library is a letter from Wilberforce expressing his regrets at being unable to attend the inaugural meeting. In the early 1800s, the word "ecumenical" was hardly known but the Bible Society sought to embrace all Christians. From the first, the General Committee was composed of 36 laymen, of whom 15 were Anglicans, 15 were members of the "Free Churches" and 6 were of "foreign residence in London." The lay character of the Bible Society was evident even then, though it always had the support of many clergy as well. From the beginning the Society had the policy of publishing the Scriptures "without note or comment," and this made it possible to serve churches with a great variety of theological convictions.

Canada has the distinction of being the first country for which the BFBS published a Gospel in a language other than English. The Gospel of John in the Mohawk language was published in 1804, the year the Society was founded. This translation was the work of Teyoninhokarawen, a Chief of the Six Nations in what is now Southern Ontario. The British called him Captain Norton. He was well qualified for the work, having an excellent knowledge of English and of his own language. An earnest Christian, Chief Teyoninhokarawen believed the book to be of great value to his people. Missionaries of the Society for the Propagation of the Gospel, who had been at work in Canada for over 100 years, would have preferred to have the translated Gospel accompanied by a written "spirited address to the Six Nations." But the Society's policy of including no "note or comment" prevented this.

From September 26 to October 3, 1996, the United Bible Societies World Assembly was held in Mississauga, Ontario. This was the first time the World Assembly had been held in Canada, and the occasion afforded an opportunity for the significance of the first BFBS publication to be recognized. On Sunday, September 29, at a service in the 211-year-old Mohawk chapel (St. Paul, Her Majesty's Chapel of the Mohawks) on the Six Nations Reserve, Brantford, a hand-sized, leather-bound copy of the Gospel of John in Mohawk was presented to Chief Wallington Staats. The presentation was made by Douglas Scott, Chair of the British and Foreign Bible Society and the Right Reverend Eduard Lohse, President of the United Bible Societies. This book is permanently on display in Huron College, London, Ontario, where it can be viewed and studied by students of both theology and the Mohawk language.

Wales, a major inspiration for the founding of BFBS, also quickly received the attention of the Society. In 1806, a new edition of 10,000 Welsh New Testaments was sent to Wales and, two years later, 20,000 complete Bibles were printed. Each year large quantities of Bibles and New Testaments reached Wales. Other parts of the British Isles needed the Word of God as well. Gaelic Scriptures were issued for Scotland and, in 1806, the Hibernian Bible Society was founded to meet the needs of Ireland. At the same time the activity of the BFBS was being extended to many other parts of the world.

In China, for example, Robert Morrison was busy translating the Bible into Chinese in Canton, where he was an employee of the East India Company. When word of this reached London, BFBS provided £3,000 to enable the translation to be completed. In India, William Carey, the father of the modern missionary movement, had been at work for over a decade, and his team at Serampore was diligent in

Scripture translation. Translation was also going forward in Bengali, Hindustani, Persian, Marathi and other languages, and BFBS assisted these translators with an annual grant of £1,000. Not surprisingly, this led to the establishment of an Auxiliary of the Bible Society in India. The Auxiliary grew and eventually became the Bible Society of India.

Similarly, other Bible Societies were soon established, inspired by the "Parent Society." Two major ones were the Netherlands Bible Society, founded in 1814, and the American Bible Society, now the largest in the United Bible Societies, founded in 1816. As early as 1809, Bible Society Auxiliaries were begun in Scotland, but they severed their connection with BFBS in 1825 because they objected to publishing Bibles which included the Deuterocanonical books, commonly called the Apocrypha. BFBS agreed to discontinue this practice, but the Scottish Auxiliaries proceeded to establish the National Bible Society of Scotland in 1861. Bible Societies gradually appeared on all continents, and all were founded on principles similar to those of the British and Foreign Bible Society.

On the Canadian scene, a crop of different Bible Societies sprang up in the years following 1804. The Bible Society in Pictou, Nova Scotia was organized in 1807 and the one in Truro, Nova Scotia in 1810. The Bible Society of Newfoundland began in 1812, and the Nova Scotia Bible Society dated from 1813. In 1817 the Bible Society of Upper Canada appeared in Toronto, but it did not continue and was reorganized as the York Upper Canada Bible Society in 1828. The New Brunswick Bible Society had its beginnings in 1819 in Saint John. It is remarkable that, at the remote Hudson's Bay Company Trading Post at York Factory, in what is now Manitoba, an Auxiliary of the British and Foreign Bible Society was started as early as 1821.

In 1833 the Ottawa Bible Society began, and in 1835 the Hamilton Auxiliary of the British and Foreign Bible Society was formed. In 1840 the Hamilton organization changed its name to Gore District Bible Society, Auxiliary of the British and Foreign Bible Society, and in 1847 it became part of the Upper Canada Bible Society. The Western Ontario Bible Society at London, Ontario was started in 1879. In 1904, the Upper Canada Bible Society turned over its Manitoba and Saskatchewan Auxiliaries, colporteurs, and Bible Depots to facilitate the formation of the Manitoba and Saskatchewan Bible Society.

Among the challenges facing the Bible Societies begun in Canada, as well as the Parent Society, was the translation of Scriptures into the languages of Canada's First Nations. One of the most captivating stories in this regard concerns the Rev. James Evans and the production of the Scriptures in Plains Cree.

Evans is very much part of the history of the Bible Society, even though he was never on the Society's staff. Born in Hull, England in 1801, he came to Canada as a young man. He became a teacher at L'Orignal on the Ottawa River, where he taught First Nations pupils, who interested him greatly. In 1828 Evans joined the Rice Lake Wesleyan Mission as a teacher. There he found great opportunities to spread both education and the Gospel among the First Nations. His next move was to the St. Clair Mission, and finally in 1840 to Norway House at the north end of Lake Winnipeg.

As Evans learned the Plains Cree language spoken by the people of the area, he found it had 36 principal sounds. This led him to develop a whole new way of writing. He made a table of the 36 sounds, placing them in an order that could be easily remembered because of its musical character. The next step was to make a simple sign or figure for each of the sounds. When these signs were placed side by side and the sounds for which they stood were uttered, words would be formed; anyone who spoke the language would recognize these words.

Evans had no paper so he scratched the signs on birchbark. Eventually he wrote verses of Scripture on birchbark, and was delighted to find the Cree people could read them with ease. But a better way of writing was needed, so he set about manufacturing a printing press. He made forms for the signs out of clay. Into these forms he poured melted lead, which he got from the insides of tea chests. When the lead cooled, he had "type" for printing. For ink he used soot from lamp chimneys, mixed with sturgeon oil. Evans' press was a jack screw used by the fur traders in bailing furs. His primitive printing method worked, and soon Plains Cree Syllabic came into common use throughout a large area of northern Canada. It continues to be used today, and has been the means of thousands of Indigenous Canadians becoming literate.

Among other translations into First Nations languages during the 1800s were:

- 1810 – Gospel of John for the Inuit of Labrador, among whom Moravian missionaries were working. It was published by the British and Foreign Bible Society, and was soon followed by translations of other books of the Bible. The Rev. C. F. Burkhart of the Labrador mission was the pioneer translator. The Inuit expressed their gratitude by collecting seal blubber to give to the Bible Society.
- 1844 – Gospel of Mark for the Micmac of the Atlantic area. Translated by Native evangelist Paul Osunkhirine.
- 1853 – Gospel of Matthew into Swampy Cree, widely used in the lower valley of the Saskatchewan River. Translated by the Rev. James Hunter, Church Missionary Society.
- 1863 – Scripture Portions for the Maliseet of New Brunswick. Translated by the Rev. S. T. Rand.
- 1880 – The Gospels for the Iroquois of Quebec Province. Translated by Chief Onasakenrat.
- 1886 – Gospel of Mark for the Beaver people of the Peace River area (Alberta). Translated by the Rev. A. C. Garrioch.
- 1891-1899 – Three Gospels and the Book of Acts translated for the Haida people of Canada's west coast.
- 1900 – First five books of the New Testament translated for the Kwakiutl people of Canada's west coast.

Besides translation, another major concern of BFBS, as well as of Canada's "homegrown" Bible Societies, was distribution of the Scriptures in English and, where appropriate, in French. Especially in the early years, much of this was done through colportage – travelling about, giving away Scriptures or selling them at nominal prices that people could easily afford. The story of early colportage in Canada is told in *The Bible in Canada: The Story of the British and Foreign Bible Society in Canada* by E. C. Woodley (1953):

> The importance of colportage was recognized in Canada from the beginning of Bible Society work. The reference to it in early reports of the Parent Society, which made grants for such work, shows the emphasis placed upon it. In a new country like Canada, where settlers were often located some distance from a trading centre in which a local Christian dealer might keep a few Bibles on one of his shelves, it was necessary for the colporteur or the travelling agent to seek them out. This work was

done by a company of earnest Christian men and women who bravely faced innumerable hardships and dangers in their faithful labour for the spread of a knowledge of the Kingdom of God through the Scriptures.

In these modern days of rapid and easy transportation . . . it is difficult to visualize the problems that the traveller had to face.

In his journal of his travels in the Eastern Townships of Quebec, in 1815, Bishop Mountain describes his experiences in the following terms: "From St. Armand to the river St. Francis, we travelled in waggons over high mountains and through deep valleys and woods, on roads composed of rocks and roots, only exchanged occasionally for short, but deep, black swampy soil. Nobody would believe before I tried it that it could be accomplished although we sometimes could not advance more than 12 miles (19 km) a day, and though we ourselves frequently thought the obstacles insurmountable." Today the same journey may be made comfortably over paved roads in three hours.

Mrs. Anna Jameson, the author of *Winter Studies and Summer Rambles in Canada,* published in 1836, records unhappy memories of the roads in Upper Canada along which she travelled. She describes the road between Port Talbot and Chatham in these words, "The road was scarcely passable; there were no longer cheerful farms and clearings, but the dark pine forest and the rank swamp, crossed by those terrific corduroy paths (my bones ache at the mere recollection!) and deep holes and pools of rotted vegetable matter mixed with water, black bottomless sloughs of despond."

Later, describing a journey of 25 miles (40 km) west of Hamilton, which occupied nine hours, she declared that she arrived at her destination "dreadfully weary, fevered and bruised, and my limbs ached woefully."

It was along such roads, sometimes in the crude carts of the time but generally on foot, that the colporteurs carried on the visitation in the country districts. There were, of course, moments of relief and even of exaltation as they were warmly received in the homes of settlers who had not forgotten their Christian past and were glad to obtain a copy of the Bible and to talk about the deep things of life.

In the city the situation was different. The problems of travel largely disappeared but they were replaced by the monotony of door to door calls, with the certainty that, in too many cases, their kindly approach would be met by a harsh rebuff. But here again there were many open doors, especially among the poor and those to whom life was hard and its rewards few. The colporteur was welcomed, and in the comfort . . . offered from God's Word, the burdens of life seemed to grow lighter and eyes shone with a new hope.

Then, on country roads, in village shops or on city streets there were the chance meetings with other travellers and the opportunity of a word of cheer and the handing out of a Scripture portion. It was a case of casting bread upon the waters which, not infrequently, was found after many days.

Where there were Ladies' Bible Associations in affiliation with the Auxiliaries, these often engaged in colportage work of a very interesting kind in addition to their efforts to raise funds. Thus in Montreal from 1862 to 1883 the Ladies' Bible Association engaged Bible Women for colportage and general welfare work. This was a fine example of Christian service. The Bible Women were successful in discovering and aiding worthy destitute people in the slum areas of the city and also engaged in rescue work for delinquent girls and needy sick women and children. Their work was Christ-centred and wherever they went they carried Bibles and portions which they sold at the lowest possible price or gave away, when necessary. But they were not satisfied with disposing of Bibles. In all kinds of homes, and sometimes under distressing conditions, they would read passages from God's Word which would bring comfort and cheer to sad and weary hearts. The record of their efforts is an heroic chapter in the history of welfare work in this country. . . .

Moved by a missionary interest in their neighbours across the international boundary, the American Bible Societies frequently made donations of Bibles and Testaments to various groups in Canada. In 1822 the Vermont Bible Society gave a supply of Bibles, including some in French, for distribution in Canada. In 1828 and again in 1834, further donations were made to be used at the discretion of the Montreal Bible Society. Missionary Societies of the Methodist Episcopal and American Baptist Churches received grants of Bibles and in 1838 the American Bible Society sent 6,400 Bibles and Testaments for free distribution to those needing them. In 1840 a grant of 500 French Testaments was made by the same Society and, in several years following, French Testaments were sent in considerable number to Madame Feller and her associates in the French-Canadian Missionary Society, which had established a centre at Grande Ligne on the Richelieu River. . . . The assistance of the Bible Societies in the United States was greatly appreciated by those seeking to spread a knowledge of God's Word among all racial and religious groups in Canada.

In their enthusiasm for the work that they were doing and as proof that it was a worthwhile Christian enterprise, the colporteurs submitted lengthy accounts of their experiences to the Auxiliaries that engaged them. These accounts occupy many pages in the Annual Reports of the Auxiliaries and contain countless stories of the deepest human interest.

Colporteur Campbell (for example), who worked in the Eastern Townships of the Province of Quebec in 1858, has this to say regarding the value of colportage: "It would be almost impossible for anyone to conceive of the amount of destitution as to spiritual matters. In some places there is much lack of means of grace and, in others, when the means are within their reach, the people do not avail themselves of these opportunities. I frequently endeavour to think of the best plan to get the people interested in the things which belong to their soul's salvation. The more, therefore, I know, the more I am convinced of the utility of the system of colportage, because the colporteur has a better chance of getting at the people, than if he should go as a minister and, unless some method of this nature be continued, many of the people will settle down in utter carelessness and indifference." Mr. Campbell was a man whom nothing could deter from his chosen task: "I borrowed a saddle to visit five families who were in backward places; in finding the roads so bad my old man would be apt to rebel, but the thought that the Saviour comes to seek and to save that which was lost made me proceed quietly in the path of duty; and I found wretched families in every sense of the term. It would be a first-rate place to teach some ungrateful people who are better circumstanced. I gave three Testaments and sold two Testaments. In returning, my horse lost his feet coming through a swamp, and I was thrown off him into the mud, where I was almost buried alive, but fortunately my horse stood still till I got up, by rolling myself quickly out of his way. The kind lady with whom I lodged the night before had all my clothes washed. This took place in the forenoon and I was ready to proceed on duty in the afternoon." *Report, 1858.*

In the Report for 1861 an interesting statement is made with special reference to work in the Kingston area: "During the summer months and in mid-winter, our colporteur is constantly employed in the remote townships, visiting regularly every house and shanty and never leaving a family unsupplied where an entrance for the Bible can be found. . . .

Quietly and unostentatiously is the work performed; every new township was thoroughly explored and, as far as possible, supplied, and at the great day when the secrets of all hearts shall be revealed, may we not trust that the seed thus sown will be shown to have borne an abundant harvest? During those portions of the year when the remoter townships were inaccessible, the colporteur is employed in the older districts, and in these his labours are not in vain. It is only by house to house visitation that the religious wants of the country can be known. Often in the midst of our most flourishing townships and in villages where churches have long been established are families found without a copy of the Scriptures."

Reference has been made to the work of the Bible Women under the auspices of the Ladies' Bible Associations. The reports of their visitations are often painful reading, as they devoted their efforts especially to women and children in desperately needy circumstances. Their desire to lift up those who had fallen by the way and to bring to them the message of divine compassion and forgiveness led them into many darkened homes. Their work in the gaols (jails) is reminiscent of that of Elizabeth Fry in England, and the motivating force was identical.

There can be few more human documents than the journals of the Bible Women.

"Many whom I visit show their value of God's Word by stopping their work while I am reading, even when their living depends upon it. Mrs. E. and family stop their washing and ironing, by which they earn their earthly bread, to hear a portion of the bread of life and sometimes, when the man of the house comes in and I fear to be in the way, I am encouraged to go on and gladly do so, in the hope of being led to give a word in season.

"Far different was the case of a young girl (in gaol for the first time) who replied in answer to my enquiries, that she never before had been spoken to about her soul, or personally warned to 'flee from the wrath to come.' It was the last visit I made before leaving town for the summer and, as I turned to leave the ward, said you will never again be able to say 'no one has cared for my soul.'

"My daily visits from house to house extend over five or six hours. I read a portion of God's Word and pray, and they always ask me to come again soon. A number of sick people look for my visits. May the Master guide me with his Holy Spirit! I have been much encouraged by one woman who 12 months ago was a poor drunkard but now seems to have given her heart to Christ, and by several others who are trying to lead Christian lives. An old man, who has been bedridden for 12 years and is very poor, is very glad to see me from day to day. I read and pray with him; he is a true child of God. And so the work goes on. There is much misery through intemperance in the district but, with God's blessing on our efforts, we expect great things."

Source: Woodley, E. C. The Bible in Canada: The Story of the British and Foreign Bible Society in Canada. *Toronto: Dent, 1953, pages 71-79.*

For years it was the British and Foreign Bible Society that dominated all Bible Society work in Canada. While other Societies were at work in the world, it was BFBS that was the most significant worldwide provider of Scriptures in the languages of the people. It has been said that, with the exception of the Christian Church, the Bible Society has been the most significant Christian activity in the past 2,000 years. The decline of the British Empire, the emergence of the United States of America as the foremost world power, and the growth of the Christian Church throughout the world have diminished the role of BFBS today, but the significant role it played for a century and a half makes it one of the world's truly great Christian enterprises. The Canadian Bible Society will always be indebted to the Parent Society for the inspiration it provided and the foundation it laid.

CHAPTER 3

Canadian Bible Society: Birth and Early Work 1904 to 1946

Since childhood, you have known the Holy Scriptures that are able to make you wise enough to have faith in Christ Jesus and be saved. Everything in the Scriptures is God's Word. All of it is useful for teaching and helping people and for correcting them and showing them how to live. The Scriptures train God's servants to do all kinds of good deeds.

2 Timothy 3.15-17

For a century, 1804 to 1904, all Bible Societies in Canada were linked in spirit, if not in organization, with the British and Foreign Bible Society. They did not, however, all bear the name British and Foreign Bible Society. Bible Societies from Newfoundland to British Columbia bore a variety of names. While they all had the same origin and purpose, when people moved from one part of Canada to another, they did not know that the Bible Society in their new community had any connection with the one where they had lived before.

By 1904 there were 14 Auxiliaries of the British and Foreign Bible Society scattered across Canada. Strongest among these was the Upper Canada Bible Society, based in Toronto and overseeing the work of some 600 Branches. At the time the steady tide of immigrants entering the country from the United States, Europe and elsewhere emphasized the need for a more coordinated effort in distributing the Scriptures. People who valued the maintenance of Christian principles in the growing Canadian population faced the challenge of sharing the Christian message with the newcomers.

A first conference to consider a union of Bible Society Auxiliaries and regional Bible Societies had been held in 1903. In 1904, on September 14 and 15 in Toronto, at the second conference held for this purpose, the final decision was made. The federation motion was proposed by Professor H. M. Tory:

> Resolved that whereas there are in Canada 14 Auxiliaries of the British and Foreign Bible Society, totally disconnected, having no fair knowledge of each other's operations, and what is of more importance, failing to cover the entire territory of our Dominion, we approve of the policy of Federation, and consolidation of the same, on a basis to be agreed upon hereafter.

This motion was carried after the following words were added: *due regard being had to the wishes of the contributing Auxiliaries.*

The first meeting of the General Board was held April 26, 1905. The new Society took the name Canadian Bible Society, Auxiliary to the British and Foreign Bible Society. Royal Assent to the Act of Incorporation of this Society was given on March 22, 1906.

With the formation of the Canadian Bible Society (CBS), an important change took place respecting the relationship of the Canadian Auxiliaries to the Parent Society – though this was not always recognized in the years that followed. Up until the founding of CBS, all Auxiliaries in Canada had been linked to the British and Foreign Bible Society in London, England. After the founding of CBS, however, all Auxiliaries were linked to the new National Society in Canada which was itself, in turn, linked to BFBS.

Name Changes Reflect Changing Times

When the Society was founded, there was intense debate as to what the name should be. Canada was still a colony of Britain, so some wanted to call it simply An Auxiliary of the British and Foreign Bible Society. The pro-British, United Empire Loyalist sentiment was lacking in Western Canada, however, and it was the West that prevailed over the East and had the name Canadian Bible Society accepted. Nevertheless many in Central and Eastern Canada maintained strong British sentiments and, in 1929, when the General Secretary, Dr. J. B. M. Armour, proposed that the name become British and Foreign Bible Society in Canada and Newfoundland, approval was given. This change obtained Royal Assent on May 30, 1930.

After Newfoundland became part of Canada in 1949, the name was again changed by dropping "and Newfoundland." In 1960 there was still another change, and it became "Canadian Bible Society, Auxiliary to the British and Foreign Bible Society." In 1980 "Auxiliary to the British and Foreign Bible Society" was dropped and since that date the name has been simply "Canadian Bible Society." In 1980 the name was also registered in French: *La Société biblique canadienne.*

Almost immediately after its founding in 1904, the Canadian Bible Society turned its attention to the tide of immigrants who had provided much of the impetus for its existence. In 1906, for example, 215,912 immigrants entered Canada, including over 6,000 from Asia. In 1907 the number of immigrants reached 277,376. Succeeding years saw ebbs and flows, with a high of 400,000 in 1912. The response of CBS is described as follows in *The Bible in Canada: The Story of the British and Foreign Bible Society in Canada* by E. C. Woodley (1953).

> The Bible Society was fully cognizant of the opportunity and responsibility of this situation. The Report of 1906 contains this pertinent statement: "The Bible, in whole or in part, is in the native tongue of all these polyglot immigrants. . . . It is used or called for in 60 versions in Canada. In a number of cases, it can be had with the English and the foreign versions side by side (in effect, in a diglot or two-language edition); and it can thus be the means of assisting foreigners to acquire the language which they and their children must learn and at the same time the means of teaching them the words of everlasting life. Large numbers . . . are without a copy of the Bible; many of them have never had a copy in their hands. In view of all such facts, the dissemination of

the Scriptures in all the tongues spoken receives a new inspiration. Here is the manifest and urgent mission of the Canadian Bible Society."

The challenge was met to the limit of the Society's resources. Vessels were met on their arrival, and the first gift received by many a newcomer was the Bible in his (or her) own mother tongue. Bible stands were set up at convenient points in the immigration sheds and in railway stations. Colporteurs visited lumber and mining camps and followed the immigrants to their new homes. "The colporteurs have been searching out those in lonesome farm buildings and isolated shacks; visiting the towns in the Kootenay, devastated by fire; tracking in New Ontario and the prairies and penetrating the bush – everywhere appearing as much Christian friends as the carriers of the Word of God." *Report, 1908.*

. . . . The value of the diglot editions of the Scriptures was recognized early by workers among immigrants. The average immigrant is baffled by the strangeness of the new land to which he has come and is suspicious of the elaborate procedures to which he is subjected before he can enjoy his new freedom. He hears officials discussing his case in a language unknown to him and does not know what it is all about. Then comes a friendly man or woman offering a copy of the Scriptures. He receives the book with some hesitation at first, until his eye lights on words in his loved language. All is changed in a moment as he realizes that the tie with his old home is not completely severed and that there are those in Canada who are ready to share with him, in his own tongue, the truth that makes men free indeed. To many the Scriptures in this form have proved their first intelligent introduction to the English language.

A large percentage of the newcomers to Canada belonged to English-speaking peoples, with their forebears in Great Britain and Ireland or in the United States. These brought with them English ways and traditions. But they were nonetheless strangers to this land. To many of them the Bible was a familiar book in earlier days; others knew little about it beyond the name. Among these the colporteur also moves with . . . hand outstretched in welcome and . . . pack of Bibles. On the churches also these new Canadians laid a heavy responsibility and Home Mission Boards of all the churches shared in missionary work among them. Where the missionary went, the Bible went also.

In 1912 an English lady contributed £100 to be expended among English-speaking settlers in Canada. By arrangement with the Manitoba and Saskatchewan Auxiliaries, Mr. P. McGregor, depository at Winnipeg, was set free for work in the Peace River district during the summer. He travelled widely in the region and scattered the seed of the Word wherever he went.

Source: Woodley, E. C. The Bible in Canada: The Story of the British and Foreign Bible Society in Canada. *Toronto: Dent, 1953, pages 247-249.*

With the outbreak of World War I in 1914 came a sudden drop in the number of immigrants entering Canada. With the beginning of the war also came a whole new set of challenges for the Canadian Bible Society. The Society's response is described as follows in *The Bible in Canada* by E. C. Woodley (1953).

At the outbreak of war, the Government at Ottawa was approached by the Canadian Bible Society with the request that it might be allowed to present a New Testament to every man in the Canadian Expeditionary Forces. The Militia Department graciously and gratefully accepted the Society's offer. A special edition bound in khaki was prepared, bearing a suitable inscription and the Canadian Coat of Arms. The inscription read, "Presented by the Canadian Bible Society (British and Foreign Bible Society) to the Canadian Soldiers in the War of 1914. 'Be strong and of a good courage.'" Short presentation services, often of an impressive character, were held at many military centres throughout Canada, with the full cooperation of the commanding officers. Copies of the New Testament in French were given to members of the French-speaking units. When a Japanese Canadian Battalion was formed in British Columbia, some Vancouver citizens made it possible for each soldier in it to receive a New Testament in the Japanese language. Canadians of other racial origins were, in due course, provided with New Testaments in their own tongues.

During the calendar years 1914, 1915 and 1916, 270,000 volumes were distributed to men going overseas who, in nearly every case, received them with gratitude. . . .

No field of service was overlooked. In 1917 many thousand copies of the Gospels were supplied to Lady Drummond and her helpers, for the Comfort Bags of wounded Canadians reaching the hospitals of greater London.

The following striking tribute to the war effort of the Bible Society appeared in the *London Daily Telegraph* at this time (1917): "Few indeed will realize how great have been the activities of this learned and uncontroversial society since the first days of the war.

"How many of us can grasp, much less visualize, totals in millions! Yet it is in millions that the labours of the Society have got to be expressed. These little books have been carried through bayonet charges and bombing attacks, in air reconnaissances and submarine feats of daring. Upon the blood-stained fly-leaves, dying hands have traced their last messages to mother or wife; at Loos there was hardly a wounded man brought in that had not a khaki-bound Testament upon him."

One of the beautiful tributes paid by soldiers to the Bible is told in the Report for 1917. A number of men returning to Canada were about to land at Saint John, NB. With their non-commissioned officer they were marching along the deck, easy and jovial, when the sergeant observed the Bible Society colporteur busy distributing Gospels to a group of immigrants. "Whissht," he commanded, "Caps off! It is the Word of God," and the men marched past in silent reverence. That was the feeling caught from the reverence with which the New Testament was handled by their comrades at the front. . . .

The testimony of . . . well-known chaplain and author, the Rev. C. W. Gordon, DD, familiar to thousands as 'Ralph Connor,' is also worthy of record. "My experience as chaplain with our soldiers at the front has given me a more profound sense of the value of the Bible to men in their hour of greatest need. The light from the lurid flames of war seems to reveal deep and hidden meaning in the old words. Many men discovered anew the Bible for themselves, and literally hundreds of thousands of soldiers found in it that perfect revelation of God through Jesus Christ, that alone satisfies the mind and heart of man."

During the struggle, the British and Foreign Bible Society supplied millions of copies of the Scriptures to men and women of the Forces. From the beginning of the war to the end of 1918, the total number of Scriptures presented to the soldiers of Canada by the Canadian Bible Society was 434,814 in 18 different languages.

Source: Woodley, E. C. The Bible in Canada: The Story of the British and Foreign Bible Society in Canada. *Toronto: Dent, 1953, pages 276-279.*

After World War I ended in 1918, large numbers of immigrants again began entering Canada. Port work again became an important part of the Canadian Bible Society's activities. For example, during the year 1925 at the port of Quebec, nearly 45,000 copies of the Scriptures were distributed in 30 languages. In the same year, over 22,000 copies were distributed at Saint John and Halifax.

During the Great Depression of 1929 to 1939, mass unemployment led to a dramatic drop in the number of new immigrants entering Canada. Nevertheless the Society, renamed the British and Foreign Bible Society in Canada and Newfoundland, continued to be active. It occupied itself with colportage and translation. It was also quite successful, in spite of the Depression, at raising funds for the Parent Society. In 1931, for example, funds raised in Canada permitted the Parent Society to issue the world's cheapest English Bible. Called the English Shilling Bible, it had sold 8,000 copies by 1933.

It was during the 1930s, as well, that the National Society began concentrating more on publicity. For example, it made its activities known to the public through radio, magazine advertisements, leaflets, lantern slides and moving pictures. In 1932 it started publishing its annual *Reports* in a style designed to have more popular appeal, with titles such as *The Book of Good Cheer, Many Diadems* and *With Unhurrying Chase.*

In 1939 the beginning of World War II brought the Depression to an end, and imposed upon the Bible Society a challenge similar to the one it had faced in the earlier World War. E. C. Woodley described the Society's World War II work as follows in *The Bible in Canada* (1953).

> The Society entered upon its great mission in the war years with the advantage of its experience gained a quarter of a century earlier. Its purpose was (a) to present New Testaments to all on active service with His Majesty's Forces, men and women alike; (b) to supply the Scriptures in the required speech to those in prison and internment camps. Jewish members of the Forces were to be given copies of the Psalms.
>
> The Bible Society immediately established a War Emergency Fund, which was registered in Ottawa according to the provisions of the War Charities Act. The Minister of National Defence approved the distribution of Scriptures, and the Chaplaincy Staff heartily cooperated.
>
> The work of distributing Scriptures was extended in 1940 to Training Camps. Norwegian airmen, of whom there were many, received Norwegian New Testaments.

In the internment camps German chaplains expressed their gratitude for assistance. The American Bible Society generously gave 2,000 Gospels in German and, in view of the difficulty of obtaining adequate supplies from England, allowed purchases to be made from its stock at very low prices. The attitude of the Society was that of Lord Nelson, who once said of the enemy, "When they become my prisoners, I become their protector," and protection covers not only the physical but also the spiritual welfare of the prisoner. . . .

A summary of the effort of the Canadian Bible Society during the years of the second World War appears in the 1946 Report. . . . The total number of volumes distributed by the Canadian Bible Society during the war was 797,860, of which 730,000 were presentation New Testaments in khaki, navy and air force blue bindings and bearing a special message from His Majesty, King George VI to those in the Services. Of this number 44,000 were drawn directly from our London office, with which arrangements had been made to meet all requests for Scriptures from chaplains serving the Canadian Forces overseas. Distribution of 2,260 copies of the Book of Psalms, in special binding, was made to those of the Jewish faith, and requests for 1,000 New Testaments in Dutch and 1,336 in Norwegian were met. 4,460 Testaments and Gospels, sealed in waterproof envelopes, were supplied for lifeboats and Carley floats. 1,727 copies of the complete Bible were supplied, many in a large type edition, for permanent use in religious services in hospitals and aboard Canadian vessels. Organizations and individuals authorized to carry on work in prisons and internment camps received 6,826 volumes in 15 languages, of which 6,203 were in German.

From surplus stocks on hand at the close of the war, 2,800 Gospels in German and 3,132 Gospels and New Testaments in Norwegian were despatched to Europe to help meet pressing needs in these languages.

Source: Woodley, E. C. The Bible in Canada: The Story of the British and Foreign Bible Society in Canada. *Toronto: Dent, 1953, pages 283, 284, 286, 287.*

CHAPTER 4

How the West Was Won

A nation that repudiates or distorts its past runs a grave risk of forfeiting its future.

Canadian historian Donald Creighton

God is pleased with everyone who worships him and does right, no matter what nation they come from.

Acts 10.35

The Canadian Bible Society has been able to attract to its staff people of unusual competence and commitment. The contribution made by staff and the significance of their work generally has not been sufficiently recognized. District Directors and other staff should be credited with much that has been achieved. Volunteers, officers and board members have played a part but the staff who, day by day, laboured long hours and made untold sacrifices have been the mainstay of the Society. For example, the role played by the Rev. E. J. B. Salter in pioneer Bible Society work on the prairies is one of the highlights of its history.

In July 1904 Mr. Salter arrived in Winnipeg from Iowa to become pastor of Central Congregational Church. At that time Winnipeg had a population of 60,000, and was the gateway through which thousands of immigrants passed to take advantage of the free land being offered in the "Last Best West." Salter had spent 10 years as a pastor on the Iowa prairies, and he looked forward to the challenge a Winnipeg congregation would present.

That same year the Rev. Dr. J. H. Ritson, MA (Oxford), General Secretary of the British and Foreign Bible Society, was in Winnipeg to take part in the 100th anniversary of the founding of BFBS. He proposed that an Auxiliary (District) of the Bible Society be formed in the West with Winnipeg as its headquarters. The confederation of the various Bible Societies and Auxiliaries of BFBS in Canada was imminent and Dr. Ritson envisaged the Western Auxiliary as being part of the new confederation. In Winnipeg he also sought support for the worldwide 100th anniversary appeal for a birthday gift to BFBS of 250,000 guineas. He spoke in several churches.

At a mass meeting in the YMCA on Portage Avenue, he proposed that a Bible Society Secretary be appointed for the prairies with the office in Winnipeg. The city's ministers all supported this and, at a citywide meeting in Grace Church, it was agreed to appoint a Secretary for the West.

The way Mr. Salter was chosen to fill that position is an example of how "God moves in a mysterious way His wonders to perform." One of the strongest supporters of appointing a Bible Society Secretary for the West was on his way to Grace Church when a violent storm made it impossible for him to proceed. He was forced to take shelter in Central Congregational Church and, as the storm continued to rage, he remained for the service. He was so impressed with Salter's preaching that he asked to meet with him the next day. The result was that he invited Salter to become the first Secretary of the newly formed Bible Society Auxiliary. Shortly after that the appointment was made.

Mr. Salter was no stranger to BFBS. His father had been a missionary with the London City Mission and, as a boy in London, young Salter had often accompanied him when he visited BFBS headquarters to obtain Scriptures for his work. Now Salter took up his Bible Society responsibilities with enthusiasm and passion. He was to lead the work for over 35 years, and establish the Bible Society in the West as a great Christian enterprise.

Every day in the early 1900s (with the exception of the war years 1914-1918), 1,000 immigrants were settling on the prairies and in new communities. In the space of a single generation, 1904 to 1921, the population of Western Canada grew from 400,000 to two million. The West was the Promised Land. In 1901, 11.1 per cent of the population of Canada lived west of Ontario. By 1921 it was 28.2 per cent.

Under Salter's dynamic and creative leadership, the enormous challenge of providing the newcomers with the Word of God in their mother tongues was largely met. He built a strong organization in Winnipeg with Thomas Ryan as President, William Gibson as Vice-President and J. W. Driscoll as Honorary Treasurer. The work was supported by His Grace Archbishop Matheson, DD, the Venerable Archdeacon Fortin, DD, the Rev. J. W. Sparling, DD, the Rev. C. W. Gordon, DD (author Ralph Connor), the Rev. D. B. Harkness, MA, the Rev. C. C. Heathecote and other church leaders.

In the early 1900s, before additional Auxiliaries were organized in the three prairie provinces, the vast territory for which Mr. Salter was responsible covered 922,958 square miles (well over two million square kilometres). There were few bridges across the Saskatchewan River, and most crossings were made by ferries. The territory's hills, valleys, prairies and mountains were inhabited by First Nations – Sioux, Assiniboine, Cree, Blackfoot and others, many on reserves by this time. Increasingly, however, the area was being settled by immigrants from Britain, the United States and Europe. Their religious backgrounds ranged from Presbyterian, Church of England, Methodist and Lutheran, to Roman Catholic, Ukrainian Orthodox and Jewish, to Baptist, Mennonite, Moravian, Mormon and Doukhobor. Small numbers of Chinese and Japanese people were also part of the population; many of them had Buddhist, Confucian, Taoist and Shinto traditions. Added to the mix were a few Black immigrants from the United States and the West Indies; many of these belonged to Methodist and other Christian churches. All these people brought their beliefs and customs with them, and hoped to pass them on to succeeding generations.

The Bible Society wanted them all to read the Scriptures in their own languages, so they would see that God made of one blood all the nations of the world. The Society believed that, through distribution of the Scriptures, many would embrace the Christian faith for the first time, or become better grounded in it.

To win the West, the Bible Society decided to meet the people where they first set foot in Western Canada. A Bible stand, with John Scott in charge, was set up in the Canadian Pacific Railway station in

Winnipeg. Scott also found time to visit the immigration sheds where the people were pouring in from Europe. During those years the Scriptures were provided in Ruthenian, Russian, Slavonic, Polish, Hungarian, Romanian, Lithuanian, Croatian, Bohemian, Norwegian, Swedish, Finnish, Icelandic, Yiddish and 20 other languages. Since many of the immigrants came from the Ukraine, BFBS published a special edition of the Gospels in Ukrainian. Some 70,000 Ukrainians settled in the Saskatchewan River Valley, and many of these Gospels found their way there.

Mr. Salter's work in the West was of great interest to people in Eastern Canada. The Rev. R. E. Welsh, MA, was appointed by the British and Foreign Bible Society to be the General Secretary of the Bible Society in Canada and to represent the Parent Society. In September 1905 he arrived in Canada, taking up residence in Toronto and immediately showing a great interest in the new Western immigrants, especially the Doukhobors. Unfortunately, however, Bible Society work in Canada proved to be too strenuous for Welsh, and he resigned to teach at McGill University in Montreal. In 1907 Rev. W. B. Cooper, MA, was appointed by BFBS to succeed Welsh. His first journey to the West was made in April 1908. Mr. Salter described that visit in the lengthy report he wrote upon his retirement:

> He, too, wanted to see the Doukhobors. A community of them had just settled a mile (1.6 km) west of the Manitoba town of Benito . . . in the Swan River Valley. So we went to Swan River town to visit these people. A journey of 25 miles with horses was necessary, so we started early. It was in the spring of the year. Just at dawn, the whole town was aroused by a great noise and the ice went out of the river with thundering reverberations. The roads also began to break up. We crossed ditches which suddenly let us through the ice and brought the water into the democrat waggon in which we rode. The mud became deeper and deeper. We put up at a farmhouse to rest and feed the horses, after which we returned to Swan River, leaving the Doukhobors to themselves. It was the only trip that Mr. Cooper undertook in the country parts of Manitoba. I think it haunted him ever after, and indeed, I do not wonder. It was too severe an initiation. He rejected all later attempts to inveigle him into anything which would be likely to repeat this unpleasant experience.

Source: E. J. B. Salter's Final Report.

Though the Canadian Bible Society, with the Rev. R. E. Welsh as General Secretary, had been formally inaugurated in 1905, Salter continued to look to the Rev. Dr. J. H. Ritson in England for direction. When the first Bible House was acquired, it was London that advised on, supported and approved the new venture. Dr. Ritson was present at 6:30 a.m. on August 15, 1912 when the Board of the Manitoba and Saskatchewan Bible Society and several Bible Society supporters gathered for the sod-turning for the new building. Thomas Ryan, the President, read from 2 Chronicles 6.32, where reference is made to "the stranger that is come from a far country." Ryan said, "This building is to be erected that the stranger in our land may be supplied with the Word of God which has guided our way through life, and that it may be supplied to every nationality in this country in his own tongue without note or comment."

Raising the money for the building proved difficult, but with perseverance the project advanced and on January 27, 1919 the building was dedicated. The building and stock of Bibles was fully paid for at that time and this was a proud achievement. BFBS gave a grant of $22,000 towards the new building. The address of that first Bible House was 483 Main Street, Winnipeg, opposite the City Hall. The next address was 224 Alexander Avenue, and then Bible House was at 19 Martin Street, where there was a large warehouse. After that the Bible House was located at the following addresses, one after the other: 294 Smith Street, 184 Alexander Avenue, 308 Kennedy Street, 419 Graham Avenue and 952 St. Mary's Road.

Mr. Salter seized every opportunity to promote the Bible and to obtain financial support for the work of the Bible Society. He used celebrations of significant anniversaries to spread information about the work. In 1911 he marked the 300th anniversary of the King James Version by writing a booklet with the title "Tercentenary." 7,000 copies of this were distributed. In 1925 William Tyndale and the 400th anniversary of his translation of the Scriptures into English were celebrated with an essay-writing contest and special services. In 1929, throughout the West, special services marked the 125th anniversary of the founding of BFBS. That year the Winnipeg office had the Bible Society in London issue a special edition of the King James Version with a commentary on the title page. In 1935 came the 400th anniversary of Martin Luther's translation of the Bible. Salter also used the memory of this significant event to keep the Bible Society's work before the people.

The resourceful Salter faithfully served the Bible Society almost continuously until his death in 1942. The hardships he endured are described in his summary of those years, and the best way to demonstrate his dedication is to quote from his own writings:

> Indeed, early travel tried the hardiest. A few examples would perhaps be appropriate. All travelling was primitive. There were no gravelled roads. The most of the western country was romance. Everything was new. The railways were beginning a policy of expansion and it is no exaggeration to say that places, that were part of a farm today, would, in a few days' time, have rails laid down, a townsite fixed, a store and café. The least said about accommodation the better, for even I would rather go hungry than eat in them for obvious reasons or sleep outdoors than indoors for still more obvious reasons. Those conditions have long since passed away. Each railway made every effort to be the first in a place, because the railway that crossed another's path, had to furnish a continual switchman at the junction. The ties would seem to me to be laid on the top of the prairie. The hotels of these speedily erected villages would often be merely a shell of bare boards to secure protection from the elements, while the work of finishing the rooms would proceed after the place was opened for business. As wells were difficult to dig and water uncertain, a ditch, 100 feet (30 m) long, 50 feet (15 m) wide and 15 feet (4.5 m) deep, would be dug. Rain and snow formed a hard clay bottom which would hold water during a whole season. Snow would gather in winter and rain in summer. Sometimes a brick filter would be built at the bottom of this improvised lake and a pump connected. The prairie schooner too was seen over the land, bearing a new settler and all his effects.
>
> One winter night, after holding a meeting in Estevan, I travelled over the whole town to secure a place of shelter, but found none. I crawled into an implement shed and lay down. At 1:00 o'clock in the morning, I awoke so stiff that I could hardly move sufficiently to get circulation but, after much effort, I made my way to the railway station to wait till a train came along. I found 10 men stretched out on the floor and benches. A good fire was blazing in the Cannon stove, which derives its name from its shape. There was only room enough to stand. To go

into the cold again was unthinkable. Wearing a heavy winter coat which I could not remove, I stood till morning. The only standing place was uncomfortably near the stove and I was sleepy almost beyond endurance. About 5:30 a.m. a train arrived going north and I boarded it and fell asleep. I had to take three trains that day to arrive in Saskatoon, where I visited around till meeting time, trying to secure as large an audience as possible. After the meeting, I went to every boarding house and hotel in the city, but could not secure a lodging. I sat in a chair in Flanigan's Hotel till morning. Then I took a train for Lumsden and worked up a meeting. But when, after the meeting, I discovered that there was no accommodation to be had, I decided I would not spend the third night out of bed if I could avoid it. So I went to the livery man and got him out of bed. He himself said he had been two nights without sleep but would drive me the 22 miles (35 km) to Regina. So he dressed and we hitched up two horses and started out. A bitter wind was blowing and the snow was drifting heavily. The tracks were covered and the horses plunged. We did not converse any for conversation was impossible and we were wrapped in heavy robes. At about 1:00 o'clock the driver, who had been asleep, awakened and, looking around him, announced that he was lost. He drove on until we saw a sod hut made of prairie turf. Driving up we awakened the bachelor inhabitant and asked the way to Regina. He told us that we were 20 miles (32 km) away. It appeared that the horses, being left to themselves, had turned their backs to the wind and taken a wrong path. Once again we started and, keeping awake, came through many high drifts to our destination. I do not know how we did it, but we arrived between 6:00 and 7:00, and I caught a train and came through to Winnipeg.

On another occasion, in a similar plight, two of us left Alameda after the evening meeting to drive to Oxbow. The night was clear but intensely cold. The road lies for 10 miles (16 km) through a valley without any landmarks. We lost our way and wandered on. There was nothing to do but to continue travelling until the horses gave out, or until we saw some house, but no house appeared in sight. In travelling with horses and sleigh or cutter in winter, it is not possible to keep the face exposed yet it is necessary to keep a vigilant outlook, first with one eye and then with the other, taking our bearings for a short distance. After meandering, however, the horses struck a path and followed it. We found ourselves suddenly in Oxbow, our destination.

The coldest day I ever experienced was at Saltcoats. I stepped off the train at 6:00 a.m. The hotel was so cold I could not stay indoors. A notice on the desk informed me that all rooms were taken. The thermometer registered 58 below zero Fahrenheit (49 below Celsius). Wind was blowing, which is unusual with such a low temperature. I crossed the lake to wander in the calm of the woods till I saw smoke issue from a chimney. I went to the house and, sitting by the fire in the kitchen, fell instantly asleep.

The question of washing was, at first, difficult of solution. My first experience was at Tantallon where, arriving in the afternoon, and having nowhere to go until the evening meeting, I went into the woods to make myself presentable. Rubbing snow on my face, I made a lather and shaved with a straight razor without a looking glass. I strapped the razor on the inside of my Bible.

During all the period of my service, the country has been expanding. We were usually one step ahead of train service, and went into the Carrot River Valley as pioneers. We travelled north of Nipawin before there was a bridge over the Saskatchewan River, and travelled over 100,000 square miles (259,000 square kilometres) between Prince Albert and Onion Lake as it was being settled. We were very interested in the immigration and boasted that we were often the first in the field. I well remember my jealousy when the government of Manitoba sent nurses into the north country beyond where we were organizing Branches of the Society or doing colportage work. We soon remedied that, however.

The railways were not as well equipped in the early days. One Sunday I ministered in Hamiota. On Monday there were three engines frozen up between there and Brandon, and I was booked to hold service that night in Souris. I hired a livery. Mitchells Bridge being out, we had to detour for a considerable distance. At Kenton I took another livery and drove to Griswold. There I engaged a driver who undertook to bring me to Souris. It was an awful day and the roads were very heavy. We lost our way and landed in a ditch just as the sun went down. It was one of the very few times I have missed an appointment. Driving once from Pierson to Elva, I had to drive along the railway track. All trains were blocked and I felt safe, but I saw a snow plough coming along the track and had to get quickly into the ditch. The driver of the snow plough could not see me and he nearly deluged me with snow. I had some difficulty to get out with the horses but succeeded, and made my engagement.

Winter travel was, of course, a nightmare. I have so often been overturned in the covered cutters that I prefer the open ones, although colder. On one occasion I was upset just at the railway track at Sidney. A telephone pole blocked the whole entrance of the cutter and but for timely assistance I could not have escaped injury.

Speaking of injuries, I was only once in a train wreck. Between Elgin and Fairfax the train left the track and a broken rail came up through the floor of the car. I was stunned; but when I resumed consciousness, my arms were around the rail and the train was in the ditch. I was considerably damaged, especially in the face where I carry the scar. A special train was sent to bring us into Winnipeg, about 200 miles (322 km).

In the course of Bible Society work, I have been snowbound on the train several times, but only twice seriously. At such a time the engine dies and the fire cannot be revived. On one such occasion, we opened the emergency kit of food in the car and I took the place of a waiter, distributing cold baked beans and biscuits. I persuaded the passengers to ask the blessing, with the remark that those who did not do so in such an emergency did not deserve any. But I did not ask "A long grace over the short commons," and we existed till rescue came. One time we spent 24 hours in a drift and held religious discussions for many hours at a time.

We have a prosperous Branch of the Bible Society in Lloydminster. Very few people remember its inception as Archdeacon Lloyd and Mr. Barr led a party of pioneer Englishmen across the untried district west of Saskatoon. For their amusement the settlers refused to give them correct information and made much capital of it afterwards. Though they told the newcomers to hobble their horses when they went down hill and persuaded them to buy things they never could use, yet against all the false directions given them, both Archdeacon (now Bishop) Lloyd and his men made good, and both the Church and the Bible Society can testify that they did not lose their vision. The Archdeacon himself, I believe, had no small part in the Saskatchewan University which was ultimately established in Saskatoon in 1909. The Barr Colony ultimately took the name of the Archdeacon and is now Lloydminster. Archdeacon Lloyd was perhaps the most enterprising of the clergy in the early days. His splendid vision foresaw a country evangelized in its formation. He visited England and invited individuals to pay for a church costing £50 each and was able to build many of these churches throughout northern Saskatchewan. They were called "50 Mathilda pound Churches." These were placed on the prairie away from the towns; each church had seven pews, the place of the eighth being taken up by a small organ. The residence for the student had one room with a one-sided roof and also a stable for a pony. Young men came out from England and gave three years of their service for bare expenses to establish this work.

I had good fellowship with these young men and together we worked on the prairies. Sometimes they gave rise to comments on their experiences and I can vouch for many things which called for the mirth of the onlookers. One especially where one of these young men, being called a long distance to take a funeral and arriving the day before the funeral, slept in the bed with the corpse, and another who led his horse over a trestle bridge and got into difficulties as the horse fell through the bridge. Another who, in preaching on the text "They all began with one consent to make excuses," remarked that a Western man would not buy oxen without first examining them to ascertain whether they were good workers and good MILKERS. (The young Minister did not know that oxen are never female.) But these were all on the side. These were men who did spade work and I honoured them then and honour them now.

The romance of the country is well illustrated by a meeting which was held in North Battleford in the early days. I listened to an account given of a country which is now well settled. Although I had travelled over the country, I felt romantic as I heard of the distances without inhabitants where population was just beginning to pour in. I made up my mind that the Bible Society should also be a pioneer in a larger sense than before. This led to our wagon enterprise. There was no way to reach the new settlers without special equipment. There were 900 school districts in Manitoba and Saskatchewan and many hundreds in Alberta. I outlined them all and placed them on a map with full description of their location and officers. I proposed to hold a meeting in every schoolhouse or, where it refused, to erect a tent and hold a meeting as near as possible to the school. . . .

While we were able to pay our own way from the first day of our organization, and decided that the West can carry its own expenses, perhaps we carried this policy beyond the day of its usefulness. It was long after the formation of the Canadian Bible Society that we realized that National Office in Toronto should have been charged with many of our expenses. If this had been done we would have been able to send much more of the gifts of donors to Toronto. We bought four farm wagons and eight 1,300-pound (590-kg) horses. In each of these wagons we had a tent capable of seating 100 people. We had folding beds, collapsible stoves and tables and folding organs. We made seats of boards with legs that doubled under on hinges and made seating accommodation for 100 people in each tent. Then, making out a programme, we invited the people to come to our meetings. Locating each evening's meeting by section, township and range, a programme was printed which gave the whole meeting without intermission. Two meetings a day was a usual thing, Saturdays included. On Sundays where possible, we went with a Pastor on his circuit. During the week, we preferred to have the cooperation of the Pastor and people and use their facilities instead of setting up at another place near by. . . . We did not leave one school out of our calculations and nothing but a storm caused any school house to be passed by. Two men went with each wagon and there were two trunks of Bibles for sale with each equipment. Each outfit weighed about 3,500 pounds (1,587 kg). Thus for several years we travelled from the time that travelling was possible in the spring, until the snow drove us under cover in the winter. Our stoves heated the tents well in the cool weather. Farmers furnished much of our living by the way. We spent the forenoon canvassing for funds and gathered in considerable amounts.

These meetings were unique. We carried our own hymn sheets, led our own singing, played our own organs, had our own gasoline lanterns for services, and perfected our organization till we had about 2,300 Branches altogether. It was a marvel where all the people came from, but we kept up a continual correspondence inviting them to come, and each neighbourhood was filled with curiosity and interest. Later some other institutions copied this method but with little success. Our main difficulty was the crossing of the rivers. Where Riverhurst now stands we crossed the Saskatchewan River, taking about four days. The wagon floated across itself and the small boat we hired was deep down in the water to the gunwale. We would land on the other side about one or two miles (1.6–3.2 km) down stream, so swift was the river. The shifting sands also made it difficult. We reached Lucky Lake, now a town, and held our meetings. Here I left two men in charge of the rig. They drove me back to the river and I crossed it on the ferry at midnight. We had to portage across a sand bank newly formed. At 1:00 a.m. I started on foot for Riverhurst. The bank was very steep and I had not gone far before I met a lynx, or wildcat. I had a heavy valise in each hand, but I paused long enough to draw my knife to be ready for emergencies. Then, advancing with my gruffest voice, I quoted appropriate words, "Back to your punishment and to thy speed add wings," etc. I passed him with more misgivings than my bold words would suggest and did not look behind. I did not need to do so for the whining of the animal assured me he had not moved. I arrived in Riverhurst and took the train out at 5:00 o'clock in the morning.

While engaged in this type of work, we decided to visit every house on the prairies. To that end, we got together a band of workers who would combine colportage and deputation work and who would cover the whole country systematically. We were able to say at one time that every township had been visited and nearly every house in every township.

I cannot refrain from giving a feeble and, of course, unheeded protest on the introduction of cars as the beginning of travelling sorrows. With horses and wagons we can go anywhere. There are places where the badger holes were like honeycomb over the country and it was long before our first gravelled roads helped out. Even today more than half the country is inaccessible most of the time because of mud or snow. Many country points, where services used to be held with a large congregation, have been closed down, ostensibly because cars make the town churches more easily reached. It is a permanent loss. But I am a voice in the wilderness so will not prolong my Jeremiad.

Source: E. J. B. Salter's Final Report.

These excerpts from Salter's report provide a picture of the extent of Bible Society work in the early years of the West. The zeal and energy that Salter and others displayed, and the hardships they endured, are a challenge to us who enjoy so many comforts and conveniences today.

CHAPTER 5

The Districts and Branches: An Overview

Forget what happened long ago!
Don't think about the past.
I am creating something new,
There it is! Do you see it?

Isaiah 43.18,19

Several of the Canadian Bible Society's Districts, called Auxiliaries until 1960, have a history far older than that of the National Society. The detailed history of each District and of a number of the local Branches is very interesting, but those details would be outside the scope of this book. Therefore only a brief survey of the Districts is presented here, followed by a short description of the organization and character of the Branches.

Newfoundland and Labrador District – 1812

As noted in Chapter 2, the British and Foreign Bible Society published the Gospel of John for the Moravian missionaries on the coast of Labrador in 1810. A report of 1811 states that when the Inuit received the Word of God in their own language, they were moved to tears and exclaimed, "Jesus is worthy of thanks and our friends are worthy of thanks, who loved us so much though they have never seen us." The Newfoundland and Labrador District, established soon after, in 1812, has the distinction of being the oldest District in Canada, as well as one of the oldest Bible Societies in Canada and the

New World. From the beginning it depended upon the churches to provide volunteers to administer and sustain the work. It was not until 1966 that property was bought in St. John's, a Bible Society office was established in Newfoundland, and the District had its own District Secretary. Newfoundland has the distinction of being, on a per capita basis, the most generous province of Canada for giving to charitable organizations such as the Bible Society.

Quebec District – 1813

As early as 1804, the Rev. Francis Dick, a minister of the Congregational Church, established a Bible Society in Quebec. However, there is no indication that it had any connection with the British and Foreign Bible Society, and it does not appear to have survived many years. By 1813 the Parent Society was active in Quebec and its chief responsibility was colportage. The present Bible House in Quebec City opened in 1924.

Nova Scotia District – 1813

Some of the earliest records of Bible Society activity in Canada can be found in Nova Scotia. From there, from small beginnings, the Bible Society movement spread. As mentioned in Chapter 2, a Bible Society was active in Pictou by 1807, and an Auxiliary of the Parent Society was formed in Truro in 1810. The Bible Society has always been held in high regard by the churches and people of Nova Scotia. Today the Truro Branch of the Canadian Bible Society is the oldest continuous Branch in Canada.

Central Ontario District (formerly Upper Canada Bible Society) – 1818

For most of its long and distinguished history, this District was called the Upper Canada Bible Society. For many years it was the dominant Bible Society in Canada, responsible for practically all Bible Society work in Canada from the Quebec border to the Pacific. It was instrumental in the formation of other Auxiliaries. In 1960 it changed its name to Canadian Bible Society, Upper Canada District. With the formation of new Districts with offices in Hamilton, North Bay and Peterborough in 1962, its territory was considerably reduced. In 1981 the name was changed again, this time to Canadian Bible Society, Central Ontario District.

Bermuda Bible Society – 1818

Bermuda continues to be a British colony, but it is very much part of North America and has long had close links with Canada through the churches, the military and business. Bible Society work in Bermuda has always depended on volunteers. One of them, L. Erskine Campbell, was treasurer for 55 years. The Bible Society secretary for the British West Indies served Bermuda until 1968 when, at the Annual General Meeting, the decision was made to become part of the Canadian Bible Society.

New Brunswick District – 1819

As early as 1808, before a Bible Society was officially organized, a grant of Bibles was made to the town of Burton by the British and Foreign Bible Society. In 1819 the Bible Society was officially formed. In 1844, as noted in Chapter 2, a translation of Mark's Gospel by Native evangelist Paul Osunkhirine was published in the Micmac language. In 1863 Scriptures for the Maliseet people of New Brunswick were printed in Bath, England. In 1825 the Ladies' Bible Society of Miramichi provided Scriptures for the victims of the Great Miramichi fire that swept from the Miramichi River to Chaleur Bay, reducing 5,000 square miles (12,950 square kilometres) to ruin and killing 160 persons.

Montreal District – 1820

Seven years before an Auxiliary was officially formed in 1820, a report of the British and Foreign Bible Society states that a grant of 100 French Bibles, 400 French Testaments, 250 English Bibles and 250 English Testaments had been made to the Rev. Austin of Montreal. Colportage was the chief interest of the Montreal Auxiliary. The

Montreal Ladies' Bible Auxiliary was formed; in 1906 it was directing the work of seven Bible Women.

Prince Edward Island District – 1837

The Prince Edward Island Auxiliary was organized in Charlottetown December 13, 1837. One colporteur was employed and he travelled 10 to 12 miles (16 to 19 km) a day, often selling 50 Bibles and giving away a few to those too poor to buy one. The PEI District has a large number of volunteers and giving per capita to the Bible Society has always been among the highest in Canada.

Eastern Ontario (formerly Ottawa District) – 1855

Called Bytown in its early years, Ottawa was founded near the juncture of the Ottawa and Gatineau Rivers in 1827. In 1837 an agent of the British and Foreign Bible Society formed a Branch in Bytown, but it ceased to operate in 1843. The Branch was revived in 1846 and engaged in the usual activities of the Society. The first President of this Branch was the Hon. Thomas McKay, who helped construct the Rideau Canal, and who was the builder and first resident of Rideau Hall, where Canada's Governor General now lives. The Ottawa Auxiliary was founded in 1855. In 1869 the Perch Auxiliary linked with Ottawa and in 1876 a Bible Women's Mission employed a woman to visit throughout the District, engaging in Bible reading and colportage.

Western Ontario District – 1879

A Branch of the Upper Canada Bible Society served this area until a separate Auxiliary was established in 1879. The chief interest of this District, situated in one of the world's finest agricultural areas, has always been spreading the Scriptures across the globe. Local colportage was not stressed, and the District Secretary and others have engaged primarily in raising money to translate, publish and distribute the Word of God overseas. Not until 1960 did the Canadian Bible Society provide a Bible House for the Western Ontario District. Until that year the work of the District was administered from private homes and rented quarters.

Manitoba District – 1904

Until 1904 Bible Society work throughout the West was carried on by the Upper Canada Bible Society. In that year a separate District for Manitoba and Saskatchewan was formed, with headquarters in Winnipeg. For the next 18 years, this District comprised both Manitoba and Saskatchewan. The great Bible Society work in the early years was colportage, carried on with energy and imagination. As immigrants flooded the prairies they were provided with the Scriptures in their own languages. The work of the Bible Society in the West, in the early years of this century, is one of its great achievements.

British Columbia District – 1908

The Bible Society's first work in British Columbia was during the Gold Rush of 1858-1861, when the Upper Canada Bible Society sent Scriptures in several languages to miners panning gold on the Fraser and other rivers. The Upper Canada Bible Society maintained an interest in the area and in 1863 sent a Bible Society agent to organize Bible Society Branches. This was before the cross-Canada railway was built, so the agent travelled by way of Panama and San Francisco. In 1899 a Branch began in Vancouver and, as interest increased, the District was established in 1908. Colportage was a major aspect of the work: records show that in 1913 three women were employed as Bible Women, and nine men were employed as colporteurs.

South Alberta District – 1908

In 1908, three years after the formation of the Province of Alberta, it was decided at a meeting in Calgary to form an Auxiliary of the Canadian Bible Society to serve the whole province. Colportage, to provide Scriptures for the thousands of homesteaders, was the main function of the Auxiliary. Bad roads, great distances and uncertain weather created severe hardships for the colporteurs but they travelled continually and distributed thousands of Bibles in many languages.

For the first 22 years the Rev. H. D. Maar was the District Secretary and his work is still spoken of today. With the discovery of oil, Calgary became the oil capital of Canada and the work of the Bible Society changed but its importance has in no way diminished.

North Alberta District – 1918

In 1917 it was decided that the growth in population warranted forming a separate Auxiliary for the northern part of the Province, with headquarters in Edmonton; in 1918 the North Alberta Auxiliary was officially established. During the first year of its existence, this new Auxiliary distributed almost 4,000 Scriptures in 34 languages. For some years the Canadian Bible Society bookstore in Edmonton was the largest Christian bookstore in Canada.

Saskatchewan District (formerly North Saskatchewan and South Saskatchewan Districts) – 1922

The Bible Society Auxiliary, with headquarters in Winnipeg, served both Manitoba and Saskatchewan until 1922. That year saw the formation of the South Saskatchewan District with office in Regina and the North Saskatchewan District with office in Saskatoon. The Bible Society was very much a part of the life of the Saskatchewan pioneer communities and closely linked with the work of the churches. After 64 years, the two Districts joined in 1986 to form the Saskatchewan District with headquarters in Saskatoon.

South Central Ontario (formerly Hamilton District) – 1962

The Hamilton Branch of the Bible Society, founded in 1835, 11 years before the city of Hamilton, was the forerunner of the South Central Ontario District. From the founding of the Upper Canada Bible Society in 1818, Bible Society work was directed from Toronto. In 1962, when the boundaries of the Upper Canada District were changed, the Hamilton – now South Central Ontario District – was formed. In 1962 the Canadian Bible Society bought 196 Main Street East to serve as headquarters for the District, and this proved to be a good location for several years. It was sold in 1985. Now the District

Office and Bible Centre are in rented spaces in Hamilton and a Bible Centre has also been established in Kitchener.

Northern Ontario District – 1962

When the Upper Canada District was divided in 1962, the Northern Ontario District was officially incorporated. This District includes five major cities – North Bay, Sudbury, Sault Ste-Marie, Timmins and Thunder Bay. The area stretches from Quebec to Manitoba, and to James Bay and Hudson Bay in the north. The Bible Society property at 847 Main Street West, North Bay, which housed the District Secretary and the Bible Depot for many years, was sold in 1985. The Bible Centre is now located in a plaza in North Bay.

Bay of Quinte District – 1962

The headquarters of this District, formed when the size of the Upper Canada District was reduced, was first located in Peterborough and then moved to Belleville. However, it was found that the work could be done more economically and satisfactorily by enlarging the Eastern Ontario and Central Ontario Districts, so this District was dissolved in 1980.

North West District – 1969

This District only existed for 20 years, but it provided the Scriptures for a large area of northern Canada. The District Secretaries had to travel continually so no office was ever established in the North. In 1975 the Rev. Samuel B. Nafziger became District Secretary and with his wife, Martha, brought not only the Scriptures but a wider vision to pastors, congregations and communities throughout the region. When the Nafzigers retired in 1989, the District was discontinued and the area is now served from the Toronto headquarters of the Society.

A plaque honouring Mary Jones, who at the age of 16 walked 25 miles (40 km) from her village to Bala for a Welsh Bible. The difficulty she had in obtaining a Bible was an important factor in the founding of the British and Foreign Bible Society in 1804.

This statue in Bala, Wales perpetuates the memory of the Rev. Thomas Charles, to whom Mary Jones went in search of a Bible.

In 1914 the Canadian Bible Society began distributing Testaments and Bibles to members of the Canadian Armed Forces. The Society has continued this practice. Here Navy Chaplains present Service Testaments to sailors.

Photo: National Defence.

The Rev. Dr. E. J. B. Salter, who was Bible Society representative in Manitoba from 1904 until shortly before his death in 1942, is buried in the cemetery of Old Kildonan Presbyterian Church. A special plaque was placed in the cemetery to honour Dr. Salter. Seen with the plaque are the Rev. Donald Collins, Manitoba District Secretary, Mr. Ivan Bickell, President and the Rev. James Marnock, Minister of St. John's Presbyterian Church, Winnipeg.

Photo: John's Photo Studio, Winnipeg.

Bishop Eivind Berggrav (left) of Norway talks with the Rev. Dr. John R. Temple (centre) and another representative at the founding meeting of the United Bible Societies at Haywards Heath, England, May 9, 1946. Bishop Berggrav was Chairman of the Haywards Heath meeting and served as United Bible Societies President from 1949 to 1957, when Dr. Donald Coggan (later Archbishop of Canterbury) became President. Dr. Temple attended Haywards Heath as General Secretary of the British and Foreign Bible Society. He served as the first General Secretary of the United Bible Societies from June 1947 until his death in 1948.

Archbishop Donald Coggan and his wife Jean, with Dr. Kenneth McMillan and his wife Isobel at Lambeth Palace, official residence of the Archbishop of Canterbury. Dr. Coggan was President of the United Bible Societies for many years.

Photo: British and Foreign Bible Society.

Dr. Olivier Béguin
of Switzerland served
as General Secretary
of the United Bible
Societies from 1949
until his death in
April, 1972.

Mr. L. Erskine
Campbell,
Honorary Treasurer
of the
Bermuda Bible Society
for 53 years.

The Rev. Ulrich Fick, General Secretary of the United Bible Societies from 1972 to 1990. During the years when Dr. Fick was General Secretary, the office of the United Bible Societies was in Stuttgart, West Germany.

Photo: Bildtechnik/Kirschner.

The Rev. Dr. John D. Erickson, General Secretary of the United Bible Societies from 1990 to 1997. Prior to 1990 Dr. Erickson was a General Secretary of the American Bible Society. The office of the United Bible Societies is now at Reading, England.

Photo: UBS/Maurice Harvey.

The Salvation Army has long been an active supporter of the Bermuda Bible Society, which was organized in 1818. Major Albert Benjamin, MBE, President of the Bermuda Bible Society, and a fellow officer greet Dr. Kenneth G. McMillan and his wife Isobel, as they arrive for the Annual General Meeting in 1980.

The Bible Society float in the parade observing the bicentennial of Truro, Nova Scotia. The Truro Branch of the Canadian Bible Society celebrated its 150th anniversary in 1960.

The Rev. Dr. J. A. Raymond Tingley was British Columbia District Secretary from 1946 to 1974. During his 28 years of outstanding service, he became one of the best known Christian leaders in the province.

The Rev. Dr. Leonard W. Schnell and his wife, Dr. Nellie Schnell. Dr. Leonard Schnell retired in 1965 after serving as North Saskatchewan District Secretary for 28 years. He covered his large territory with enormous speed and energy.

The Rev. Emmanuel J. Heuer was North Alberta District Secretary from 1944 until 1957, when he was appointed visual education production secretary, a position he held until 1974. Ably assisted by his wife Mercy, he produced audio-visual materials and Bible Society films that were widely used in Canada and around the world.

Photo: Castor-Sigerist Studios, Edmonton.

The Rev. Dr. Allan J. Barrett, Newfoundland District Secretary from 1966 to 1973.

The Rev. Alex Cowan, Upper Canada District Secretary of the Canadian Bible Society, presenting a copy of the New Testament to the Hon. William G. Davis, Premier of Ontario from 1971 to 1985.

Photo: Beta Photos, London, Ontario.

In 1978, the Rev. Wallace Howlett, on the right, succeeded the Rev. J. C. Thompson as Western Ontario District Secretary.

The Rev. Andrew Brndjar was on CBS staff from 1962 to 1985, first as Western Ontario District Secretary and then in the Central Ontario District. He was not only one of the most productive District Secretaries, he also had the distinction of consistently operating with the lowest expenses of any District Secretary.

The Rev. Howard G. Zurbrigg was on CBS staff from 1969 to 1985, first as District Secretary in Hamilton, then in the National Office as Scripture production, supply and distribution secretary. His artistic talent enabled him to produce exceptionally attractive publications. While on Bible Society business in Haiti, he was robbed and severely injured. Unfortunately he received a transfusion of AIDS-infected blood, which led to his death on September 6, 1994.

The Organization and Character of the Branches

People are amazed to learn that in the mid-1900s there were Branches of the Bible Society in 3,500 Canadian communities. In 1967, Canada's Centennial Year, when many towns and villages wrote their local histories, they often found that the Branch of the Bible Society was the oldest continuous community organization.

The Bible Society Branch had a simple structure and purpose. The officers were the President, the Vice-Presidents, the Secretary, the Treasurer and the organizer of the annual canvass to raise funds for the translation, production and distribution of the Scriptures. The officers were usually lay people and it was customary to have all the ministers and pastors in the community serve as Vice-Presidents. In the early years the Roman Catholic priest seldom participated in the work, but following Vatican II (1962-1965), it became quite normal for the local priest to be a Vice-President. The District Secretary of the Bible Society made annual visits to as many Branches as possible, and was often present for their annual meeting.

Most of the Branches were small and the officers met only once or twice a year. However, some Branches were larger, met regularly and had a Bible Depot in the home of a volunteer. Some Branches kept detailed records, and have written histories of their activities. For example, branches in St. Thomas and Hamilton (Ontario), Moose Jaw and Regina (Saskatchewan), and several other communities have compiled such histories. Many of the officers served continuously for several years, and it was not uncommon for the Presidency to pass to a son or daughter and then to a grandson or granddaughter. The officers were deeply committed to the objectives of the Bible Society and they served with great pride.

On November 2, 1996, a special service in Dominion-Chalmers United Church, Ottawa, celebrated the anniversary of the Bible Society Branch in Bytown (now Ottawa). As noted above, it had been established 150 years earlier. The Rev. Dr. Kenneth G. McMillan was the special speaker at the anniversary service. The following account of that Branch's organization indicates the importance the founders placed on the event.

> At a Public Meeting held in the Free Church, Lower Bytown, on the evening of the second day of November, 1846, called by notices given

from the Pulpits; Mr. Donald Kennedy in the Chair. The meeting having been opened with prayer by the Rev. J. C. Davidson, the following resolutions were unanimously passed:

Moved by the Rev. J. F. Wilson, seconded by the Rev. James Musgrove:

First – That the Bible being the only revealed will of God to man, and that alone wherein is made known the way of Salvation through a Redeemer; this Meeting rejoices to know that efforts are being made to disseminate throughout the earth, this precious treasure.

Moved by the Rev. James Milne, seconded by the Rev. J. T. Byrne:

Second – That this Meeting cordially approves of the object and Constitution of the British and Foreign Bible Society, and gladly embraces the present opportunity for joining with that Institution, for the purpose of aiding in the grand work of giving the Bible to all mankind in their own tongues throughout the world.

Moved by the Rev. J. C. Davidson, seconded by Mr. Milne:

Third – That a Society be now formed in this town, in accordance with the preceding Resolutions, and that it be conducted in conformity with the following rules:

1. This Society shall be called the "BYTOWN BRANCH BIBLE SOCIETY," and shall embrace as the field of its operations the Townships of Napean and Gloucester.

2. This Society shall act on the principles of the British and Foreign Bible Society namely, that of circulating the Holy Scriptures without note or comment, and shall be a Branch of the Montreal Auxiliary Bible Society, which is in connection with the Parent Institution above named.

3. Every person paying annually the sum of five shillings currency, shall be a member of this Society: and those paying five pounds currency shall be members for life. The smallest contributions will be thankfully received.

4. This Society shall be under the management of a Committee, consisting of the President, Vice-President, Treasurer, Secretary, together with not less than six other Members. This Committee shall meet once

every month, or oftener, if judged necessary; five of whom shall constitute a quorum.

5. There shall be an Annual Meeting of the Members and Friends of this Society, to be held in the month of February, or at such other time as the Committee may especially appoint. At this Meeting a Report shall be read, showing the operations of the Society during the past year; the Accounts shall be presented, duly audited, and a new Committee shall be elected.

6. The Funds of this Society, arising from general contributions, and the sale of Bibles and Testaments, shall, after paying necessary expenses, be remitted to the Treasurer of the Montreal Bible Society, in payment of books received, and in aid of the Parent Institution.

7. This Society shall use diligent means in order to effect a general distribution of the Scriptures within the sphere of its exertions, by introducing a copy of the Word of God early into every family, and also as soon afterwards as possible, into the hands of every one able to read.

8. This Society shall endeavour to procure an Annual Subscription, more or less, from every individual possessed of the Scriptures, for the purpose of aiding in the general circulation of the Bible, throughout the whole world, in all languages.

9. No alterations shall be made in these Rules, nor any new ones formed, except at the Annual, or some other General Meeting of the Society duly called.

Part II

Relationships International and National

Chapter 6

Bringing the National Societies Together:
United Bible Societies

Chapter 7

Cooperating to Resolve an Issue:
Inclusion of the Deuterocanon, or Apocrypha

Chapter 8

Coming of Age:
The Canadian Bible Society and the Parent Society

CHAPTER 6

Bringing the National Societies Together: United Bible Societies

Your Word is a lamp that gives light wherever I walk. Your laws are fair and I have given my word to respect them.

Psalm 119.105

Bringing the various historic national Bible Societies together was achieved with considerable difficulty. While some key figures in the British and Foreign Bible Society promoted the formation of the United Bible Societies, there was also great resistance. James S. Roe, in his history of BFBS 1905-1954, says on page 437:

> No society had as much to forego as had the BFBS. . . . An international Bible Society in itself, it was under increasing pressure to restrict its outlook to that of a "National Bible Society," of listening where it had been accustomed to speak, and of concurring where it had been accustomed to instruct.

As early as 1919, the American Bible Society had proposed a "World Federation of National Bible Societies." The Rev. Dr. John Ritson of the British and Foreign Bible Society rejected this, saying BFBS was much more than a national Bible Society. This attitude is quite understandable, for the British Empire had spread around the globe and BFBS was active everywhere the Union Jack was flown. The Netherlands Bible Society, sensing tensions between BFBS and the American Bible Society, had proposed occasional conferences to enable the leading Bible Societies to consult with one another. But it took many years for anything concrete to develop.

Leaders often play a crucial role in initiating substantial changes and, when new men assumed office, the possibilities of greater cooperation became possible. In 1928 the Rev. Dr. Eric North, a Methodist with an impressive background of missionary and ecumenical work, became General Secretary of the American Bible Society. In 1929 the Rev. Dr. Arthur Wilkinson became a General Secretary of BFBS, and in 1931 the Rev. Dr. John Temple was appointed the second General Secretary in London. Soon a new relationship of national respect and trust developed between the two largest Bible Societies of the world.

In July 1932, at a historic conference in London – attended by representatives of the American Bible Society, the British and Foreign Bible Society and the National Bible Society of Scotland – it was agreed to eliminate competition in several mission areas of the world. ABS and BFBS agreed to establish a joint agency for all the West Indies and the Guianas. All three Bible Societies were working in China, and there had been tensions between them in that country, so it was decided to try to form the China Bible Society.

The Netherlands Bible Society had been serving the churches in many parts of the Dutch Empire, and was very much interested in the elimination of competition between Bible Societies. In July 1939, as part of its 125th anniversary celebration, it invited several Bible Societies to attend a conference in Woudschoten, Zeist in the Netherlands. The world was on the brink of World War II, the World Council of Churches was about to be born, and there was an acute awareness of the need for greater cooperation.

John R. Mott, the great American missionary statesman, eloquently and convincingly pleaded for joint action in the translation, production and distribution of the Word of God. The Rev. Dr. W. J. Platt, who later became General Secretary of BFBS and very well known across Canada, was in attendance at the Woudschoten conference. Hendrick Kraemer, the translation expert, was one representative of the Netherlands Bible Society. H. C. Rutgers, General Secretary of NBS, pressed for a "Council of Bible Societies" and this was grudgingly accepted. In less than two months, all the plans were put on hold as World War II broke out.

In 1940 the Ecumenical Commission for the Chaplaincy Service to Prisoners of War was founded, and Olivier Béguin became its

Secretary. One of the Commission's functions was to supply Bibles to the hundreds of thousands of prisoners taken during the war. The United States was not at war until 1941 and the American Bible Society, after consulting with the Rev. Dr. W. A. Visser 't Hooft, made Béguin an agent of the American Bible Society. At that time it was not known that this would be part of Béguin's preparation to become a future General Secretary of the United Bible Societies, once this organization was finally founded after the war. Neither was it known that the Rev. Dr. Ulrich Fick, who was to succeed Dr. Béguin as General Secretary, would, as a German prisoner of war, receive a Bible from the organization of which Béguin was the wartime Secretary. Truly, "God moves in a mysterious way His wonders to perform."

There are many stories of Bible Society workers' heroism in Europe during the war, for it became very difficult for them to carry on their activities. Enormous hardships were endured by Alexander Enhole, superintendent of the Bible House in Warsaw, and also by his wife. The work was carried on in spite of the war. At the end of the war, Enhole wrote in his report:

> In the early days of the German invasion, a bomb dropped near the Warsaw Bible Depot, blowing out the windows and doors. One little pane of glass only remained, on which were the words, "Heaven and earth shall pass away, but my word shall not pass away." Those words remained on that small fragment and, through the long months and years, people as they passed by took off their hats, signing the Cross and saying, "It is a miracle."

The Society's war workers showed an amazing spirit of dedication and selflessness. For example, the Rev. Carl Uhl, General Secretary of the Bible Society in Austria, was a prisoner of war. The day he was released, he sent a cable to BFBS: "Arrived home today, will start work tomorrow."

As the war drew to a close, Dr. North of ABS and the Rev. John Temple of BFBS began to make plans for postwar work. The first nongovernmental international conference after the cessation of hostilities was the historic gathering of May 6-8, 1946, at which the decision was made to form the United Bible Societies (UBS). It took place in the conference centre of the Diocese of Chichester, "Elfinsward," in Haywards Heath, England. The Right Reverend

G. K. A. Bell, Bishop of Chichester, was one who saw the need for all the world's Bible Societies to work together, so his Diocese was a most fitting location for the meeting. Bishop Bell was a driving force for reconciliation following World War II, and he had a passionate concern for making the Bible more widely available.

Some of the world's great Christian leaders participated in the founding of UBS. Dr. Hanns Lilje, later to become Bishop (Lutheran) of Hanover, and Bishop Eivind Berggrav, Bishop (Lutheran) of Oslo and Primate of Norway, were but two of them. Lilje had spent years in prison for his opposition to Hitler. Berggrav was also a prisoner for years and faced the threat of execution on several occasions. It was said he had such a powerful Christian influence that his captors were obliged to change his guards continually, to prevent them from being converted. A young man from the American Bible Society, Eugene Nida, who was destined to play a large role in Bible Society translation work, was appointed one of the conference secretaries at "Elfinsward."

Delegates were present from the American Bible Society, the British and Foreign Bible Society, the Netherlands Bible Society, the National Bible Society of Scotland, and from the Bible Societies in Czechoslovakia, Denmark, Finland, France, Germany, Norway, Poland, Sweden and Switzerland. It may seem ironic that the Bible Societies in Australia, Canada and New Zealand were not represented at the meeting, for they were Societies of significantly larger stature than some who were present. The reason was that the Bible Societies in Australia, Canada and New Zealand, along with all others in the British Commonwealth, were considered an integral part of the British and Foreign Bible Society. BFBS assumed it represented the interests of all Bible Societies in the Commonwealth. So, while Canada was not present at the founding meeting and is not recognized as a charter member of UBS, the Canadian Bible Society nevertheless considers itself a charter member.

The Rev. Dr. John Temple was appointed the first General Secretary of UBS, assuming the office in June 1947 while also retaining his position as General Secretary of BFBS. On November 30, 1948, Temple died suddenly in Hong Kong. UBS did not have far to look for his successor. They appointed Dr. Olivier Béguin, mentioned earlier in connection with the war work. A Swiss teacher and a man of ideas, he had a background of working with the Bible Societies. Dr. Béguin served until his premature death from cancer on April 1, 1972. For nearly a quarter of a century, he guided the world work of the United Bible Societies and, under his leadership, that work assumed ever increasing significance.

Béguin was succeeded by the Rev. Dr. Ulrich Fick who, as a German prisoner of war, had received a New Testament which transformed his whole outlook on life. By this time a German Lutheran pastor with missionary experience, Dr. Fick proved to be a most able successor. When he retired in 1990, the Rev. Dr. John D. Erickson, a Lutheran pastor and a key member of the American Bible Society's staff, was appointed as General Secretary of UBS. In a period of unprecedented change, Dr. Erickson guided UBS with Christian discernment. The Rev. Fergus MacDonald, General Secretary of the National Bible Society of Scotland, succeeded Dr. Erickson upon the latter's retirement in early 1998.

Over the years the United Bible Societies has developed and grown in importance. It divided the world into four regions and all national Bible Societies, while retaining their independence, also recognized their interdependence. A World Service Budget was established, to which national Bible Societies in the developed countries contributed, and from which Bible Societies in the developing countries drew support. At first the Canadian Bible Society's contributions were simply part of the British and Foreign Bible Society's donations, and there was no indication that Canada had provided some of the funds. Later CBS became the third largest contributor to the World Service Budget, gradually assuming standing in UBS. Dr. Kenneth McMillan, CBS General Secretary 1957-1983, played a significant role, serving in several capacities including Chair of the General Committee. Dr. Floyd Babcock, CBS General Secretary 1989-1997, represented the Canadian Bible Society on several UBS committees.

For many years, to enable the Bible Societies to work with churches of many traditions, the United Bible Societies published the Scriptures "without note or comment." In 1955 Bishop Eivind Berggrav, UBS President, promoted a change in this historic policy. The Bible Societies continued to support the concept that preaching and teaching people to read the Bible are the concerns of the churches; but UBS said that the Bible Societies should help the churches in this work.

Over the next few years, the United Bible Societies appointed Study Secretaries to study the use of the Bible and promote people's understanding of it through publications and by other means. A UBS office was opened in Geneva. The Study Secretary there became a link between the World Council of Churches, the International Missionary Council and UBS.

Canadian churches did not favour the Bible Societies entering the churches' role of interpreting and teaching the Scriptures. Nevertheless the Canadian Bible Society, as a member of UBS, went along with the idea to some extent, promoting the distribution of UBS publications among the churches. Bibles and Testaments with introductions and footnotes were published and distributed. The Canadian Bible Society also continued to publish its annual list of Daily Bible Readings. Its main concern, however, always remained the basic, vital mission of translating, publishing and distributing the Scriptures.

The CBS Annual Report for 1963, in a statement on "Promoting the Use of the Bible," gives the Society's position:

> Distribution of the Scriptures alone is not enough. They must be read and understood. The Bible Society is constantly seeking to provide the Scriptures in attractive formats, in legible print and with illustrations which will induce people to read them. Experience has shown that Gospels and Selections of Scripture are often read while whole Bibles, which people already possess, gather dust on shelves. The reading of a Gospel, time and again, awakens an interest in the reading of the Bible and leads people to open their Bibles and to read the Word of God.

Among Study Secretaries appointed by the United Bible Societies was G. H. Wolfensberger. From his office in Geneva, from 1962 to 1967, he produced a series of six booklets under the general title *The Bible in Our Time*. William Visser 't Hooft, General Secretary of the World Council of Churches, was a supporter of Wolfensberger's work and of the Bible Societies. During his term of office, a close relationship developed between WCC and UBS. With the retirement of Visser 't Hooft, however, the Bible no longer held a central place in the life of WCC. When Study Secretary Wolfenberger completed his service in 1967, he was not replaced. UBS continued to have an office in Geneva, but cooperation with WCC in the use and understanding of the Bible greatly diminished.

The history of the United Bible Societies has been chronicled in an inspiring and factual manner in *Taking the Word to the World* by Edwin H. Robertson. This 338-page book, by a gifted writer who has a long time association with the work, was published in 1996 for the 50th anniversary of UBS's founding. For an appreciation of the Bible Society movement, Robertson's book is essential reading. In his final chapter, he quotes Dr. Kenneth McMillan regarding confidence for the future of UBS:

> There is every reason to believe that the greatest days of the Bible Society movement are in the future, not the past. Rapidly changing world events which make traditional work difficult can be new opportunities for the Bible Society. Look what happened in China. In recent years its iron broom cleared the way for Christianity to spread as never before and for the Scriptures to be provided. The painful revolutionary changes made way for a miraculous explosion of Christianity in China and for an enormous demand for the Word of God. This will be true in country after country.
>
> Even in the post-Gutenberg age the printed page *will* communicate in a unique and distinctive way, *but* the Bible Societies will be involved also and increasingly in electronic publishing. . . . The greatest challenge the Bible Society movement faces is meeting the modern world with the same vision and faith with which the founders met their world.

Source: Robertson, Edwin H. Taking the Word to the World: 50 Years of the United Bible Societies. *Nashville, Tennessee: Nelson, 1996, page 306.*

CHAPTER 7

Cooperating to Resolve an Issue: Inclusion of the Deuterocanon, or Apocrypha

The Law, the Prophets and the later writers left us a wealth of valuable teachings, and we should praise Israel for the instruction and wisdom they provide. But it is not enough that those who read them should gain understanding for themselves. Anyone who values learning should be able to help others by what he himself says and writes. That is why my grandfather Jesus devoted himself to reading the Law, the Prophets and the other books of our ancestors. After he had mastered them, he was led to write a book of his own in order to share his wisdom and learning with others, so that anyone who shared his love for learning should have his book available as well, and be all the more able to live according to the Law.

Foreword to Sirach or Ecclesiasticus

When the King James Version of the Bible appeared in 1611, it contained the books known as the Deuterocanon, or the Apocrypha. These books have, however, proven to be a problem for Bible Societies over the years. They are a part of the Bible for Roman Catholic and Orthodox churches. Anglicans accept them as devotional reading, but not for doctrine. Most Protestant churches do not regard them as part of the Canon of Scripture. The 39 books of the Old Testament and the 27 books of the New Testament comprise the Protestant Bible.

The British and Foreign Bible Society, in its early years, published the Bible with the additional books included. From Scotland came strenuous objections to the Bible Society's publishing books that many considered a source of heresy. In 1825 the Scottish Auxiliaries severed their connection with BFBS. Feelings were so strong that BFBS adopted a policy of publishing only the 39 books of the Old Testament and the 27 books of the New. The policy of the British and Foreign Bible Society also applied to Bible Society work in Canada. Though the position was taken largely to satisfy Scotland, the Scottish churches proceeded to establish their own Bible Society, the National Bible Society of Scotland, in 1861.

By not publishing the Deuterocanonical books, the British and Foreign Bible Society limited its effectiveness, since the Roman Catholic and Orthodox churches did not want what they regarded as an incomplete Bible. Thus, for many years, BFBS did not provide the Old and New Testaments for the churches which had most of the world's Christians. The translation, publication and distribution of the Deuterocanonical books continued to be a contentious issue. Many would not support the Bible Society if it published these books, and others would not support the Bible Society because it did not publish them.

At Vatican II (1962-1965) the Roman Catholic Church officially declared that the Scriptures should be made available to all people. This confronted all members of the United Bible Societies with the need to change their policies on the Deuterocanonical books. The General Committee of the United Bible Societies, meeting in Edinburgh in September 1969, adopted a statement which became the policy of the Canadian Bible Society and all Bible Societies. The main points of this statement are as follows.

> 1. When the Authorized Version of the English Bible was published in 1611, all copies contained the Apocrypha. The same is true of most of the early translations such as Luther and Valera. Subsequently, however, editions without the Apocrypha appeared from time to time. From its formation in 1804 down to about 1826, the British and Foreign Bible Society's circulation of Scriptures included editions with the Apocrypha: but in view of the controversy at that time, regulations were adopted excluding such circulation. Most, but by no means all, Bible Societies have since operated under a similar limitation until recent years.
>
> 2. In June 1964 a world conference of church leaders and Bible Society representatives, meeting at Driebergen in Holland, urged that

the Bible Societies should undertake their task of worldwide circulation of the Scriptures with renewed vigour, and recommended that "where the churches desire and specifically request it, the Bible Societies should consider the translation and publication of the books commonly called the Apocrypha."

3. It should be noted that the churches desiring to have the Apocrypha are not only (as sometimes supposed) the Orthodox and Roman Catholic; but also (for example) Anglicans and Lutherans, who value the Apocrypha as supplementary to the Old and New Testaments, though they do not regard its books as part of the Canon.

4. It needs to be stressed that each member Society remains an autonomous body within the UBS family. Subject, therefore, to the basic aims and conditions of the partnership, each Bible Society makes its own decisions as to the texts which it will or will not publish or distribute. This freedom applies, of course, in relation to editions with the Apocrypha.

5. It continues to be the normal policy and practice of the Bible Societies as a whole to publish the Holy Scriptures without the Apocrypha. When editions with the Apocrypha are published, this is usually subject to the following arrangements.

(a) That there should be a specific request from the responsible body of the church community desiring such an edition;

(b) That the Deuterocanonical books should be included as a separate section, between the Old and New Testaments;

(c) That the full additional cost of providing this separate section should be carried by the requesting church or in some separate way, so that in any case there is no subsidy for the Apocrypha from UBS funds.

6. The Committee feels it desirable that, when Bible Society editions of the Bible include the Apocrypha, it should be preceded by a clear explanatory note which indicates the difference of value attributed to these books by the different churches.

7. A categorical assurance can be given that no group which has *not* requested an Apocrypha edition will receive one, and that no one will be involved in translation or distribution of the Apocrypha against his wish or conscience.

CHAPTER 8

Coming of Age: The Canadian Bible Society and the Parent Society

The old order changeth, yielding place to new,
And God fulfils Himself in many ways.
Alfred Lord Tennyson, *The Passing of Arthur*

Don't let anyone look down on you because you are young, but set an example for the believers in speech, in life, in love, in faith and in purity.

1 Timothy 4.12

In 1905, when the federation of Bible Societies and Auxiliaries in Canada took place, the General Secretary of the newly formed Canadian Bible Society, Auxiliary to the British and Foreign Bible Society, was appointed by the British and Foreign Bible Society as their personal representative on the General Board in Canada. At the beginning of the century, there were British colonies throughout the world, with British Governors appointed by Britain, and the Bible Society was simply following the pattern of the Empire. The British and Foreign Bible Society followed the Empire as it expanded over one-third of the globe, and adopted its administration policies.

The Bible Society benefited from the leadership of the Parent Society in the same way the colonies did from direction given by

Whitehall in London. Sound policies were put in place, and strong national Bible Societies emerged.

The colonial pattern may have been followed too thoroughly and for too long, however. For example, when Mary C. Urquhart joined the staff of the British and Foreign Bible Society in Canada in 1950, she was shocked by the extent of the colonialism that still prevailed at that late date. The London office still had to approve practically every detail of the work including appointment of District Secretaries and other staff, salaries, retirements, pensions and property purchase. All property acquired was held by the Parent Society. Only Bibles and Testaments produced by the British and Foreign Bible Society were to be sold in Canadian Bible depots, and the "without note or comment" policy had to be followed.

The General Secretary of the Canadian Bible Society, Auxiliary to the British and Foreign Bible Society, was appointed by London, paid by London, participated in the British pension plan, lived in a residence owned and maintained by London, and was responsible for making sure all funds for world work were sent to the British and Foreign Bible Society for them to allocate. It was a system that worked well for some years. The Rev. R. E. Welch, the Rev. W. B. Cooper, the Rev. Dr. J. B. M. Armour and the Rev. W. H. Hudspeth – the first four General Secretaries – were all Britishers. BFBS minutes indicate that London was aware of Canada's desire to have a Canadian appointed as General Secretary, but this did not happen until 1952, when the Rev. A. H. O'Neil was appointed to fill that office.

By the time the Rev. Dr. Kenneth McMillan became General Secretary in 1957, there was a growing feeling in the Canadian Bible Society that it needed a stronger Canadian identity and more independence. Dr. McMillan found the name British and Foreign Bible Society to be out of step with this feeling and the prevailing spirit of the nation. Even the Church of England in Canada had changed its name to the Anglican Church of Canada. An even greater problem was the multiplicity of names by which the Society was known across Canada. Did the Nova Scotia Bible Society, for example, have any relationship with the Upper Canada Bible Society? In fact, both were part of the National Society but their names in no way indicated that. This was also true with regard to the Montreal Bible Society, the

Western Ontario Bible Society, the Ottawa Bible Society and others. National advertising was impossible with such a multiplicity of names.

One would think the need for a name which suited the Canadian nation and which was the same from coast to coast would have been readily agreed to. Change is never easy, however, and there was a long struggle and many debates before the name was changed.

The Rev. Dr. W. J. Platt, one of BFBS's General Secretaries, had a close and warm relationship with the Bible Society all across Canada. He was responsible for the Dominions (Canada, Australia, New Zealand and South Africa). The minutes of the April 24, 1958 meeting of the BFBS committee indicate his understanding and conciliatory spirit. They quote him as follows.

> (There is a) rising tide of nationhood which Canada experiences along with other members of the British Commonwealth. . . . Our friends in Canada will accept cooperation with and loyalty to London so long as these are sought with tact and we can supply their requirements.

The July 7, 1958 minutes of the London committee dealt with the change of name of the Society in Canada as follows.

> In view of the trend of Bible Society affairs in Canada as reported by Dr. Platt following his visit to the Dominions, and in response to a formal request from the Rev. Dr. Kenneth G. McMillan on behalf of the 16 local Auxiliaries in Canada, the subcommittee agreed that the Society's lawyers should be consulted concerning the proposed change of name from "British and Foreign Bible Society in Canada" to "Canadian Bible Society, Auxiliary to the British and Foreign Bible Society."

As is often the case, the debates that took place on this matter are not reflected in any of the minutes. The West and Quebec were quite pleased with the change, but United Empire Loyalist Ontario and New Brunswick were opposed. To downgrade the name of the great British and Foreign Bible Society seemed preposterous. The idea was looked upon by some as a loosening of the ties of Empire. The objective was not only to change the name of the National Society, but to have each of the Auxiliaries also change its name to Canadian Bible Society. Many of these Auxiliaries were incorporated by provincial legislatures, and the alteration required extensive legal work. After long debate, however, all Auxiliaries agreed and there was one name from coast to coast.

Many wanted to have the name just "Canadian Bible Society" so it would conform to other members of the United Bible Societies such as the American Bible Society, the Netherlands Bible Society and the Norwegian Bible Society. But this was too much for some to accept so, as a compromise, "Auxiliary of the British and Foreign Bible Society" was added.

The Society's solicitor, H. Donald Langdon, QC, and Dr. McMillan went to Ottawa in 1960 to appear before a committee of the Senate to support amendments to the Act of Incorporation regarding the change of name. A Private Member's Bill approving this change, among others, had been passed by Parliament but, before it became law, Senate approval was required. Senators came from every province of Canada, and some held the same convictions about ties with the "Motherland" as had been expressed within the Bible Society. The Senators were assured, however, that CBS would continue to be a partner with the British and Foreign Bible Society, and the new name eventually became law that same year, 1960. It was a struggle that extended over several years, but the change was vital for the welfare of the Canadian Bible Society.

(For a complete list of the Canadian Bible Society's name changes since its inception, please see Chapter 3.)

When the sympathetic Dr. Platt retired, the new leadership in London did not understand as well as he had that the days of Empire were gone, and that the United Bible Societies was the way of the future. The dominant role of the British and Foreign Bible Society was threatened when several Bible Societies wanted to provide services in countries where only the British were at work. The American Bible Society was a vigorous and energetic enterprise which offered new translations of the Scriptures and had the resources to provide Bibles where they were in short supply. As several members of the United Bible Societies enlarged their spheres of influence, BFBS felt increasingly threatened. They felt that the Bible Society in Canada was too friendly with the American Bible Society and that there was a danger of Canada, as a member of the United Bible Societies, exercising too dominant a role in comparison with its Parent.

The Rev. Wilfred Bradnock, translations secretary of the British and Foreign Bible Society, found it difficult to adjust to the new translation approach of Dr. Eugene A. Nida of the American Bible Society. Nida, a world-renowned linguist, pioneered the use of dynamic equivalence in translation, and rapidly became a world leader. Mr. Bradnock visited the Bible Society Districts in Nova Scotia, New Brunswick, Montreal, Quebec and Ontario, and then the American Bible Society in New York in the winter of 1961. Upon his return to London, eager to maintain allegiance to the Parent Society and its approach, Bradnock suggested that Canada was no longer loyal to BFBS. He reported that CBS General Secretary, Dr. McMillan, was too friendly with the American Bible Society, and should be removed from office. Bradnock assured the British and Foreign Bible Society that, if he were appointed General Secretary in Canada, he would restore Canada to its proper place in BFBS. On the basis of Bradnock's report, the British and Foreign Bible Society decided to send a strong delegation to Canada to implement changes.

On a June day in 1961, three officials of the British and Foreign Bible Society arrived in Halifax. Two of them, the Rev. John Watson and the Rev. Dr. Norman Cockburn, were the General Secretaries of BFBS. The third was Professor George Kilpatrick, a New Testament professor at Oxford University, who was a member of the BFBS Board in London and a friend of the Rev. Wilfred Bradnock. The three men asked to meet with the Board of the Nova Scotia Bible Society Auxiliary. There they presented arguments for the removal of Dr. McMillan from the position of General Secretary of the Canadian Bible Society, Auxiliary of the British and Foreign Bible Society. They accused him of disloyalty to London and of being too friendly with the American Bible Society. The Rev. M. C. P. Macintosh, District Secretary of the Bible Society in Nova Scotia, telephoned Dr. McMillan to alert him of the visit of the officials from England and of their mission.

The British delegation then travelled to Saint John, New Brunswick, to meet with the Bible Society there. From Saint John they went to Montreal to continue their mission. The Rev. Dr. Stuart Johnston, District Secretary of the Bible Society in Montreal, flew to Toronto to warn Dr. McMillan about what the officials from the UK planned to do. They planned to visit all the Bible Societies across

Canada in order to obtain support for the removal of Dr. McMillan from the office of General Secretary.

Though the three visitors from England advised Dr. McMillan that they were coming to Toronto, they did not divulge to him the purpose of their visit. They stated that they did not need his assistance in any way, and that they had arranged their own accommodation in Toronto – at Trinity College, University of Toronto. On the day the trio arrived in Toronto, Dr. McMillan was the theme speaker at a London, Ontario missionary conference under the auspices of the Department of Overseas Missions of the Canadian Council of Churches. This was an appointment he could not cancel. In her husband's absence, Mrs. McMillan met Cockburn, Watson and Kilpatrick at the airport and took them to the McMillan home for tea. She then drove them to Trinity College.

The British officials told Mrs. McMillan that they did not need to see Dr. McMillan. Instead they began contacting members of the Bible Society's Board. Some Board members informed them they should see Dr. McMillan, but they refused to do so. The Sub-Executive Committee of the General Board made arrangements to meet the delegation from England, and on June 22 a dinner meeting was held at the University Club on University Avenue, Toronto. Dr. McMillan was present for the dinner, but then left as the meeting continued.

The three visitors each spoke at length in a guarded manner about their visit to Canada, avoiding the real reason why they had come. As the evening progressed, it became obvious that the BFBS men had vastly underrated the members of the Sub-Executive. The President of that Sub-Executive was the Hon. Mr. Justice Dalton C. Wells. One Vice-President at that meeting was the Very Rev. Dr. J. S. Thomson, former moderator of the United Church of Canada and at that time Dean of the Faculty of Divinity at McGill University. The other Vice-President was the Very Rev. Dr. John McNab, former moderator of the Presbyterian Church in Canada and at that time editor of *The Presbyterian Record*. The Honorary General Treasurer was Dr. Reginald H. Soward, a prominent Toronto lawyer and chancellor of the General Synod of the Anglican Church of Canada. All in attendance that evening were prominent in fields of business, and were people of stature.

It was a long evening, and finally the members of the Sub-Executive insisted on knowing the purpose for which Cockburn, Watson and Kilpatrick had come to Canada. The men from the UK eventually stated that, according to the Constitution, CBS General Secretary Dr. Kenneth McMillan had been appointed by the British and Foreign Bible Society and could be removed by them. Mr. Justice Wells replied, "Then we'll change the Constitution." The men from England were severely chastised, told to see Dr. McMillan, and to pack their bags and go home. They did as they were told.

This event is reported in detail since it was a decisive moment in the life of the Bible Society in Canada. The Society immediately began to amend the Constitution and the Act of Incorporation in several ways. One was to permit the election of outstanding Canadians who were not representatives of the Districts as officers of the Society. (From 1960 the Auxiliaries were called "Districts.") Another change was the removal of restrictions on the right to hold property. A third was to have the appointment of the General Secretary made by the Canadian General Board rather than by London. Through such changes the Canadian Bible Society became an equal partner with the British and Foreign Bible Society and an active member of the world fellowship of Bible Societies – the United Bible Societies. CBS had come of age.

CHAPTER 9

The Canadian Bible Society, The Upper Canada Bible Society and the Constitution

Two objects cannot occupy the same space at the same time.
A Principle of Physics

The following inscription, set up by a Roman centurion, was found in the Libyan desert: *I, serving as a captain of a legion of Rome in the Libyan desert, have learned and pondered this thought: IN LIFE THERE ARE TWO PURSUITS, LOVE AND POWER, AND NO MAN CAN HAVE BOTH.*

The Upper Canada Bible Society, founded in 1818, played a distinguished role in distributing Scriptures in Canada and in supporting the worldwide work of the British and Foreign Bible Society. For many decades the Upper Canada Bible Society was responsible for all Bible Society work in Canada west of Montreal, except for the limited work of the Ottawa Bible Society and the Western Ontario Bible Society. It carried out extensive and effective colportage and established Bible Depots, not only in Ontario but in the West.

In many ways the Upper Canada Bible Society was already a national society when the Canadian Bible Society, Auxiliary to the British and Foreign Bible Society, was founded in 1905. From that date the Upper Canada Bible Society felt its influence and power to be threatened by the new national organization. This feeling was understandable. In hindsight it appears that, had a way been found for the Upper Canada Bible Society to evolve into the National Society for the whole of Canada, many years of tension would have been avoided.

The first Constitution of the National Society was designed to assure the Auxiliaries that the National Office had little authority. Each Auxiliary, or Bible Society, that became part of the National Society jealously guarded all Bible Society work in its territory, and the National Society played an ill-defined role. With the exception of the Bible Society properties in Montreal, Ottawa and Toronto, all were held in the name of the Parent Society in London. At the beginning the National Society's ability to hold property was limited to the insignificant amount of $25,000. It also had no authority to solicit financial support.

Furthermore the Board of the National Society was composed of people appointed by the 13 Auxiliaries – the Bible Societies that made up the new confederation. The number of representatives each Auxiliary could appoint to the National Board was determined by the number of Branches each constituent part had. This meant that the Upper Canada Bible Society, by far the largest Auxiliary, had many more representatives than any other. Also, for reasons of geography and travel, most officers and committee members of the National Board consisted of representatives of the Upper Canada Bible Society. Financially the Upper Canada Bible Society towered over all the others comprising the National Society, and this further served to provide it with power and influence.

In 1928 the British and Foreign Bible Society appointed the Rev. Dr. J. B. M. Armour as General Secretary of the Canadian Bible Society, Auxiliary to the British and Foreign Bible Society, and as BFBS representative on the General Board. Dr. Armour's position, however, was severely limited by the power and influence of the Upper Canada Bible Society. It was with great difficulty that he succeeded in having the National Society's Constitution changed so that the choice of officers and committee members would not be limited to individuals the Auxiliaries sent to be members of the General Board. This change would make it possible for outstanding lay people and church leaders to serve, even if they were not representatives of Auxiliaries. It also meant that the officers and committee members would no longer be largely representatives of the Upper Canada Bible Society.

The Upper Canada Bible Society challenged the legality of this change. It had eminent lawyers on its Board, and they argued that the Act of Incorporation did not permit anyone to be an officer or committee member who was not a representative of an Auxiliary. The Upper Canada Bible Society was indeed correct in this claim. The Constitution and Act of Incorporation were thus brought into conflict.

The British and Foreign Bible Society was well aware of the long-standing conflict between the Upper Canada Bible Society and the National Society. Dr. William J. Platt of BFBS, mentioned in Chapter 8 of this book, was a friend and supporter of the Canadian Bible Society, and he provided constant guidance and help. In 1958, as discussed in Chapter 8, Dr. Platt supported Canadian General Secretary Dr. Kenneth McMillan in his efforts to change the National Society's name from "British and Foreign Bible Society in Canada" to "Canadian Bible Society."

Upper Canada Bible Society representatives, however, strenuously opposed this proposed change, as well as any other constitutional changes. Their opposition was so vehement that Dr. McMillan delayed action. The London Committee's minutes of November 12, 1958 state that:

> The Sub-Committee were informed that, since the Upper Canada Bible Society opposes the idea of changing the Constitution, the Advisory and Finance Committee in Toronto has decided to limit action at this juncture to changing the Act of Incorporation for the Society's work in Canada. The effect of this decision is to suspend constitutional changes until the legal ambiguities of the present Act have been made good.

The name change finally did occur in 1960. Opposition continued, however, particularly from the Upper Canada Bible Society. As a compromise, and to achieve limited success, the name became "Canadian Bible Society, Auxiliary of the British and Foreign Bible Society." The March 16, 1960 minutes of the BFBS Committee include this reference to Canada:

> Dr. Platt informed the Sub-Committee that Dr. Kenneth McMillan had been successful in easing some of the tensions which had existed for the past 50 years between the Upper Canada Bible Society in Toronto and the National Office of the British and Foreign Bible Society in Canada.

In 1979 Dr. McMillan was able to have the Act of Incorporation amended by a Private Member's Bill in the Parliament of Canada. With the Act's amendment, the Constitution was finally no longer in conflict with the Act of Incorporation – as it had been ever since the Upper Canada Bible Society's challenge to Dr. Armour's constitutional changes some 40 years earlier. The 1979 amendment also removed all limitations on the amount of property the National Society could hold. When the British and Foreign Bible Society handed over to the National Society all property it held in Canada, including the residence of the General Secretary (69 St. Leonard's Avenue), the National Society gained more jurisdiction in the Districts (called Auxiliaries until 1960).

From a position of relative weakness in 1905, the Canadian Bible Society had, by 1979, made gains in clarifying its role and establishing its influence as a true National Society. Some of these gains, as well as CBS's changing relationship with the Upper Canada Bible Society, are reflected in the following listing of head office locations from 1905 to the present.

Locations of the Canadian Bible Society Head Office

In 1905, when the National Society was founded, the National Office was located in a tiny room in property belonging to the Upper Canada Bible Society, at 102 Yonge Street, Toronto.

In 1910, when the Upper Canada Bible Society moved to its fine new building at 14 College Street, Toronto, the National Office rented a small office at this new address.

In 1945, with the purchase of a residence at 122 Bloor Street West, Toronto, the National Office was able to have an office separate from the Upper Canada Bible Society. The building was purchased for $35,000 with funds raised in Canada, and was owned by the British and Foreign Bible Society.

In 1959, 122 Bloor Street West was sold for $117,300, and the National Office moved to a residence it purchased for $45,000, at 32 Jackes Avenue, Toronto.

In 1962, 1835 Yonge Street, Toronto was purchased for $250,000.

In 1963, 32 Jackes Avenue was sold for $65,000.

In January 1963, the Upper Canada District of the Canadian Bible Society moved from 14 College Street to the National Society's new property at 1835 Yonge Street. This was an historic move. Until 1945 the National Office had been located in property owned by the Upper Canada Bible Society, but now the Upper Canada District occupied space owned by the National Society.

On January 9, 1964, the National Office moved from 32 Jackes Avenue to 1835 Yonge Street, Toronto. The National Office, the Central Stock Depot for all of Canada, and the Upper Canada District office were now in the same building. The Yonge Street property, with fine display windows, was ideal for a Bible Depot, and it also had a large meeting room which was used by the Society and other organizations.

On June 12, 1980, 1835 Yonge Street was sold for $1,150,000 cash.

In 1980 the National Society purchased 10 Carnforth Road, Toronto, for $1,200,000. The Carnforth Road property provided office space for the National Society, office space for the Upper Canada District, room for a Bible depot, and 43,000 square feet (3,995 square metres) of warehouse for the Central Stock Depot. It also provided space for tenants who paid rent sufficient to cover half the cost of taxes and utilities. Located on over two acres (0.8 ha), it provided parking for 72 cars. This property, purchased in 1980, continues to meet the needs of the Society.

The political unity of Canada is continually in jeopardy, threatened by separatist sentiments in Quebec, the West and elsewhere. Unfortunately the same kinds of centrifugal forces are strong in the Canadian Bible Society, in spite of the enormous gains the Society has made. For example, having all District Secretaries appointed and paid by the National Society, as specified by the Constitution, gave the

National Society a role in the life of the Districts. However, if a District Secretary chose not to cooperate with the National Society, that Secretary often found it easy to persuade the District Board to adopt policies not in keeping with those of the National Society.

For many years Bible Society Auxiliaries in Canada felt a much greater loyalty to London than to Toronto. The only real factor promoting the unity of the Canadian Bible Society was the District Secretaries' dedication to national policies and their cooperation with the National Office. If a District Secretary chose to act independently, there was little the National Office could do to prevent it. The District Secretaries were the key people on the staff of the Canadian Bible Society. When the General Board determined policy, the input of the District Secretaries was essential. When policy had been determined, everyone was required to put aside his or her own personal preferences and the desire to act independently, and give full support to the General Secretary and the National Office. Only then could the Canadian Bible Society function effectively under its Constitution.

A positive aspect of the Constitution was that it required all staff and Board members to exhibit the Spirit of Christ and behave as Christians should. It is a high tribute to the members of the General Board, to the staff of National Office and to the District Secretaries that the lack of control and accountability provided by the Constitution did not prevent the Society from being an important provider of God's Word for Canada and the world.

Recently centrifugal forces have become even stronger, and major changes have occurred in the Society's Constitution. At a meeting of the General Board on May 28 and 29, 1997, a new structure was adopted. It is designed to give the Districts power and authority to direct their own affairs without interference from a National Society. The National Society is now permitted to do only those things which the Districts decide they cannot do by themselves. The National Office is now called the National Support Office and the General Secretary is called the National Director. The National Support Office exists to support the Districts, to do on a National basis those things District offices cannot do well on their own and to set overall policy. Districts operate much like the branches of a National organization, but do not exist to execute National Support Office directives. The National Support Office does not play an authoritarian role in relation to the Districts, but rather a coordinating and integrating role. The relationship is one of collaboration and consultation, not power and control.

The General Board has been replaced by a Board of Governors consisting of one representative from each of the 16 Districts. It will meet five times a year. There is no longer an Executive Committee to function between meetings of the Board of Directors, and the Personnel and By-Laws Committees have been eliminated. The Finance and Audit Committees are now one committee, and a Nominating and Governance Committee has been established. District Secretaries are now called District Directors.

Part III

Continuing the Good Work

Chapter 10
New International Responsibilities

Chapter 11
Scripture Translation:
An Ongoing Challenge

Chapter 12
Scripture Production and Distribution

Chapter 13
French Canada,
the Roman Catholic Church
and the Bible Society

Chapter 14
The North West District

CHAPTER 10

New International Responsibilities

In a world in which the very foundations are being shaken, in which all faith, all ideologies are called in question, in which it is loudly proclaimed that God is dead and that man's existence has no meaning – the one and only important theme is surely to proclaim the Gospel of the loving God and to call men to that repentance which leads to newness of life.... And does that not imply that direct personal evangelism comes first and that the issues of life in society are secondary? Can a new and better world be built with men who have no faith, no hope?

Dr. W. A. Visser 't Hooft,
for many years General Secretary of
the World Council of Churches

Over the years previous to the 1960s, the Bible Society in Canada had from time to time enjoyed some involvement with areas of the world administered by the British and Foreign Bible Society. For example, the Manitoba and Saskatchewan Bible Society had made a special appeal for $18,000 to pay for a Bible House in Lagos, Nigeria. This money was sent to the Parent Society for them to forward to Nigeria. Western Canada had a special interest in Nigeria, as the Rev. A. W. Banfield had translated the Scriptures into the Nupe language. Banfield, for many years secretary of the Bible Society in West Africa, had eloquently promoted western Canadians' involvement in foreign missions.

There are other isolated examples such as this. However, it was not until the 1960s that the Canadian Society was able to have sustained direct involvement with work beyond its borders. This was over a century and a half after Bible Society work began in Canada.

In 1962 the Canadian Bible Society requested that the West Indies and Bermuda be administered by Canada. The request appears in the London minutes of September 12:

> That in our work of cooperation with the British and Foreign Bible Society and in regard to our financial contributions, we request the Parent Society to commit areas of work to the Canadian Bible Society with particular reference to the West Indies and other designated areas, in which areas the Canadian Bible Society would take special responsibility for the appointment of Secretaries, the payment of their salaries, and the direction and supervision of the work there, always having close consultation with the Parent Society.

The minutes further state:

> Mr. Watson recalled that the joint agreement concluded at Buck Hill Falls (Pennsylvania, April 1962) between the executive officers of the American Bible Society and the BFBS envisaged that CBS be invited to be the administering Joint Agency partner in Cuba, and he had no doubt that this would be accepted. . . . Mr. Watson explained that there was a certain urgency in the case of Cuba because the present Secretary is due to retire and the ABS is encountering difficulty in getting Scripture supplies into Cuba.

Eventually the Canadian Bible Society was permitted to administer the work in the West Indies and Bermuda. The Secretary for the West Indies and Bermuda lived in Kingston, Jamaica, where BFBS provided him with a residence. The office was in a congested area of Kingston, where there was little space for keeping a supply of Scriptures for the region. One of the first changes the Canadian Bible Society initiated was the purchase of property away from downtown Kingston, at Half Way Tree, and the erection of a building to provide a warehouse for Scriptures, an office for the Bible Society, and also space to rent to other organizations. The rent paid by the tenants provided sufficient income to cover some of the cost of operating the region. One of the Canadian Bible Society's projects for 1964 was raising the $60,000 for the new property in Jamaica.

Later, recognizing the desirability of Bible Society work in the West Indies being administered by the West Indies, and not by Canada, the Canadian Bible Society initiated establishing the Bible Society of the West Indies as an autonomous Bible Society within the United Bible Societies. The new Bible House in Jamaica was considered adequate to serve the wider region. (Indeed it has proved to serve the Society well for over three decades.)

Jamaica, Barbados, Trinidad, Tobago and other former British and French colonies of the region were all included in the new Bible Society of the West Indies. The Society had its own board of directors and its own staff. However, local and ethnic concerns were strong. The widely scattered islands were concerned about maintaining their own identities. As a result the region was soon divided into separate societies, for the eastern and western Caribbean.

Contrary to popular opinion, Bermuda never considered itself part of the West Indies. It has quite a different history and culture. It has had a long and close relationship with Canada. For example, the Canadian navy maintained a base there for several decades. Canadian shipping companies served Bermuda. Several church congregations in Bermuda belong to a Presbytery of the United Church of Canada. The Salvation Army in Canada and Bermuda are under the same Commissioner. The Presbyterian Church in Canada has a congregation in Hamilton, Bermuda. In February 1968 Mrs. Isobel McMillan, wife of the Canadian General Secretary, was the speaker at the Annual General Meeting of the Bermuda Bible Society. At that meeting the decision was made that Bermuda would become part of the Canadian Bible Society. This has proven to be a happy and successful arrangement.

The story of CBS involvement in Cuba is quite a different one. For many years the economy and much of the life of Cuba was dominated by the United States. Cuban congregations of several of the large American denominations belonged to the Conferences or Synods of the American churches. The Bible Society in Cuba was closely linked with the American Bible Society and under its jurisdiction.

In 1956 Che Guevara and Fidel Castro arrived in Cuba and waged a three-year war against the corrupt dictatorship of Fulgencio Batista. In 1958 Batista was overthrown and Fidel Castro began establishing a Communist regime on the island.

As a result the United States broke off diplomatic relations with Cuba in 1961. Canada, however, did not; the Canadian Embassy continued to function in Havana. The American missionaries had to return home, and most of the Roman Catholic priests were deported to Spain. When the American Bible Society could no longer administer the work in Cuba or provide the Scriptures required, the Canadian Bible Society was asked to assume responsibility for Cuba.

When the General Secretary of the Cuban Bible Society fled to the United States, Dr. A. Perdomo, a Cuban who was a Baptist pastor, became General Secretary. He found it increasingly difficult to obtain import licences for Bibles, even though they were provided free. In 1962 a shipment of Bibles was shredded by the Cuban government. Steps had to be taken to try to get Bibles to Cuba. Since Canada continued to enjoy diplomatic relations with Cuba, it was thought that the CBS General Secretary might be able to persuade the Cuban government to be more accommodating. It was possible to airlift Bibles into Cuba through Mexico but, like all Communist regimes, the Castro government was very hostile to the Bible. With many churches closed and Cuban jails full of people suspected of being against Communism, providing Bibles became one of the chief ways of supporting the persecuted Christians and the largely leaderless churches.

Recognizing the danger of a visit to Cuba, CBS General Secretary Dr. McMillan consulted with Mr. A. J. Pick, head of Latin American Affairs in the Canadian government's Department of External Affairs. Since Canada and Cuba still continued to enjoy good relations, the Department of External Affairs advised Dr. McMillan that it was possible for him to visit Cuba, but that such a visit would not be without risks.

The Canadian Department of External Affairs advised the Canadian Embassy in Havana that Dr. McMillan was travelling to Cuba by way of Mexico, and that he would arrive December 2, 1963. Dr. Perdomo made an appointment for Dr. McMillan to meet with Dr. Jose Delipe Carnead, head of the Department of Religious Affairs in the Cuban government. Perdomo was at the airport to meet McMillan. He did not see him, however, for immediately upon arrival McMillan was placed under arrest and escorted to a jail in Havana.

Fortunately Mr. John Graham, an officer in the Canadian Embassy in Havana, was at the airport. When he heard of the arrest, he followed

McMillan to the jail. Conditions in Cuba were very unsettled at that time. The whole nation was on alert for an American invasion. The jails were crowded. There was no justice in the courts. Prisoners' convictions were determined before they were even tried. People were executed daily. It was difficult to obtain the release of anyone in prison. Graham went to extreme measures to have the Canadian General Secretary released. He told the officials that it would create a diplomatic incident if such an innocent and important person were detained any longer. Through Graham's persistence and threats, Cuban officials finally agreed to release McMillan into the custody of the Canadian Embassy.

Dr. McMillan spent several days in the Canadian Embassy waiting for the return of his passport and for an exit visa. During those days he had a constant stream of visitors from the churches. He heard not only of the need for Scriptures, but of the oppressive conditions under which Christian work was carried on. Eventually the Canadian Embassy was able to obtain McMillan's passport and exit visa. Canadian officials personally escorted him onto the plane to make sure he got safely out of the country.

For the next several years, it was only with the greatest difficulty that any Scriptures entered Cuba. Eventually the Bible Society office and its contents were confiscated and its bank funds seized. Dr. Perdomo, General Secretary of the Cuban Bible Society, was placed in a labour camp. In time, however, the Canadian Bible Society succeeded in obtaining exit visas for him, as well as for his wife and two young daughters. They were permitted to take nothing with them except the clothes they were wearing. Their route to Canada was by way of Spain. In Canada they began a new life and Perdomo eventually began working with the Cuban refugees who were arriving in the USA in large numbers.

When the Canadian Bible Society was assigned responsibilities for work outside Canada, it had no idea that it would encounter hostile conditions such as it did in Cuba.

CHAPTER 11

Scripture Translation: An Ongoing Challenge

Translation it is that opens the window, to let in the light; that breaks the shell, that we may eat the kernel; that puts aside the curtain, that we may look into the most holy place; that removes the cover of the well, that we may come by the water.

Introduction to the
Contemporary English Version of the Bible, 1995,
quoted from "The Translators to the Reader,"
King James Version of the Bible, 1611

Up until the 1900s, Bible translations tended to be literal, word-for-word renderings. As the theory of translation developed, it became clear that such translations were often difficult to understand and sometimes even conveyed the wrong meanings. It is ironic that Bible translators who had a deep concern about producing an accurate rendering of the Scriptures often actually produced wordings that distorted the meaning.

In one of the languages of Liberia, for example, a word-for-word translation, which did not take into account the people's culture and the idioms of their language, gave a totally wrong meaning to the Lord's Prayer. After the translation was in use for several years, it was found that the people were reciting it as "Don't let us get caught" rather than "Lead us not into temptation."

Language is more than words. For a number of years now, the Bible Society has sought accuracy not only by basing translations on the original languages – Hebrew and Greek – and by using translators whose mother tongue is the language of the new translation, it has also taken into account the culture of the people so the meanings, not just the words, of Scripture are conveyed. The term that describes this approach to translation is "dynamic equivalence."

The Bible Society movement has been richly blessed by having a pioneer of this approach, the Rev. Dr. Eugene A. Nida, as the Translations Secretary of the American Bible Society. He joined ABS in 1943 and has now retired, but continues to be actively engaged in translation. Dr. Nida is a truly remarkable person. He is a Bible scholar, a committed Christian, a great communicator, a storehouse of knowledge on a wide range of subjects, and a person of abounding energy. Over the years he has provided a great deal of help to the Canadian Bible Society and to all other members of the United Bible Societies. He is respected and honoured worldwide. Dr. Nida is fluent in several languages and has a working knowledge of many others. One of his great bequests to the Bible Societies is the training of men and women for Bible translation.

In his book *God's Word in Man's Language,* published in 1952, Dr. Nida gives an example of the use of the "dynamic equivalence" principle. The Bible translators were having great difficulty translating the word "redeem" into Bambara, a language of West Africa. Eventually this word was rendered as "God took our heads out." This sounds strange to us but, in the Bambara language, it accurately conveys the meaning of redemption. The history of the Bambara people includes the era of the slave trade. Slave-traders travelled into the interior and captured people. The captured individuals had iron collars fastened around their necks, and they were chained together. Then they were made to walk out to the coast, where the slave ships were waiting for them. From time to time, as the lines of slaves passed through a village, a local chief might see some friend being led away and would want to free him or her. This could be done by paying the slave-trader in gold, silver, brass or ivory. To redeem a friend, a chief would literally "take the person's head out of the iron collar."

Bambara Christians know that God's redeeming love in Christ Jesus frees people from the slavery of sin and self, and from the control of the Devil. God sent His Son that people might live. Christ has redeemed us; He "took our heads out." Also, just as in ancient times a redeemed slave felt an obligation to serve the one who had redeemed him, we become volunteer slaves of Jesus Christ.

In Canada, as discussed in Chapters 1 and 2 of this book, a major concern of Bible Society work has been translation of the Scriptures into the languages of the First Nations. When Europeans arrived, there were about 500,000 Native people in what is now Canada. Generally, the Indians – Micmac, Cree, Ojibwe, Blackfoot, Chilcotin and other First Nations – lived south of the tree line, and the Inuit lived north of it.

In the years following the arrival of Europeans in Canada, the number of Native people declined due to war, starvation and disease. During the last half century, however, Native Canadians have been increasing in number, and in an awareness of their history and culture. They know the importance of language in preserving their culture, and this has created an increased interest in Scripture translation. Mary C. Urquhart, BA, BD, who was on the Canadian Bible Society staff for 27 years (1950-1977), was for many years responsible for Scripture translation and production for Native Canadians.

The work of Mary Urquhart embraced a wide range of responsibilities. She joined the staff as secretary for audio-visual education, but that soon became only one of her many responsibilities. She immediately began to assist historian E. C. Woodley in writing the history of the Canadian Bible Society, *The Bible in Canada,* published in 1953. She became chief assistant to the General Secretaries, who were for many years responsible for all that the National Office was expected to do.

Urquhart's work embraced not only Scripture translation and production for Native Canadians: she was also involved in all Scripture production, all promotional material, the writing of the Annual Reports, all Canadian Bible Society publications, and a host of other activities. She played an active role in the Toronto Institute of Linguistics. Her academic training, missionary background and vast knowledge of a wide range of subjects were a tremendous asset to the Society. She was a brilliant and competent person whose contribution to the Society deserves greater recognition.

The following comments, quoted from Mary Urquhart's 1973 report to the Canadian Bible Society's General Board, give some idea of the Society's work with respect to Native peoples at the time.

> After the Conference on Cree and related languages held in the autumn of 1971 and the Translators' Institute at Medicine Hat in the summer of 1972, the events of 1973 were of a more routine nature. However, the "mini-Institute" described in the report on Ojibwe/ Saulteaux may have found a more useful pattern . . . than bringing widely diversified groups together regularly.
>
> It has been the traditional policy of the Canadian Bible Society to sell Scriptures at a price those who need them can afford. In most Indian and Eskimo (Inuit) editions, this meant selling below cost, frequently at as little as half a normal price. In some areas it is now obvious that Indians and Eskimos have sufficient regular income to pay a normal price for Scriptures so that neither a large subsidy for Scriptures in their own language or half price sales of recent English translations are necessary.
>
> They can convey an image of the Bible Society as wishing to show the detested paternalistic attitude. In some areas the churches are still not as aware as they might be of the need to avoid this type of approach. There are still, however, many reserves where dire poverty continues and many Indians moving to the city who cannot afford to pay full price during the time they may need them most while they are getting established in a new way of life. . . .
>
> There is still very little direct contact between the Bible Society and Indian Christians, as our policy has always been to work through the churches. As band councils have a more decisive voice in which workers are released to give time to translation work and who shall publish the Scriptures which are translated, it may be necessary to find other channels of communication as well as working through the churches.
>
> Difficulty in finding Christian Indians, competent in their own language, who will take up the challenge of translating Scriptures for their own people, continues. At present both the non-Indian missionaries and Indian leaders in the field of literature in their own language are frequently involved in preparing literacy materials to teach adults and children to read their own language, in preparing dictionaries and other language tools.

On July 1, 1974, the Rev. Howard G. Zurbrigg became Secretary of Scripture production, supply and distribution. The provision of Scriptures to Native peoples was thus included among his duties. (For more information on the Rev. Zurbrigg's valuable contribution to the Bible Society, please see Chapter 12.)

In recent years the First Nations have developed an even greater self-awareness and a marked increase in ethnic pride. This has created interest in having modern versions of the Scriptures in their own languages. When Dr. Harold W. Fehderau became Director of Translation for the Canadian Bible Society in 1980, he – with his administrative assistant Hardy Schroeder – ably responded to the increased use of Native languages. Dr. Fehderau brought to his task both training in linguistics and missionary experience in the Democratic Republic of Congo (formerly Zaire). Dr. Fehderau, described as one of the world's six top Bible linguists and translators, retired December 31, 1996 and went to be with the Lord April 8, 1997, succumbing to a virus that took advantage of his body's weakened condition due to cancer. Dr. Fehderau divided Canada's Native languages into three groups:

1. The languages which are now, unfortunately, extinct and for which there is no need of translation.
2. The languages for which Scriptures translation is in progress.
3. The languages which will possibly need translation in the future.

Dr. Fehderau estimated that there have been about 65 Native languages in Canada. Over 30 of these are extinct, or nearly so; the members of these Indian bands are using English or French almost exclusively. At present there are 12 languages which will probably resist the overpowering pressure of English or French, and continue to be in general use in Canada. At least some portions of Scripture have been translated into about 35 languages and further work is in progress in about 20. In all current projects, competent Native Christians are involved in the transfer of meaning into Native language translations. Non-Native input involves exegetical checking (explanation or interpretation) and administrative coordination. In 1996, CBS was involved at one level or another with the following indigenous languages:

Algonquin (QC)
Atikamekw (QC)
Cree: Eastern (QC)
Cree: Moose (QC, ON)
Cree: Swampy (MB)
Cree: Western (MB, SK, AB)
Dogrib (NWT)
Inuinaktun (Western Arctic: Copper)
Inuktitut (Eastern Arctic)
Inutitut (Labrador)
Micmac (NB/NS)
Naskapi (QC)
Ojibwe/Cree (ON)
Ojibwe/Saulteaux (ON)
Slavey (AB)

Many of these language populations require relatively small print runs to meet their Scripture needs. Thanks to computerized publishing, CBS is able to offer this service economically. The translation department has its own typesetting unit (CAP: Computer-Assisted Publishing, with Ed Peters as manager), because of the highly specialized nature of Scripture publishing in general, and because of the special scripts used by many Native languages. Some syllabic fonts were developed by Canadian Bible Society CAP personnel.

Not all Native language projects will end up with a complete Bible. The translation department has worked out a plan of action for the next decade. It involves providing Scriptures of different kinds and in different formats for different groups: Selections (pamphlets), Portions, audiocassettes, video Scriptures, New Reader Scripture booklets, Scripture Comics, New Testaments, Bibles and Study Bibles.

Notes on Some Individual Native Languages

Algonquin

The translation of the New Testament was published in 1998. Some booklets in the *Walking with Jesus* series are available, and others are ready for printing. Preparations are being made for doing a Gospel of Luke video in Algonquin.

Carrier

The New Testament was recently completed in the language of the Carrier people of north central British Columbia.

Chilcotin

This is a language of northern British Columbia, spoken in the Alexis Creek area. The Gospel of Mark was prepared and recently published with the help of Wycliffe Bible Translator Randy Radney.

Cree: Eastern

Spoken on the eastern shore of James Bay and east into the interior of Quebec, Eastern Cree is divided into the northern and southern dialects. Mr. and Mrs. Ron Bartlett of Wycliffe Bible Translators are nearing completion of their work on the New Testament in the southern dialect. Initial work on the northern dialect began a number of years ago in Great Whale, with the effort being coordinated by the Rev. Tom Martin. The Gospel of Matthew is almost completed. There are plans to complete the entire New Testament. Several of the six booklets in the *Walking with Jesus* New Reader series are ready for printing.

Cree: Moose and Western (or Plains) Cree

Moose Cree is spoken in Ontario at the southern tip of James Bay (Moosonee), as well as in parts of Quebec. Western Cree is spoken in Manitoba and across northern Saskatchewan and northern Alberta. Moose Cree and Western Cree translations continue to be important dialects for Scripture use in the churches. The Moose Cree New Testament has been reprinted recently using new computer technology, as has the New Testament in Western Cree. And efforts are under way for a new contemporary translation of the Bible in Western Cree. Native translator, the Rev. Stanley Cuthand, has been working on passages of the Old Testament during the past number of years. The Western Cree Bible will be made available in both roman and syllabic scripts.

Dogrib

The Dogrib are one of the peoples of the Northwest Territories. Work on the New Testament is under way under the coordination of Jaap Feenstra of Wycliffe Bible Translators. The first three New Reader booklets in the *Walking with Jesus* series have been published, and work continues on the remaining three.

Inuinaktun (Western Arctic: Copper)

The goal of the Right Reverend J. R. Sperry, Anglican Bishop of the Arctic (retired), is to complete the translation of the entire New Testament. Recently a video Scripture production was completed, using the wording of the translation of the Gospel of Luke. It was prepared by the Rev. Sperry and CBS translation consultant Hart Wiens.

Inuktitut (Eastern Arctic)

The entire New Testament was printed in a new translation in 1992, and work is continuing on the Old Testament. A 40 per cent edition 'Shorter Old Testament' is being planned, to be followed later by the publication of the entire Bible. The Rev. Ben Arreak is the local Native translator-coordinator of the project. Work has been completed on a Gospel of Luke video. Also, the first Scripture Comic in Eastern Arctic Inuktitut *(Joseph)* is being printed, with work continuing on other booklets in the series.

Inutitut (Labrador)

The entire Bible was translated many years ago and published in a series of separate books. A request has come to CBS for assistance to print the entire Bible under one cover. Work on this project is under way.

Micmac

The complete New Testament in Micmac has been translated and is in the last stages of final revision.

Naskapi

The first four booklets of the *Walking with Jesus* New Reader series have been published, with work continuing on the remaining two. Also, work has begun on the translation of Genesis.

Ojibwe/Cree

The entire *Walking with Jesus* series is being prepared.

Ojibwe/Saulteaux

Ojibwe/Saulteaux is spoken in Northwestern Ontario, Manitoba and northern Minnesota. The Ojibwe New Testament was completed and printed in 1988 with the important help of Native speaker Jim Keesic, who worked with Charles Fiero of the Christian and Missionary Alliance Church as project coordinator, and Dr. Fehderau as translation consultant. Since then work has continued on the Old Testament by Native translators Jim Keesic and Tom Cameron, with the help of coordinator the Rev. Henry Hostetler of Impact North Ministries and CBS translation consultant the Rev. Bob Bryce. A 40 per cent selection of Old Testament texts will be published as an initial overview of Old Testament materials.

Slavey

The Slavey are among peoples of the Northwest Territories. Like a number of others, this Native population has become bilingual, with English as the predominant language. For this reason a New Testament prepared under the direction of Victor Monus of Wycliffe Bible Translators was never published. An effort is under way, however, to present the Scriptures in a video format in which the Gospel material will be dramatized.

The Canadian Bible Society's translation department has also been asked by the United Bible Societies to provide a world service ministry in a number of areas. For example:

1. Translation consultancy work for English-speaking and French-speaking countries in the West Indies and South America (Haiti, Jamaica, St. Lucia, Guadeloupe, French Guiana).

2. Typesetting and other computer-related assistance to projects from several areas (Lao, Haitian Creole, Brazilian Portuguese, Jamaican Patois, Antillean Creole).

3. Training for translation projects in the Americas Region – training in the use of computers for preparing electronic Scripture manuscripts.

Some of CBS's Recent International Publishing Projects

- Haitian New Testament and a Haitian diglot (two-language) Gospel of Mark
- *Walking with Jesus* New Reader booklets in Antillean Creole
- Scripture selections in Hindi and in Gullah
- American sign language: Almost 30 per cent of the Bible is available on video cassettes, with plans calling for the completion of Exodus and additional Pauline letters soon.

Translation of the Scriptures is a task that will never be completed. The Word of God does not change but the cultures of the readers change, the meanings of words change, and there are new insights into the meaning of the Scriptures. At one time people sang, "O for a thousand tongues to sing my great Redeemer's praise." Now at least one book of the Bible has been published in well over 2,000 languages, and each year Christ is praised and adored in additional tongues.

Some people may wonder why there seems to be a continuing need for new English versions when some languages are still without even one book of the Bible. Resistance to new translations is nothing new. In 1611, for example, when the *King James Version* appeared, it was a "modern" translation and took some 50 years to become widely accepted. Many people preferred an older version in English.

A compelling reason for new translations in English today is that English has become the universal *lingua franca.* Mandarin is the native tongue of 836 million, Hindi of 333 million, Spanish of 332 million and English of only 322 million. However, besides the 322 million whose first language is English, another 422 million speak English as a second language – for a total of 744 million English readers.

English is now the language of academic, scientific, medical and technological research. English is the language of air traffic control. It is on its way to becoming the language of global policing and emergency response. Most conferences, business as well as academic, are held in English. Even more importantly, English is the language of advertising and tourism. The Internet is 90 per cent English. All this means that the language of the English Bible must be one that is easily understood if it is going to be read by the millions of educated people who are the leaders in every field of endeavour around the world.

No language is static. Words and phrases which are current at one time have little or different meaning with the passing of time. Archaeological discoveries and research provide better texts in the original languages and a clearer understanding of those texts. The science of linguistics, which is comparatively new, enables translators to utilize new ways of communicating. Some linguists maintain that every language requires a new translation at least every generation.

Surveys indicate that, even in developed countries, where there has been universal education for many years, a surprising number of people are able to read only the simplest language. In North America, for example, 49 per cent of adults are unable to read at a grade eight level. Where people use English as a second language, it is even more important to provide easy-to-read Scriptures. Below are the results of a survey indicating reading levels of several different translations.

VERSION	READING LEVEL REQUIRED
King James	Grade 12
New American Standard	Grade 11
New King James	Grade 8
New International	Grade 8
Contemporary English	Grade 4

The Bible must not only be read, but also understood. When the Scriptures are in the living language of the reader, the message of the Bible is clearly communicated and people are confronted by the judging-saving Word of God. When the Bible is understood, a verdict is demanded and the Scriptures become a vital link in people's pilgrimage from unbelief to a saving knowledge of Christ.

CHAPTER 12

Scripture Production and Distribution

These miracles are written so that you will put your faith in Jesus as the Messiah and the Son of God. If you have faith in him, you will have true life.

John 20.31

For many years practically no Bibles, Testaments or Scripture Portions were printed in Canada. Scriptures distributed by the Bible Society in Canada were exclusively those published by the British and Foreign Bible Society. During World War II, when the importation of Bibles was severely restricted, Ryerson Press (Toronto) did publish a *King James* Bible, but this was an exception. BFBS encouraged the policy of having only their own publications handled by the Bible Society in Canada. BFBS held the copyright for the *King James Version,* and it was assumed that only with their permission could that version be printed in Canada. (Later it was discovered that BFBS copyright did not extend to the Commonwealth.) Canadian Bible Society depots and bookstores generally ordered directly from England. It is amazing that with these restrictions the Bible Society was able to distribute large quantities of Scriptures in several languages.

The Bible Society in Canada had no warehouse or central stock depot. In time, as a result, the Districts began to order from the American Bible Society and other Bible Societies, as well as from commercial publishers. In this way they were able to obtain a somewhat wider selection of Bibles, Testaments, Scripture Portions and Selections.

In 1955 Kenneth Rhodes became business manager for the Upper Canada Bible Society, and this was the beginning of a new and better relationship between it and the National Society. Rhodes played a significant role in overcoming the Upper Canada Bible Society's opposition to the National Society. He is an example of what a great difference one person can make. Rhodes began stocking Bible Society publications at 14 College Street, Toronto, and the Bible depots across Canada began to order from this Central Stock Depot instead of from sources outside Canada. This was a major change and the beginning of a new day for Bible Society work in Canada.

Also in 1955 the Rev. Dr. A. H. O'Neil, General Secretary, conceived the idea of having the Bible Society offer a copy of the Scriptures to all new Canadians. The presentations would be part of the ceremonies at which new citizens were received at Citizenship Courts held regularly in major cities across Canada.

Immigration has been a distinguishing feature of Canadian life, since the nation's whole population, except for the Native peoples, consists of immigrants or their descendants. The nation was founded on Christian principles, and Dr. O'Neil believed new citizens should be made aware of this. Catholic and Protestant editions of the New Testament were presented, as well as Old Testaments to those of the Hebrew faith. Over the years Citizenship Court Judges have generally welcomed this presentation of the Scriptures.

From 1955 on, there was a gradual move towards the Canadian Bible Society having its own supply of Scriptures, but there was still little Scripture production in Canada. As discussed in Chapter 11, Mary Urquhart and the General Secretary, Dr. McMillan, were responsible for all Scripture translation, production and distribution. But this was only one of their several responsibilities.

What is surprising is the amount of Scripture translation, and the large number of Scriptures distributed in Canada, when the staff of the National Office consisted only of the General Secretary and four others. One of these was bookkeeper Lenore McCracken, who served the Society for a total of 45 years, working with five different General Secretaries. When she retired in January 1963, she was succeeded by Kenneth Rhodes, mentioned earlier in this chapter. By that time Rhodes had already begun to work for the National Office, since he had become manager of the newly created Central Stock Depot on January 1, 1962. It was the competence and commitment of the small National Office staff that allowed so much to be accomplished. The District offices, store managers and District Secretaries did not participate in Scripture translation, or the production of Scriptures or other materials, but they were an integral part of the Bible Society team in Scripture distribution.

A highlight of the year 1964 was the production of a booklet of Scripture passages entitled "Strength for Today." This was published for hospital chaplains to mark the 60th anniversary of the National Society.

In 1973 the Bible Society for the first time sold over a million Scriptures. Most of these were purchased through CBS bookstores. A special event of that same year was the publication of a Scripture Selection in English and French, marking the centennial of Prince Edward Island. Also in 1973, as part of the Royal Canadian Mounted Police centennial, another attractive Scripture Selection was produced in both English and French. Over 500,000 copies of this were distributed.

A red-letter day for the Canadian Bible Society was July 1, 1974, the day the Rev. Howard G. Zurbrigg, BA, BD, assumed the position of Secretary for Scripture production, supply and distribution. Mr. Zurbrigg had been a minister of the Evangelical United Brethren Church and, when his denomination became part of the United Church of Canada, he became a minister of that denomination. Following this pastoral service, he became CBS District Secretary in the Hamilton District (now South Central Ontario), and for five years was popular and highly effective in that position. He was a talented person, artistically gifted and creative.

In his new position as Secretary for Scripture production, supply and distribution, Zurbrigg soon established himself as an excellent designer of Scripture Selections in attractive formats. Some considered him the best in his field. His wife joined him as his administrative assistant and they became a highly productive team. During the 10 years the Zurbriggs were part of the National Office staff, Scripture production and distribution in Canada were completely transformed.

Howard Zurbrigg, in a very real sense, gave his life for the Bible Society. In 1984, while in Haiti on Bible Society business, he was mugged, robbed and badly injured. At that time he received a blood transfusion. Upon his return to Canada, he was diagnosed with hepatitis. The Zurbriggs resigned from the Bible Society staff in 1984, and in 1985 Howard began a very successful ministry as pastor of Pickering Village United Church, east of Toronto. His health continued to be a concern, however, and finally in 1992 doctors diagnosed his problem as AIDS, which he had contracted from the 1984 blood transfusion in Haiti. He had to resign from his congregation in 1993, and his health deteriorated rapidly. He died September 6, 1994. His ministry spanned only 29 years, and 15 of those were with the Canadian Bible Society. Far into the future the Society will continue to benefit from his work.

The year 1975 saw a new approach to Scripture distribution in Canada – the "Scripture Courtesy Centre." This program relied entirely on volunteers who were eager to make the Scriptures accessible to every person. These volunteers bought Scriptures from the Canadian Bible Society, kept supplies in their homes or places of business, and sold them at the same price for which they were purchased. By the end of the year, 28 volunteers from Newfoundland to the North West District had set up "Good News Stands" in their homes, offices or churches.

By 1976 there had begun to be significant Scripture production in Canada. For the first time, the Canadian Bible Society produced Scriptures not only for itself, but also for other members of the United Bible Societies. In 1976 the Canadian Bible Society sold the following to other Bible Societies: 1,933 Bibles, 165 New Testaments, 22,064 Portions and 62,280 Selections.

The Montreal Olympic Games opened July 1, 1976. Under the auspices of *Aide Olympique*, a fellowship of some 40 Christian organizations, more than 3,500 trained Christian young people from 60 nations, speaking more than a dozen languages, converged on Montreal. Their common purpose was to provide a Christian presence and witness at the Olympic Games. The Canadian Bible Society provided about two dozen organizations with Scriptures: 100 Bibles, 8,800 New Testaments, 1,030,000 Gospels and 357,000 Scripture Selections.

The year 1976 is also remembered as the year when the complete *Good News Bible* was published. This dynamic new translation by the American Bible Society was published in Canada on November 1, and 120,000 copies were sold by year's end.

In 1978 a record number of Bibles and Testaments were presented at Citizenship Courts: 140,027. Also, for the first time in history, over half a million New Testaments, many with the Psalms, were distributed in Canada. Most of these had been printed in Canada. Total Scripture distribution reached 8,077,432 in 1978, partly due to the "Five Year Program of Advance" launched by the Canadian Bible Society the previous year.

Scripture production and distribution in Canada continued to grow, and in 1979 total distribution was 9,998,811. In 1980 it reached 12,713,335. In that year the Canadian Bible Society joined with the other members of the United Bible Societies in the "God's Word: Open for All" program, which was launched at the world gathering of Bible Societies at Chiang Mai, Thailand. Representatives from 100 countries had agreed that this should be the theme for the 80s. In addition to promoting an increase of Scripture translation, production and distribution in Canada, the Canadian Bible Society accepted the challenge of providing 10 per cent of the cost of increased programs in Asia, Africa and Latin America.

With the appointment of Dr. Harold W. Fehderau as Director of Translation in 1980, there was an acceleration in the translation and revision of the Scriptures in the languages of Canada's Native peoples. (Please see Chapter 11 for more details.) Also the traditional programs were carried on year after year – of providing Scriptures for the visually challenged, for Citizenship Courts, for prisoners, for students training for full-time Christian work, for special mission programs, and for members of the armed forces.

By 1983 the Canadian Bible Society was a major Scripture producing organization. It had now become a major partner in the United Bible Societies, and the third largest contributor to the World Service Budget.

In 1993 *Maclean's* magazine published a survey, conducted by Angus Reid, which revealed that only 20 per cent of Canadians read the Bible or other religious material at least weekly. In September 1993, in response to this report, the Canadian Bible Society launched a program called "Faith Comes by Hearing." This program is based on the use of audiocassettes to enable people to listen to the reading of the Bible. In this post-Gutenberg era, when the electronic media are dominant and the traditional printed page less popular, the "Faith Comes by Hearing" program has a strong appeal. It enlists pastors who are willing to challenge their congregations to listen to the entire New Testament on cassette for about 37 minutes a day for 30 days. The hope is that this will establish the daily habit of listening to the Scriptures.

In 1994 the Canadian Bible Society reported that almost 800 churches had completed the program, and that the spiritual lives of the participants were enriched. Such was the enthusiasm that, by the end of 1997, close to 2,000 churches had taken part.

Total Scripture distribution in Canada reached 6,495,722 for the year 1997 and the number of languages in which the Scriptures had been distributed in Canada had reached 233. In the last three years, New Testaments presented at Citizenship Courts numbered 53,219. Bibles, Testaments and Gospels provided to prison inmates numbered 7,491. The visually challenged received a total of 19,139 large print Bibles, Braille volumes and audiocassettes of Scripture readings. There were 3,793 presentations of Scriptures to students at Bible colleges and theological seminaries. New Testaments and Gospels presented to members of the Canadian armed forces and army cadets numbered 19,552.

For several years the use and understanding of the Bible has been a concern of the world's Bible Societies. The United Bible Societies employed additional staff, and published a series of books to encourage the reading and understanding of the Scriptures. Among the Canadian Bible Society's initiatives in this direction has been the publication of annual "Daily Bible Reading Guides." These have been widely used, and have helped people read the Bible each day.

The Canadian Bible Society also recognizes that, besides having the Bible in the right language, several other important factors operate in encouraging people to read and understand it. Such factors include the format in which the Scriptures are published, their general attractiveness, and the readability of the print. Without doubt, over the years, the small print in many Bibles has discouraged people from reading the Word of God. In recent years Bibles have become much more attractive and readable, and Scripture Portions have introduced many to the Bible for the first time. The American Bible Society was a pioneer in producing the Scriptures in new formats, and the Canadian Bible Society has reproduced many of their publications.

The Canadian Bible Society continues to stock the Scriptures in some 100 languages, and to be a source of supply for both individuals and churches. Recently new equipment in the Society's large warehouse has resulted in lower costs for mailing. A greater use of computers enables the Society to keep adequate stock on hand and also to facilitate delivery. Languages are continually changing and the Bible Society is committed to providing the Bible in the mother tongue of the reader and in a format that encourages it to be read.

Unfortunately the production and distribution of the Scriptures can be adversely affected when the credibility of the Bible is questioned. Attacks on the reliability of the written Word have been made for many years, but "the Bible has proven to be an anvil that has worn out many hammers." Nevertheless the Bible Society is deeply concerned about attacks on the Bible, for they discourage many people from reading it. It is not easy for ordinary Christians to evaluate the validity of the criticisms. In the late 19th and early 20th centuries, theological liberals undertook the "Quest for the Historical Jesus." Failing to reach the stated goal of discovering "the real Jesus" behind the Gospel accounts, this was followed by "The New Quest." The latter has now been replaced by the "Third Quest," as expressed in the work of such bodies as the "Jesus Seminar" and others who speculate in a highly imaginative way.

These attacks have created, in the minds of many, uncertainty about who Jesus is. They have assaulted Biblical faith and the orthodox Christian belief that Jesus Christ is the Divine Son of God, the Second Person of the Holy Trinity. The consequences of these attacks for both individuals and society are serious.

Vandalism is a regrettably common occurrence today. The original Vandals introduced mindless destruction in Europe and North Africa in the fifth and sixth centuries. They were the ones who sacked Rome in 455 AD and carried off treasures, as well as the Roman empress and her two daughters. The Vandals were exceedingly cruel to orthodox Christians. For the Bible Society, the actions of the Vandals are significant because they were Aryan Christians, a heretical sect that denied the Divinity of Christ and rejected the authority of the Bible. Parallels can be drawn between them and more recent attackers of Scripture.

It is essential to counter the destructive consequences of denying a Biblical faith – a belief in the reliability of the Gospel narratives and their portrayal of Jesus as the Divine Son of God. Many Biblical scholars totally disagree with the findings of those who deny the historical accuracy of the Gospels. The Bible Society's production and distribution of the Scriptures is motivated by the conviction that the Bible is the inspired Word of the Almighty God.

CHAPTER 13

French Canada, the Roman Catholic Church and the Bible Society

All of this makes us even more certain that what the prophets said is true. So you should pay close attention to their message, as you would to a lamp shining in some dark place. You must keep on paying attention to their message, as you keep on paying attention until daylight comes and the morning star rises in your hearts. But you need to realize that no one alone can understand any of the prophecies in the Scriptures. The prophets did not think these things up on their own, but were guided by the Spirit of God.

2 Peter 1.19-21

In 1763, at the end of the Seven Years' War, Quebec – or New France – became a British possession. The adjustment was difficult for the people of Quebec. However, by the terms of the Quebec Act of 1774, they were guaranteed the right to maintain their traditions, institutions, French language and Roman Catholic faith.

In 1804, the same year the British and Foreign Bible Society was founded in London, England, a Branch of the Bible Society was organized in Quebec. But it was short-lived and there is no record of its being associated with the Parent Society. The year 1813 saw the organization of the Quebec Auxiliary of the British and Foreign Bible Society. From then on, the Bible House in Quebec City played an important part in the work. The Montreal Auxiliary from its beginning in 1820 showed a keen interest in reaching the French by employing colporteurs. This work is described in detail in *The Bible in Canada* by E. C. Woodley.

Despite encouraging beginnings, there was a sense of division between the British-based Bible Society and French Canadians. This feeling was deeply rooted in the history of the nation, and was perceived at many levels in Canadian society. Sir Wilfrid Laurier, Prime Minister from 1896 to 1911, through his understanding helped hold Canada together. But he deplored English Canadians' failure to understand the French. Laurier said:

> For us, sons of France, political sentiment is a passion, while for the Englishman, politics are a question of business. The Englishman respects your opinions but he never thinks of your feelings.

Added to the longstanding sense of French-English division was the fact that most French Canadians were Roman Catholics, and the Roman Catholic Church generally did not favour the reading of the Bible by the masses. The Roman Catholic Church is built upon the Bible, and it holds to the great central doctrines of the Christian faith. It believes that the Church's official interpretation of the Scriptures, inspired by the Christian Tradition, is the only valid one. However, the Church proclaimed this interpretation only for a limited number of texts. Since the Bible could be interpreted in so many different ways, the Roman Catholic Church felt it was not safe for the average man or woman to read it. Private interpretation was dangerous. When one sees the multiplicity of Christian and non-Christian sects based on a particular misinterpretation of the Scriptures, one is sympathetic to the concerns that the Roman Catholic Church had for many years.

When the Church was the most vital force in the life of the vast majority of French Canada's population, and when the Roman Catholic Church generally did not favour Scripture distribution, Bible Society workers were not welcomed. In fact, the people were warned about Bible Society colporteurs. In addition, for many years, the Roman Catholic Church rejected most Bible Society translations, as it insisted on translations by Roman Catholic scholars based on the Latin Vulgate. The Bible Society sought to overcome this obstacle by permitting the colporteurs to carry Scriptures which had the imprimatur of the Roman Catholic Church.

Despite the Roman Catholic Church's generally restrictive attitude towards Scripture reading, there were some early movements in the direction of change. On October 8, 1914, for example, in an encyclical letter Pope Benedict XV made the following statement.

> We strongly desire, aye and exhort also . . . the widest possible diffusion of the Gospels and the entrance of these most holy books into Christian households. . . . that all the faithful shall become habituated in the daily reading and study of the same.

In 1943 Pope Pius XII, in the encyclical *Divine Afflante Spiritu,* encouraged Bible translations into the vernacular languages, and urged the people to read the Holy Scriptures. He wanted Bible translation to be done from the original texts, Hebrew and Greek, instead of from the Latin Vulgate.

The Bible Society was heartened by such pronouncements, as it saw French Canada as a mission field to be evangelized with the French Scriptures. This did not, however, necessarily mean drawing people away from the Roman Catholic Church. The Bible Society prided itself on being a non-proselytizing movement, and always encouraged its colporteurs to avoid confrontation.

The Roman Catholic Church, in the minds of both Quebecers and the rest of Canada, was strongly associated with the French language.

Then as now, retention of the language was seen as the major way French Canadian society could preserve itself, distinct from English-speaking North America. Looking back now, it seems it might have been a good idea for the Bible Society, early on, to have considered making itself bilingual. It could have become a place where French and English were partners. But this possibility does not seem to have occurred to the British and Foreign Bible Society. No doubt some English-speaking people believed that, in time, the French language would diminish in importance, and the people of Quebec would be assimilated into English-speaking society. As we know now, this has not happened, nor is it likely to occur.

By the 1950s, as transportation and communications systems grew and developed, Bible distribution was undertaken in new ways across Canada including Quebec. The Annual Report for 1955, for example, shows that the number of Scriptures distributed by colporteurs was relatively small. The Montreal Auxiliary discontinued the use of part-time colporteurs, and appointed Mr. C. Henry Hochland as a full-time colporteur for the whole province of Quebec. Interested individuals made the Scriptures available in many communities by having Scripture depositories in their homes or shops. For many years this continued to be a valuable way of distributing French Scriptures.

In the 1960s, the Vatican II Council brought about fundamental shifts in the Roman Catholic Church's attitude towards a wide range of Christian concerns. Among the changes was a new approach to the Scriptures. Vatican II declared that all people ought to have easy access to the Bible.

Encouraged by this development, the Bible Society began giving somewhat greater recognition to the place of the French language in its activities. In 1969 the Rev. Robert R. Richardson, BTh, was appointed director of French work. He was given oversight of all French activities in Quebec, and also of Bible Society work among the more than one million French-speaking people in other parts of Canada. Before taking on his new responsibilities, Richardson had been manager of the Canadian Bible Society bookstore in Quebec City for three years, and then assistant manager of the Montreal Canadian Bible Society bookstore. A pastor of the Christian and Missionary Alliance Church, he served with great effectiveness as Director until he returned to the pastorate in 1973.

Succeeding Richardson, the Rev. Daniel Racine, LL, MEd, joined the staff of the Canadian Bible Society on October 1, 1974. Racine was a native of Switzerland and a member of a highly regarded family. He had a real appreciation of French culture and of the significance of the Scriptures in the life of Christians. He had extensive responsibilities since he was assistant District Secretary for both the Montreal and Quebec Districts, as well as Director of French work for all Canada. With a distinguished academic career, achievements as an author, and with experience in many fields including the Canadian civil service, Racine raised the Canadian Bible Society's French work to a new level. A member of the Brethren Church, he had long been accustomed to working with all Christian Churches and engaging in various outreach programs. Under his direction French-speaking Canadians in Quebec and all across Canada became more involved in the activities of the Society.

It was during Racine's directorship that French-speaking Canadians' needs were met in several new ways. There was a need for a publication similar to *The Quarterly Newsletter* in English. Thus a French version began to be published in 1975; it later became known as *Actualités bibliques.* The same year saw the publication of the Bible translation known as the *Traduction œcuménique de la Bible (TOB).* Protestant, Roman Catholic and Orthodox scholars united in the translation of this new Bible. It became very popular in Canada. A Canadian edition of 61,000 copies was published, but some people were so anxious to obtain the new translation that they could not wait for this edition, and 33,000 copies of the European edition, which had been made available sooner, were distributed. At a Roman Catholic Charismatic Congress in Montreal in June 1977, 10,000 copies were sold. Within a 48-hour period, orders were taken for an additional 8,000. A total of 58,000 copies of this French Bible were sold in Canada that year.

The same year, 1977, the Canadian Bible Society received the largest order ever for Scriptures – 100,000 *TOB* New Testaments and Psalms for the Sisters of St. Augustine at Chicoutimi, Quebec. Hundreds of additional copies were also printed at the same time for sale in retail stores.

Advances such as these notwithstanding, the Bible Society and French Canadian Christians had continuing difficulties in gaining a sense of unity. It was not until 1980, fully 75 years after the National Society was incorporated, that its name was officially changed to include "*Société biblique canadienne (SBC)*" in addition to "Canadian Bible Society (CBS)."

In 1983 Racine, who had done so much to involve francophones in Society work, was relieved of his duties by the General Secretary, the Rev. William Russell. This was done without consulting the informal French Committee, or *Conseil francophone,* which had been formed in 1981. Following Racine's dismissal, a special committee prepared a written report that served as a basis for the formation of the *Secteur francophone,* or French-language sector, of the Canadian Bible Society.

Among the many distinguished members of the Board of Directors of the Canadian Bible Society, Sister Gertrude McLaughlin of Montreal deserves special mention. A Roman Catholic nun belonging to the Order of the Holy Names of Jesus and Mary, she was a prominent and influential member of the Board of the Montreal District from 1974 to 1986. She also served on the General Board of the Canadian Bible Society and was elected a Vice-President. Sister Gertrude had a profound understanding of the Roman Catholic Church, the Protestant faith and both French and English cultures. She made an enormous contribution to a better understanding between the Canadian Bible Society and the francophone people. She continually underlined the fact that the Canadian Bible Society was seen among the francophone people as exclusively Protestant and anglophone. At a time when the Canadian Bible Society was facing these two major obstacles to becoming a part of French society, her wise counsel was of tremendous value.

Sister Gertrude was an outstanding Bible scholar and produced weekly notes for Bible study for a large constituency of the Roman Catholic Church. She prepared the material and mailed it to parishes and individuals. Through these notes, hundreds of people became Biblically literate and had their Christian faith deepened. Her death while undergoing heart surgery was a great loss to the Bible Society and to the whole Christian community. Her Christian character and invaluable service will long be remembered.

In 1983 Daniel Racine was followed by Mr. Serge Rhéaume, who was given the title "Directeur du Secteur francophone" (Director, French-speaking Canada). Rhéaume immediately began establishing good relations with the General Board of CBS and with churches and Christian organizations. He provided information about Bible Society work, and asked the churches and Christian organizations for their support and advice. His ministry included the one million French-speaking Canadians outside of Quebec, as well as Quebecers.

In 1984 the *Secteur francophone* moved from the CBS Montreal office to its own quarters at 4050, avenue du Parc-Lafontaine in the French section of Montreal. This demonstrated the self-directing character of the *Secteur francophone.* On January 3, 1985, for the first time, the Quebec District was given its own full-time District Secretary, the Rev. Roger Robert. By 1986 *Secteur francophone* Director Serge Rhéaume was able to visit all the Districts and meet with many French-speaking people across Canada. He was encouraged by the full support he received from all the District Secretaries and he rapidly became accepted as a valuable member of the cross-Canada Bible Society team.

The composition of the *Conseil francophone* (the Board of the *Secteur francophone*) demonstrates the national character of the French work. The *Conseil* is comprised of members-at-large who are elected by the Districts. Currently this *Conseil* consists of two members from the Quebec District, two members from the Montreal District, one member from the New Brunswick District (representing Eastern Canada), and one member from the Alberta District (representing Western Canada).

The election of *Conseil* members is rotated among the Districts and, in the past, *Conseil* members have also come from Saskatchewan and Manitoba. The President of the National Society, the National Director and the District Directors of the Montreal, Quebec, New Brunswick and Eastern Ontario Districts are all ex-officio members of the *Conseil.* This provides it with a distinct national character.

One method the *Secteur francophone* has employed in publicizing CBS work and promoting fund-raising is the French "Expo-Bible." Expo-Bible is a display consisting of 12 panels with the following themes.

How people have always communicated
The spread of writing systems
The lands of the Bible
God speaks through the prophets and their writings
Scriptures of the Jewish people
The Greek Old Testament
The New Testament (Christian Writings)
Ancient Greek manuscripts

Latin manuscripts of the Bible
First translations of the Bible
The Bible in German and English
The Bible in French

Accompanying the panels were a replica of the Rosetta Stone, a papyrus, a leather script and samples of the Bible in different languages.

This exhibition became very popular in churches, schools, conventions and other special events. Three such exhibitions were in use across Canada soon after its introduction and, by popular request, were also made available in English.

Under Rhéaume's leadership production of Scriptures in French increased dramatically. He discovered that there were many Canadians capable of producing French Scripture materials. Soon these Scriptures were being produced in Canada not only for Canada, but also for French Bible Societies around the world. Canadians with academic competence began to make a valuable contribution to CBS.

Thirty national Bible Societies in the United Bible Societies serve French-speaking populations in their own countries. *Francosec* is a UBS committee involved in the translation, production and distribution of Scriptures for French-speaking countries. Canada has been well represented in this field of endeavour. Serge Rhéaume was Vice-President of *Francosec* for three years, and was then elected President. The Canadian Bible Society has worked on joint projects with the French, Belgian and Swiss Bible Societies, as well as with the UBS Africa Regional Centre. It is significant that the *Secteur francophone* of CBS is among the top three Bible Societies in the world in Scripture distribution.

Scriptures in the vernacular are common in many languages. The need for one in French was met by the publication of *Parole de Vie* in the early 1990s. This easy-to-read translation, similar to the *Contemporary English Version,* was welcomed by Catholics as well as Protestants including Evangelicals.

Nowadays, the 16 Bible Centres established across Canada make French Scriptures more readily available. French-speaking staff in certain Bible Centres also provide improved service. CBS French Scripture catalogues are published from time to time. French-speaking congregations of nuns have proved to have a great interest in Scripture distribution and special editions of the New Testament are published for them. Good relations with the French Protestant and Roman Catholic School Boards in Quebec have enhanced the image of the Bible Society and increased Scripture distribution. Friendly relations with the *Société catholique de la Bible* (Catholic Bible Society) have brought a new degree of cooperation in Scripture distribution. With Roman Catholics the most popular versions have been *Français courant* and the *TOB*.

The Secteur francophone is more effective if personnel and supporters can communicate in French. Fortunately, some District Directors are now bilingual, as is the National Director appointed in 1997, the Rev. Fr. Gregory Bailey. Several staff members at the CBS National Office are also adept at communicating in both French and English.

From 1804, when the first Branch of the Bible Society was established in Quebec, to the present, when CBS is serving a bilingual nation, the Bible Society has made enormous progress. In addition to serving the French-speaking people of Canada, CBS shares in the work of 30 other national Bible Societies throughout the world. In a period of history when some 25 ethnic wars are being fought and language has become a divisive factor, CBS is a shining example of Christian tolerance and cooperation.

CHAPTER 14

The North West District

We can do no great things, just small things with great love.
Mother Theresa

Pioneer missionaries in Canada's remote northwest were mostly Anglican clergy from England, with a small number of Roman Catholic priests and nuns. As a result, many of the Inuit became evangelical Anglicans. The Roman Catholic missionaries made most of their converts among the Indians. As discussed in Chapter 2, the Bible Society was serving the missionaries and churches of the northwest from the mid-1800s on. It was not until 1969, however, that CBS officially organized a North West District. Just prior to the formation of this district, the area had been served by the Rev. Dr. J. A. R. Tingley, CBS District Secretary in British Columbia, and the Rev. E. M. B. Wheelock, CBS District Secretary in North Alberta.

The North West District organized in 1969 had some responsibility for all of the Canadian north. But specifically it was to cover the area north and west of Valleyview, Alberta, and as far south as Valemount, British Columbia. Later the District was enlarged to take in parts of British Columbia as far south as 100 Mile House. This comprised an area of approximately two and a half million square kilometres (one million square miles). The District's approximately half million people were scattered over this vast land area, which had over 700 churches.

The first North West District Secretary was the Rev. Stephen J. F. Collins, BA, BD, STM, a minister of the United Church of Canada and the son of missionaries to Africa. Collins assumed his position on September 1, 1969. He was equipped with a small mobile home on the back of a three-quarter-ton truck. He lived in this humble accommodation and travelled wherever roads permitted him to go.

For many missionaries in the area, meeting Collins was their first direct contact with the Bible Society. The visit of the District Secretary was a welcome experience for them. He carried quantities of Scripture for sale and for free distribution, and he successfully solicited funds for the support of the larger work of the Bible Society.

On July 1, 1971 Bernard J. Wolfe succeeded Collins as District Secretary. For 16 months he travelled in the Bible Society mobile home, promoting interest in CBS and distributing Scriptures. Wolfe, however, found the constant travel too difficult and resigned on October 31, 1972.

Since the District Secretary was continually travelling, the office for the North West District was a "desk" in the National Office. Mrs. L. Hummel was the very efficient and devoted office secretary for the North West District. From October 31, 1972 until the next District Secretary took over on August 1, 1973, she kept in contact with Bible Society supporters in the District by correspondence, and met requests for Scriptures. Mrs. Hummel provided a great service by being responsible for the North West District's "desk" for many years.

The Rev. Gunter Flemke, BTh, a North American Baptist minister, succeeded Wolfe as District Secretary on August 1, 1973. He and his wife, Sharon, lived in the small mobile home and carried on the work that had been started. It was a difficult life for a young couple and, on June 30, 1974, they were transferred to Toronto. There Gunter became one of the District Secretaries in the Upper Canada District, and also assumed the position of Direct Mail Secretary for all of Canada.

The next District Secretary for the North West District was the Rev. Samuel Bishart Nafziger, BTh, AB, MA – a Mennonite with extensive experience in teaching in both Christian and public schools, in pastoral ministry and in administration. He was a graduate of Eastern Mennonite College, Kansas City University and Iowa State University. When he began on November 15, 1975, he was 62 years of age. For the next 14 years, he and his wife Martha lived in a "fifth wheel trailer" drawn by a truck. They travelled thousands of miles and were away from their home in LaCrete, Alberta, 95 per cent of the time.

They were a highly motivated couple. Though only Sam was officially on staff, Martha also worked full time for the Bible Society, speaking at meetings, distributing Scriptures and continually supporting her husband. The Nafzigers were true missionaries and gladly accepted all their hardships. Their spirit and devotion to service were exhibited during the years they served the Bible Society and, when they completed their time with CBS, they continued as volunteer workers, teaching the Bible and assisting the churches in many ways.

In 1994, at age 81, the remarkable Sam Nafziger and his equally remarkable wife Martha went to Russia under the auspices of the Gospel Missionary Union of Canada and for 18 months taught the Bible in Russian schools and to adults. This was a rewarding and challenging experience, and they had the joy of seeing many become Christians. The Nafzigers now live at Buffalo Head Prairie, Alberta.

Scripture distribution and financial support both increased dramatically in the years the Nafzigers served the region. On many occasions they were in dangerous situations and every day presented a challenge of one kind or another. Martha reported many of their experiences. The following firsthand accounts from her writings give some insight into their work.

Getting Started

In August of 1975 we announced our intentions to family and friends; we had agreed to work for the Canadian Bible Society and the Society agreed to have us. Daughter Linda commented, "I'm proud of you in your 60s doing something like this."

Samuel began designing a trailer to house us for our travels and collecting materials to build it. Our four sons came home at various times and for short periods friends and neighbours also pitched in and helped on the construction. The weather grew extremely cold in late November and Samuel developed chilblains in his feet. Most of the work needed to be done outside.

Before the trailer was finished Samuel considered it roadworthy. He was very eager to get started. We sallied forth on the 16th of December in spite of the temperature being -42 degrees F (-41 degrees C). When we arrived at Manning (Alberta), we discovered that a jar of beet pickle had broken and dyed the inside of the refrigerator a bizarre red – the first of many similar mishaps. Most of the pots and pans had leaped off the shelves and were holding a jamboree on the floor. (The cupboard doors had not yet been attached.) I looked at the chaos in the trailer and said, "For you, Lord. It is a part of enlarging my coast like I've been praying."

En route we made improvements: acquiring and installing a flexible pipe to the cookstove so that I could cook. We stopped at Canadian Propane and spent two hours installing a new connection so that our propane tank would accept propane. Then coaxing the bedroom furnace to operate. . . .

The tip of my nose was tender; probably frost-bitten. That evening I hurried to bed to thaw out under the electric blanket. Had I EVER been so cold before?

The next day the weather did a complete switch. The temperature rose to +35 degrees F (nearly +2 degrees C). Then we had a new concern: all those packages of frozen foods that I had brought from home and stowed in the trailer's lower compartment were now in danger of defrosting! A kind pastor's wife offered to make room for them in her freezer for two weeks.

On we went, stopping in towns and arranging for meetings for the return trip. We needed to get to Edmonton and talk with Gunter Flemke, whom we were replacing, to learn about our upcoming responsibilities for CBS.

Thus the great adventure began.

On the return trip we plunged into our new work with both enthusiasm and trepidation. It all looked so appealing but could we do it? Before many weeks we developed expertise constructing promos, preaching concise sermons, selling Scriptures, making posters, telling stories to children, and writing reports, letters and sometimes articles. We learned to love our work and this offset the disagreeable and hard things like cramped quarters, water shortages, finding sani-dumps, soothing grumpy people, battling mudholes, snowbanks, rough roads, and overcoming the vagaries of the weather. Friends commented, "It looks like this job was made for you." It was a constant challenge to our talents and abilities and it made us supremely happy.

That winter we roamed the Peace River Country doing our work. Before all the snow disappeared we ventured up the Mackenzie Highway to work in the Northwest Territories while the roads were still frozen. Samuel explained, "Firm roads save gas." He was concerned about saving every penny possible for CBS.

To Bella Coola

Not all Canadians know about a beautiful and verdant valley on the east end of Burke Channel on the West Coast. It is called Bella Coola. It can be reached by plane or boat and is also accessible by road from Williams Lake. A traveller must first cross the scenic Chilcotin Plateau, then climb the Tweedsmuir Range. In late April when we journeyed there, the mountains were still robed in deep snow. The descent into the valley is quite abrupt, dropping some 5,000 feet (1,524 metres) in approximately 10 miles (16 kilometres). Two sets of triple switchbacks with 18 per cent grades and no guard rails provide either thrills or terrors, depending on one's makeup. For a while a motor home was draped over a tree up there, but it had been removed and we did not see it. Almost suddenly winter is left behind and one journeys into glorious spring – lacy cedar trees, clear water flowing in streams with bald eagles patrolling them, deer bouncing off the highway. Farther on one sees small farms with flowering apple and cherry trees, green lawns, stocky clumps of rhubarb, ploughed garden plots, tulips and daffodils swaying in the breeze, cows and little calves grazing. Almost in a matter of minutes, one has entered a different world.

Just as interesting are the people and the churches. The little old priest who migrated from Hungary years ago takes great pleasure in showing us the chapel he has built, a work of art in itself. Three murals adorn the walls, each one taking three months to construct out of ceramic tiles.

We were blest in our visit with an independent group whose pastor is Miguel Moreno, an Argentinian. These folks were vibrant and welcoming. Seldom have I spoken to a more enthralled group of children. A complete contrast to that day's evening service where a two-year-old dominated the children's part of the meeting – absolutely exploding with naughtiness. Never have I experienced such total competition while speaking. Inwardly I begged the Lord to *do something*. Presently the child's mother came and removed the disruptive little rascal. Thank heaven, what a relief that was!

Bibles for Malawi

In late 1986 we visited Evangel Assembly in Grande Prairie. The pastor, Norman Labrenz, and his wife, although middle-aged, were getting ready to leave for Africa as missionaries. They faced a problem:

they wanted to take along articles for housekeeping, but they had heard that Scriptures were in short supply in Malawi and greatly needed. In the light of eternity, they opted for Scriptures. Just at that time we appeared and, when they looked over our display, they knew they had made the right choice. They purchased all they could afford at reduced prices, and then we also gave them additional copies outright.

Usually that is the last we hear of such a transaction. Some weeks ago a letter arrived from Malawi with this information: "The Bibles we purchased from you . . . we shipped them in barrels on October 15th. They arrived by slow boat in mid-April 1986. I go out to the Natural Resources College and teach a course on Scripture every Wednesday. Many of those young people have given their hearts to God but didn't have a Bible. Rather than give them one free (for a person doesn't value what you pay nothing for), we sold them for $2 each. My, how they treasure their Bible! Some of the earlier class have graduated but we keep in touch by mail. They have been posted at agriculture projects around the country and have written that they have started Bible studies in their villages; sometimes their Bible is the only one in that village. I thought you would be interested in what happened to 'your' Bibles."

Indeed, Pastor Labrenz, we are interested and much encouraged.

A Good Day!

We awoke with anticipation. This day we would be working in some churches out of Fort St. John, BC. After downing a nourishing breakfast of cheese omelette, we snatched up our essentials and hurried off to the first appointment 30 miles (48 kilometres) away. In the early sunshine the snow-covered earth resembled a vast brooch set with sparkling diamonds. Time was limited at this Mennonite Church. Pastor Dirks greeted us warmly and the congregation gave the Bible Society part of the Sunday School hour. Samuel gave his promotional talk and, after goodbyes, we left.

At Cecil Lake we found the young pastor standing outside in the snow and sunshine, apparently awaiting our arrival with some trepidation. (Earlier he had called the Bible Society man to ask if he believed in the new birth and other basics of the Christian faith.) If, for some reason, we failed to appear, he would be in a jam. He had gone fishing that week, and had no sermon prepared, and the place was filled with people!

We went inside. Sunday School was almost over and a great volume of noise issued from the classrooms. How would we cope with that, I wondered! Presently everyone got settled and the service proceeded. I told a children's story and was gratified to note the superb attention. Samuel followed with his promotional talk and then his sermon. The excellent attention continued. We moved back to the table where the Bibles were displayed, and then I discovered that my cash box was missing. It was not in our belongings anywhere. What could have become of that 40 dollars? We were meeting the people, selling Scriptures and rejoicing to find such an interested eager group of Christians in this rural setting. Pastor Zylstra must be doing a good work.

A young couple with three little girls invited us to their home for dinner. The pastor also invited us. Regrettably his invitation had to be declined. He and his young wife had moved from Toronto nine months before, and this had been his first holiday from preaching since his arrival. After a good country meal featuring home-made sausage, our hostess insisted we rest. Then, after more visiting, we took pictures and travelled on to Goodlow.

At Goodlow we shared a turkey dinner with the Marshall Holdstocks and other guests. The Holdstocks came from Britain to translate the Scripture into the Beaver Indian language. We found them as gracious and cordial as the other Wycliffe translators in the great Northwest. Samuel took pleasure in showing them the film *Trials of a Translator.* We longed to prolong the fellowship but another appointment compelled us to travel on. That money box. . . .

Another 30 miles (48 kilometres) took us across the Alberta border to Cherry Point. Our previous visit to this isolated Norwegian community had been outstanding and we anticipated this visit very much. This little church rarely has visitors so when guests come it is an *event* for them. We immediately sensed the warmth and appreciation, the attentive listening. We wanted to do our best for these good people. We served up a children's story, two films, a promo, plus a sermon. They absorbed it all. Afterwards they bought many Scriptures and served refreshments. When it was over, they helped us gather up our equipment and carried it out to the truck, wishing us God's blessing. They wanted us to stay for the night, which we declined since the weather and roads were good and we felt energetic enough to drive the 60 miles (96 kilometres) return to Fort St. John.

I sighed in thanksgiving. Not every time do things go so well but this time they did – fine weather, safe travelling, the mechanical items like the truck and projector functioning well, the inspiring people we met. The only flaw in a perfect day was the cash box. About 11:30 we stepped into the trailer and there on the filing cabinet sat the cash box smiling innocently! Thank you Lord, for such a beautiful day. Let me hold it to my heart a long time!

Beside the Skeena

Twice this year our trailer got into mischief. The most exciting moments of the year occurred on the stretch between Terrace and Prince Rupert, BC. The very narrow Yellowhead Highway is sandwiched between the formidable Skeena River and the CN Railway – a squeeze so tight that one wonders how a motorist could possibly cope with the emergency of a flat tire. The road was also very rough, putting extra strain on the caravan. Finally the road veered away from the river and Samuel was speeding up to climb the long steep hill ahead. A startling noise at the back end caught our attention and the side mirrors showed a shower of sparks flashing under the trailer. At once he steered to the shoulder and we leaped out to check. The hitch had broken, disengaging the trailer. Despite that, the trailer had followed right behind like an obedient camel. Had this happened earlier it could have disappeared into the Skeena River or collided with traffic. Two minutes later it could have rolled backwards down the hill or dropped off a cliff to its destruction. That it did not, is a miracle of God.

The next day a stranger offered Samuel a hitch to bring the trailer to his business place in town. After getting it repaired, he said, "That kind of thing doesn't happen twice in a lifetime. You must be praying to the right people!"

At a Gas Station

On our way into High Prairie, Alberta, we stopped at a gas station to gas up. The attendant noticed the *Bibles for Sale* sign on the truck and asked, "You got Bibles for sale?"

"Oh, yes," we assured him. He looked over our assortment, unable to decide which version or format to choose. He called the boss out to help. Instantly the boss was all interest, too, as he also wanted Bibles. He chose a Thompson Chain. As if selling four Bibles at a business place operated by Catholics on a Saturday morning was not enough happy excitement, the boss inquired about our work and, when he learned that we solicit funds for the Bible Society, he contributed a handsome $750 to the cause.

The Foot Incident

One evening after dark while walking rather smartly, Samuel's heel dropped into a hole while the toe did not. He tore a muscle in the heel so, for some time, walking flat-footed was painful. But he found that by placing a tuna fish can in the heel of his overshoe, he could manage. It wasn't elegant but it worked.

One preacher wise-cracked that maybe he had fallen off a horse.

End of Fifth Circuit

The day we completed our fifth circuit, we left Mackenzie, BC, and headed back towards Alberta. About 10:00 p.m. we stopped at a small place called Progress, perhaps 20 miles (32 kilometres) short of Dawson Creek. We pulled into the lane of a community hall to park for the night. The lane was muddy from a recent rain. We parked on a slight slope. Being very weary we fell asleep promptly. But several times during the night, I noticed that the trailer made strange groaning noises. The next morning I got up and dressed, when all at once I felt the sensation that the trailer was moving. It was! Eleven tons of caravan were slowly waltzing down the lane. I yelled to Samuel who had already leaped out of bed, and was now streaking through the door in his pyjamas and racing barefoot to the truck. On the way he fell face-down in the mud and gravel. Upon trying again he realized the truck door was locked but, by that time, the truck had reached a level stretch and stopped by itself. He came in bruised and minus some skin in spots, and pyjamas bloody. After first aid, a cup of tea and some rest, he perked up and soon we proceeded on our way to Alberta. Although he had forgotten to set the truck in gear the night before, God's good angels must have kept the caravan from moving until we were awake.

The North West District was discontinued in 1989. The area is now served by the Canadian Bible Society's National Office in Toronto. But the memory of the indomitable Nafzigers lingers on.

Part IV

Many Parts, All One Body

Chapter 15
Promoting the Work
with Visual Aids

Chapter 16
Canadian Bible Society
Bookstores and Bible Centres

Chapter 17
The Quarterly Newsletter

Chapter 18
Women's Auxiliaries

CHAPTER 15

Promoting the Work with Visual Aids

One picture is worth a thousand words.

Chinese Proverb

The Bible should be taught so early and so thoroughly that it sinks straight to the bottom of the mind, where everything that comes along later can settle on it.

Northrop Frye

July 1, 1957 was a red-letter day for the Canadian Bible Society, for on that date the Reverend Emmanuel J. Heuer, BA, BD, became visual education production Secretary. Over the next 17 years, he travelled the world gathering "footage" and stories to produce 16-mm films on the work of the Bible Society. From July 1, 1944 Heuer had served as District Secretary in the North Alberta District. His 13 years as a District Secretary had acquainted him with what was needed to effectively communicate, to supporters and potential supporters, the importance and significance of the Bible Society's work. His education at the University of Alberta and St. Stephens College, Edmonton, and his years as a minister of the United Church of Canada had provided valuable training for his new role.

During Heuer's years as District Secretary, "movies" were still something of a novelty for many people. Mani, as many called him, saw the possibilities for using this medium. The lack of electricity in much of rural Alberta meant that communities were not only without TV, but also without motion pictures of any kind. To provide power for a movie projector, Mani carried a portable generator on a small trailer behind his car. This meant he could, at any time and in any place, show a film. He was welcomed at rural schools at all times. The showing of a film was also a big attraction at Bible Society meetings in church halls. Mani's meetings were made much more interesting, and larger numbers were attracted to them. More and more people learned about the work of the Bible Society, and the number of supporters grew.

The supply of suitable films was limited, so Mani, though an amateur, undertook the production of films featuring the Bible Society's work. The best place to start gathering the material was close to home. With limited equipment he took pictures of the work of Bible Society colporteurs in the four western provinces. Colporteurs were distributing Scriptures in several languages along the picturesque Pacific coast, in the grandeur of the Rockies and to the farmers on the prairies. *Frontiersmen* was the title of the film telling the dramatic story of Bible distribution in Canada. This 28-minute film was an immediate success. There was a demand for it all across Canada and by other members of the United Bible Societies.

It became apparent that Bible Society work could be publicized more effectively if more such films were available. The Rev. Dr. J. A. Raymond Tingley, District Secretary of the Bible Society in British Columbia, spearheaded a move to draft Mani for the full-time production of Bible Society films. The General Board of the National Society gave a sympathetic hearing to the unanimous request and appointed him Visual Education Production Secretary in 1957.

The Heuer family settled into a new life in Toronto. The three musically gifted daughters had the advantage of the many facilities of a large city to further their education. Mrs. Heuer, Mercy, began a new career – working as a volunteer beside her husband in the basement workshop of their home. Their home provided all the office and film-producing facilities that they required for their work. There, scripts were written, films were edited and spliced and all the work of manufacturing high-quality productions was accomplished. One secret of the Heuers' success was their eagerness to learn, and their striving for excellence. It is a wonderful illustration of how people can develop their gifts and become highly successful by never being complacent and never refusing advice.

Several of the films featured stories of people being brought into the Christian fold. *Serango Harvest* centred on the work of Canadian

Baptist missionary nurse Anne Munroe. A missionary in India, she felt called to the people living in the hills around Serango. With malaria a constant scourge and wild tigers roaming the hills, it was a dangerous place. One night while she slept, a tiger snatched her little dog off her bed. But Munroe remained and continued to use all her skills to reach the people with the Gospel. The inhabitants were Animists, and they lived in constant fear of evil spirits. They believed that the ghosts of the dead haunted and tormented the living, if they were displeased.

One of their superstitions was that, when a mother died in childbirth, the mother's ghost would harm anyone who took the baby. As a result the babies of these mothers were taken into the jungle and left to die. Nurse Munroe told the people that Jesus Christ loved all little children. But the Good News was not accepted.

Then Munroe was given an opportunity to directly demonstrate the love of Christ in this respect. A mother of two died when her third child was born. Instead of taking the baby into the jungle to die, the father took it to Nurse Munroe. Two days later the father returned and was amazed to find that the nurse had not been harmed in any way. This became the talk of the tribe. The people began to really listen to Munroe as she told them about the love of Jesus and His power to save. The father of the baby, with great courage, became a believer and was publicly baptized. This was the beginning of a mass movement, which saw thousands in the valleys and hills of Serango become followers of Christ.

A remarkable feature of the Heuers' ministry was the low budget they required. Single-handedly, they did what others needed a whole crew to do. Mani travelled alone, carried his own equipment, operated his own cameras, researched the stories and wrote the scripts. Back home in the basement, with the help of his wife, who worked as a volunteer, the footage was edited and all the steps taken to complete quality films.

A new film was produced each year so, on September 1, District Secretaries had a fresh presentation for their deputation work. Over the years a film library was developed, from which churches, parishes and Bible Society Branch officers could obtain films for various programs. Reports, made each year on the use of films, indicate that there was a high demand year after year. To this film library were added films produced by the American Bible Society, the Bible Society of Australia and other Bible Societies in the English-speaking world.

Television stations were often looking for good material to complete their daily broadcast schedules. The Bible Society films were all strictly timed to 28 minutes, to conform to the needs of TV stations. By means of TV, a much wider audience was reached. Thousands who would never attend a Bible Society meeting or a church event learned about the work of the Bible Society. It was the high quality of the films, and the fascinating stories they told, that created a demand for them on TV. All this extra promotion was at no cost to the Bible Society.

The CBS films also attracted the attention of other Bible Societies in the United Bible Societies. They were used by the American Bible Society, the Bible Society in Australia, the New Zealand Bible Society, BFBS, the National Bible Society of Scotland, the Norwegian Bible Society, the Austrian Bible Society and others. Since the sound tracks were in English only, the films were shown without sound in some countries. In such cases they were accompanied by someone narrating the story in the local language.

An additional contribution made by Heuer was the production of 60-second "radio spots." These short tapes were appreciated by many radio stations. They were broadcast as public service announcements, at no cost to the Bible Society. Even more significant were the 30-second and 60-second TV "clips" shown as public service announcements. TV stations receive many public service announcements, and the degree to which they are used depends a good deal upon the opinions of the program directors. Directors often show what appeals to them and what they like. As a result the Bible Society TV clips received a disproportionate amount of air time. The Bible Society at no time paid for any spot announcements on radio or TV and in one year alone free time to the value of $400,000 was received. 160 English and 75 French radio stations carried the spot announcements.

Mani Heuer also contributed his talents to other facets of Bible Society work. He and his wife produced "displays" for Bible Society meetings. Together they took over the task of keeping up-to-date displays in the large window of the Bible Society building at 1835 Yonge Street, Toronto. It was encouraging to see people, at all times of the day and night, admiring the Bible Society window.

Heuer visited Bible Societies in Europe, Asia, Africa and Latin America, filming Bible Society work and collecting stories. The following partial list of films indicates the nature and extent of what was produced over a period of years.

Frontiersmen: colportage in western Canada
For Everyman: information for Bible Society canvassers
To Bala for a Bible: Wales (story of Mary Jones)
The Potter's Wheel: India
Cornerstone of a Nation: Canada
Under the Red Pagoda: Japan
Adventures of Yohan Pogum (Gospel of John): Korea
Crowded Ways: Taiwan and Hong Kong (jointly ABS and CBS)
Trials of a Translator: Dr. Eugene A. Nida
Freedom in their Souls: Africa
Three Sixteen World Street: helps for canvassers
Penzotti Pathways: South America
The Finest Gold: Thailand
Serango Harvest: India
Rejoice With Me: India (the Lost Coin and the Lost Sheep)
Two Leaves and a Bud: Sri Lanka
The Leaves of the Tree: Africa
Another Beatitude: India
The Land of the Wall: China
A New Spring in Coppermine: Canada

After the late Rev. E. J. Heuer retired in 1974, he continued to provide his services to the Canadian Bible Society. In the annals of the Bible Society around the world, many individuals have made outstanding contributions to the work, and Mani Heuer takes his place among that illustrious company. He was the right man in the right place at the right time.

Since Heuer's retirement there has been little Canadian Bible Society film production. Other Bible Societies around the world, however, continue to produce Bible Society films. Some of these, as well as those Heuer produced, may be found in the CBS film library.

With respect to visual aids, CBS has in recent years turned its attention to short videos as opposed to films. People may order these at nominal cost, to share with their families, friends and church groups. CBS videos include the following.

Let There Be Light: overall ministry of CBS at home and around the world

Light of the Amazon II: volunteers on the boat *Light of the Amazon II* minister to Brazilians both physically and spiritually

A New Day of Hope: Bible needs and Bible distribution in former Soviet Union

God Speaks My Language: translating Scriptures into Aboriginal languages in northern Canada

To Fulfil a Dream: Alaska's Yupik people fulfil their dream of enjoying the Scriptures in their own language

Good News from Behind Iron Bars: churches in Argentina start within prison walls when prisoners receive Bibles and become Christians

Challenge of India: the Gospel used as an instrument to teach spiritual truths as well as improve literacy levels

Challenge in Egypt: outreach programs help bring the Gospel as well as raise literacy levels

Rocky Mountain Ride: 12 bike riders cycle through the Canadian Rockies in 1992 to raise funds for Scriptures for Russia and Ukraine

Legacy of Love: how people can, through the Gift Annuity program, give a gift now that will provide for the future sharing of God's Word

Miracle in China: work of CBS in China

Mary Jones and Her Bible: how, through a young girl's desire for the Word of God, the Bible Society came into being in 1804

Lifestyle, Bible Is for Everyone: CBS ministry in Africa

In 1995 the Canadian Bible Society produced a one-hour television special featuring Moira Brown, former co-host of *100 Huntley Street,* as announcer. The video was aired on Vision as well as other stations across Canada, and was well received. In 1996 CBS shortened the TV special to a half-hour presentation and developed two public service spots. Again, these were aired on Vision and other stations across the country, and were well received by the Christian community. The television exposure significantly heightened awareness of the Bible Society's ministry.

CHAPTER 16

Canadian Bible Society Bookstores and Bible Centres

When people cease to believe in God, it is not that they will believe in nothing – rather they will believe anything.

G. K. Chesterton

The sky and the earth won't last forever, but my words will.

Matthew 24.35

The Bible Society in Canada has been unique among all members of the United Bible Societies since, for a number of years, it operated large and successful Christian bookstores. These bookstores, which sold books with a great variety of theological perspectives and doctrines, clearly violated the principle of distributing the Scriptures "without note or comment." CBS never made an official decision to ignore the Bible Society principle. Quite innocently, however, Bible depots selling the Scriptures in many languages found themselves meeting requests from customers for helps in teaching the Scriptures. To fulfil this urgent need, the Bible Society began to distribute more than the Scriptures.

Often it was a Sunday School teacher who wanted extra help in teaching. Bible depot managers, as a service to the community, and to keep the goodwill of Sunday School teachers, who also supported the work of the Bible Society, began to stock books to help such teachers as well as other lay people. In time the limited stock proved to be inadequate. Gradually the stores began carrying larger inventories, including theological books for the clergy. There were occasional objections to a certain book because some considered the doctrine of the author incorrect. For example, Harry Emerson Fosdick, the noted preacher of Riverside Church in New York, was considered a heretic by some. A few books were carried "under the counter" to avoid offending some, while still making them available to those who wanted them.

At one time there were several major Canadian cities that had a thriving Canadian Bible Society bookstore. The Bible Society in Vancouver appears to have been the first to break with the tradition of carrying only the Word of God in many languages. One day Mr. William Lee, a Bible Society supporter, came to the Bible depot and gave the Rev. Nelson Harkness, the District Secretary, $100,000 for the purpose of placing in the Bible depot a stock of Bible stories for children. He had been unable to buy a Bible story book for his grandchildren anywhere in Vancouver.

That $100,000 was the beginning of Canadian Bible Society bookstores. The Vancouver Bible depot began operating in 1937 and, on September 1, 1939, at Harkness's invitation, Miss Velma Cross became its manager. Her salary was $60 a month. The Book depot was a very small operation, with a $1,200 stock of Scriptures and a $200 stock of Bible story books. At that time there were no other Christian bookstores in the city. When people discovered that Christian books were available at the CBS Bible depots, they eagerly bought them and asked for more.

Miss Cross saw there was a great need for Christian books and, as a service to the churches, she began promoting the establishment of libraries in the churches. This increased the demand for Bibles as well as other books. The Bible Society was in an excellent location, and developing a retail business was feasible.

Under Cross's able management, the Canadian Bible Society bookstore in Vancouver became one of Canada's leading Christian bookstores. The volume of sales increased annually. Even when the store became a large operation, distribution of Scriptures still had a high priority, being consistently 50 per cent of total sales.

The Vancouver CBS bookstore was much more than a business. The officers of the Branches throughout British Columbia looked to the store manager for Bible Society promotional literature and for direction in Branch canvasses and Bible Society work in general. The office of the District Secretary was part of the store, and the general public saw the store and the Canadian Bible Society District as one unit. The store was a great financial asset. It generated enough profit from sales to cover not only all its own operating costs, but also all the administrative expenses of the British Columbia District. What is even more remarkable is that, during the 35 years Cross was Manager, profit from the store provided $500,000 for the translation, publication and distribution of Scriptures in the larger work of the Bible Society.

The Canadian Bible Society bookstore in Vancouver had the distinction of being the only one in Canada to be "held up." A young man once entered the store, held a knife to Cross's throat and took $270 from the till. Others in the store were unaware of the robbery, and the man was never apprehended.

All Canadian Bible Society Bookstore Managers have interesting stories to tell of their customers' requests. Then as now, people consistently asked for the impossible – a small Bible with large print, for instance. Plaques with Scripture quotations were a popular sales item. One woman seeking a plaque for a young man in prison found what she wanted in these lines quoted from a hymn:

Bless this house, O Lord we pray,
  Keep it safe both night and day,
Bless the walls so firm and stout,
  Keeping want and danger out.

The Vancouver CBS bookstore operated for 45 years. It closed in 1982, when the Society decided to return to the policy of carrying only Scriptures in the Bible depots.

The Vancouver Christian bookstore is an example of what took place in Calgary, Edmonton, Regina, Moose Jaw, Saskatoon, Winnipeg, London, Ottawa, Montreal, Saint John, Halifax and Charlottetown. The key to the success of a bookstore was the Manager, and the Canadian Bible Society was fortunate to have many who were outstanding in their field. Under the able management of Mr. David Reimer, for example, the CBS bookstore in Edmonton became the largest Christian bookstore in Canada. Each year, profit from the Edmonton store provided thousands of dollars for the general work of the Bible Society. Miss Nellie Bradley is another example. She was on the staff of the Canadian Bible Society in Regina from February 1, 1942 until December 31, 1979. Manager of the Bible Society store in Regina, she not only provided outstanding service to the customers, but was for many years the mainstay of Bible Society work in southern Saskatchewan.

Mr. C. G. Gunnar, a most conscientious Manager, worked in the Bible Society's Winnipeg bookstore for 47 years. He was ably assisted by his wife; even after their retirement in 1960 they continued to serve as volunteers. Mrs. Molly Austen managed a successful Canadian Bible Society bookstore in Halifax and also assisted the Nova Scotia District Secretary. Mr. John Brown, Manager of the CBS bookstore in Montreal, provided invaluable service to a wide constituency in Quebec. Similar comments could be made about CBS bookstore managers across Canada. They all felt they were in a Christian ministry and not just operators of a business. They were key people in the work of the Bible Society in their Districts.

The bookstore period of Bible Society work in Canada drew to a close as other Christian bookstores became more common in Canadian cities. The CBS stores had been started to meet a need that, at the time, was not being adequately met elsewhere. When people were being served by others, the Society returned to operating Bible depots where people could get the best selection of Scriptures in dozens of languages.

There were negative aspects to the Society having Christian bookstores but for four decades the positive features enhanced the Society's work. The bookstore period is one CBS can look back on with pride and with deep appreciation for the faithful managers. An essential Christian service was rendered to the churches and to the Canadian general public.

On April 22, 1982 the era of Canadian Bible Society bookstores officially ended when the following recommendation was passed.

> That the Executive Committee of the General Board encourages all Districts to operate Bible Centres which carry only Scriptures and that where a District elects to operate a Canadian Bible Society bookstore, that bookstore is requested to provide the same services as a Bible Centre and to fully participate in all national Scripture distribution programmes.

For a bookstore to change into a Bible Centre, a decision of the Board of the District was required and this meant the debate about operating Christian bookstores continued at the District level. To encourage Districts to adopt the new policy, National Office provided considerable guidance. The following are some of the communications this office sent to the Districts, along with detailed guidelines regarding the physical layout, the property and location, the staff, office hours, bookkeeping, and inventory.

A Proposal for Scripture Distribution in Canada

I. Close all Canadian Bible Society bookstores in Canada as of December 31, 1982.

II. Scripture distribution will then be carried on in three ways:

1. *Through Other Retail Outlets:* 600 English language bookstores and the almost 300 French language bookstores are already serviced by Central Stock Depot. CSD sales to these retail outlets surpasses by far CSD sales to our own bookstores. While we could go the way of the American Bible Society and sell to all customers at uniform prices (i.e. same prices both to the retailers and to churches and individuals), I believe we should maintain our services as a wholesale operation. Our service to the retail trade will continue to be upgraded and Scripture sales will be realized without any subsidies provided by CBS.

2. *Through National Office Projects:* Citizenship, Students, the Blind, the Armed Forces, etc. Also through direct marketing to churches and volunteers for some specific projects. This will have to be handled carefully, and explained to the retail trade.

3. *Through the Bible Centre:* Bible Centres are already in operation in the following Districts: Newfoundland, Ottawa, Hamilton, Upper Canada and Northern Ontario. These five differ from one another, and should now be organized on a more uniform pattern as outlined below.

What Is a Bible Centre?

General Description

1. *The Bible Centre,* operated only in locations where the Canadian Bible Society has a District Office, serves as the Scripture Distribution

Centre and information centre for the Canadian Bible Society. Only Scriptures are offered to the public for sale and for free distribution. All CBS promotional materials are also displayed. In this way we fulfil our mandate while projecting the image that reflects our objectives – the TRANSLATION, PUBLICATION and DISTRIBUTION of the Scriptures.

2. *The Bible Centre* is simply not feasible within existing bookstores, since the basic problem of operating bookstores would still be with us.

3. *Moving to the Bible Centre concept* will also give CBS a golden opportunity to reorganize the entire District operation in many locations. At a time when it is imperative for financial reasons to keep District operating costs at a minimum, the closing of the bookstores and consolidating the District Office with a Bible Centre in modest quarters could also realize a substantial saving. Savings would include reduced insurance on buildings and contents, and a reduction in payroll and staff benefits and pensions paid by National Office. Such a reorganization of District work is of prime importance.

It is not surprising that all the bookstores did not immediately cease to operate. Gradually, however, over a period of years, they changed into Bible Centres. Their inability to function without being subsidized was a major factor in persuading them to conform to the national policy and, by 1995, the transition was generally completed.

CHAPTER 17

The Quarterly Newsletter

When men turn away from God, one of two things happen: they will think they are gods and go mad, or they will turn to carnality and live like animals.

Blaise Pascal

How beautiful upon the mountains are the feet of those who bring the happy news of peace and salvation, the news that the God of Israel reigns.

Isaiah 52.7

The British and Foreign Bible Society had two main publications. Several times a year it published a small magazine called *The Bible in the World,* which kept churches and Bible Society supporters informed about Bible Society work around the world. Since the Bible Society provided missionaries with the Scriptures they needed for their work, *The Bible in the World* was widely regarded as a prime source of information about Christian missionary work in the world.

This same publication was mailed to Bible Society supporters in Canada. After a time, at the request of Canadians, *The Bible in the World* published a special edition for Canada, with the back page given over to the work of the Bible Society in Canada.

The other main publication of the British and Foreign Bible Society was the *World Report,* which appeared annually. This small book was a comprehensive survey of the Christian Church's growth on all continents. It was a resource for speakers on Christian missions and a fund of wonderful illustrations and stories for sermons. Ministers' libraries often contained several years of these *Reports*. They constituted a valuable contribution made by the Bible Society to the churches.

Shortly after Dr. McMillan became CBS General Secretary in 1957, he saw the need for a Canadian publication to replace *The Bible in the World*. If there was indeed to be a Canadian publication, consideration had to be given to writing the material, to maintaining a mailing list, to mailing the publication and to covering the overall cost. Mr. Keith Graham of Chesterville, Ontario was the publisher of the local weekly newspaper there. He had facilities to print the publication, to address mailing labels and to do the mailings. Arrangements were therefore made for him to provide these services to the Bible Society. The post office did not give reduced mailing rates for a publication mailed fewer than four times a year. This was the main reason why the publication was made *The Quarterly Newsletter*. The first issue was published in May 1960. It became an immediate success, replacing *The Bible in the World* in Canada and becoming the chief means of keeping donors informed about the work.

The Canadian Bible Society engaged the Rev. Leslie K. Tarr as a "consultant" on public relations and publicity. Les Tarr was a journalist, as well as professor of communications in a Baptist Theological Seminary. He was a wise counsellor and provided excellent advice on *The Quarterly Newsletter*, the Annual Report, press releases, monthly advertisements in religious periodicals, and information leaflets. The General Secretary, being responsible for writing all that was published, was fortunate in having the advice of a communications expert. For 20 years Tarr provided his services at the same modest rate of $1,800 a year. He knew it was important to motivate the recipients of the *Newsletter* to open it and not to simply discard it unread, as a piece of "junk mail." Tarr advised Dr. McMillan to begin writing, in each issue, an inspirational column which both clergy and donors would find helpful in a practical way. The article was not to be about the work of the Bible Society but about Christian living in general. Tarr believed that a regular feature such as this would lead people to open the publication. When they did they would then go on to read more than just Dr. McMillan's article and thus be informed about the work of the Bible Society.

The General Secretary's articles became very popular and were used for sermons by ministers, for devotions at church meetings and for private devotions. Many regular readers of *The Quarterly Newsletter* filed away the General Secretary's messages and they continue to be used years after they first appeared. A book entitled *Against the Tide,* containing a number of these messages, was published in 1984. It went into a second printing and, while copies are no longer available, people continue to request it.

Over 200,000 copies of *The Quarterly Newsletter* were being mailed every three months; for a quarter of a century it became the main means of promoting the work of the Canadian Bible Society. Each issue contained an advertisement for Canadian Bible Society Annuities or an advertisement to encourage people to remember the Bible Society in their wills. There was an encouraging response to these ads. The Bible-a-Month Club was also a regular feature.

The Canadian Bible Society Newsletter (adopting the title *Our Bible Matters* in 1998) is now published three times a year instead of four. Its circulation is approximately 125,000 copies per issue. There is also a French edition *(Actualités bibliques)* which is published twice a year, and has a circulation of about 10,000 copies per issue.

CHAPTER 18

Women's Auxiliaries

Very early on Sunday morning the women went to the tomb carrying the spices that they had prepared. When they found the stone rolled away from the entrance, they went in. But they did not find the body of the Lord Jesus, and they did not know what to think.

Luke 24.1-4

When they returned, they told the eleven disciples and the others what had happened.

Luke 24.9

Women have played key roles in the work of the Canadian Bible Society. In many Branches the officers, canvassers and main workers have been women. While women have generally not formed separate organizations to promote and support the work, some Women's Auxiliaries were indeed organized across the country. The Ladies' Bible Society of James Church, New Glasgow, Nova Scotia began in 1857. For many years it contributed to the New Glasgow Auxiliary of the Bible Society. Also in New Glasgow a Ladies' Auxiliary began in Westminster Church, and this continued in Trinity Church after Church Union in 1925. In Yarmouth, Nova Scotia a Ladies' Association was started in 1904 for the purpose of furthering the aims of the Bible Society.

In New Brunswick the Society has been greatly aided by Ladies' Auxiliaries. For example, in 1825 the Ladies' Bible Society of Miramichi helped meet demands caused by the Great Miramichi Fire.

The records of the Montreal Bible Society also refer to the work of a Ladies' Auxiliary.

A Bible Women's Mission was established in Ottawa in 1876; it engaged a competent woman to act as District visitor, Bible reader and colporteur. In western Ontario a Ladies' Bible Association was formed in 1864 to work in cooperation with the Upper Canada Bible Society, which served the whole of western Ontario at that time.

The above mentioned organizations are no longer functioning. There are, however, two Women's Auxiliaries which continue to be active.

In 1930, the Women's Auxiliary of the Upper Canada Bible Society was founded in *Ardwold,* a beautiful historic residence on Spadina Avenue, Toronto, the home of Lady Eaton. The inspiration for this organization came from a visit to Toronto of the Governor General and Lady Willingdon. They were guests at Chorley Park, the official residence of Lieutenant Governor and Mrs. W. D. Ross. Mrs. Ross, a native of Nova Scotia, expressed regret that there was no Women's Auxiliary of the Bible Society, like those in her home province. Lady Willingdon, whose father had been deeply interested in the British and Foreign Bible Society in London, encouraged the formation of the Auxiliary and consented to be the foundress.

At a second meeting, on May 12, 1930, at Government House, the Auxiliary was officially organized with Mrs. Ross as the Honorary President. That office was filled by the wife of the Lieutenant Governor for many years – until 1992, when Mrs. Isobel McMillan, wife of the former CBS General Secretary, was appointed Honorary President. From its formation in 1930 the organization was greatly respected. It attracted as its officers highly esteemed women, and to its membership prominent women from all Christian traditions.

Long before ecumenical practices were common, the Bible Society brought together church members from many denominations, and the Women's Auxiliary reflected the church life of Toronto. The Council of 25 was composed of representatives from each of the major denominations. The Council held monthly meetings. Four times a year, it held public meetings in different churches, with speakers on the work of the Bible Society. One of the organization's basic principles was to have every congregation in the city represented by a "key woman," who promoted the work of the Bible Society in her own congregation.

For many years the Auxiliary contributed about $25,000 annually to the local District of the Bible Society. It also encouraged the purchase of Bible Society Annuities and the leaving of legacies to the Bible Society. In 1965 the first Sunday in May was designated Bible Society Sunday from coast to coast in Canada, and members of the Women's Auxiliary were responsible for this becoming an annual event in their congregations. Through the work of the Women's Auxiliary, a very favourable image of the Society has been developed and many women have received valuable education about its work. Over the years the Women's Auxiliary has been a place where women from many Christian traditions have found, in promoting the work of the Bible Society, common ground on which they could work and pray.

The Toronto of 1930 has given way to the multicultural city of the present. However, the need continues for Christian women from all churches to help with the translation, production and distribution of the Word of God. In 1998, the Women's Auxiliary opened its doors to men in their Bible work efforts, becoming "The Toronto Auxiliary". To develop new and innovative fundraising events to attract both young and old, some members formed the "Toronto Project Committee".

The other CBS Women's Auxiliary that continues to be active is in Regina. It is the Women's Auxiliary of the Saskatchewan District. Even before Saskatchewan became a province in 1905, the Bible Society was well known there through the work of the Rev. E. J. B. Salter, the pioneer of Bible Society work on the prairies. Few communities in the province were without a Bible Society Branch. In the city of Regina, however, the Branch system in time ceased to function well. Regina was too large for just one community Branch, so attempts were made to establish a Branch in each congregation. Women who were active in these congregational Branches found it difficult to get people to canvass. Financial support for the Bible Society was far less than what was needed.

In September 1961 seven concerned women gathered in the lower hall of the Bible Society on Albert Street to consider ways of spreading information about the Society and increasing financial support for it. Mrs. Georgina Gill from the United Church chaired the meeting. The decision was made to form a Women's Auxiliary of the Bible Society,

The British Columbia District once received a gift of $75,000 from an anonymous donor. The District Secretary, the Rev. Dr. Raymond Tingley, and the President, the Rev. T. M. Badger, watch the Treasurer, Mr. Art Riley, write a receipt for the largest single gift received by the Canadian Bible Society.

Photo: Photo Arts Studio, Vancouver.

The fifth-wheel trailer, home of the Rev. Samuel B. Nafziger and his wife Martha, as they covered the vast North West District of Canada. They provided the Scriptures to many remote areas and presented a Christian witness to thousands.

The Rev. Dr. Gerald E. Benson left the business world in 1979 to become District Secretary in Newfoundland and Labrador. During his 17 years in this position, support for the Bible Society from church leaders and congregations reached an all-time high.

Mrs. Ruth Benson assisted her husband in his work, managed the St. John's office of the Bible Society, and supplied Scriptures to Newfoundland and Labrador.

Photo: H. Best Photography.

Isobel McMillan and General Secretary Kenneth G. McMillan at a Bible display featuring the *Today's English Version New Testament,* at a meeting of the American Bible Society in New York in Nov. 1969. In 1966 the New Testament in Today's English Version, under the title *Good News for Modern Man,* was published by the American Bible Society. The Old Testament was published in 1976 and the Deuterocanonical books in 1979.

Mr. David Reimer, manager of the Canadian Bible Society bookstore in Edmonton, with a display of Bibles. For many years the Edmonton store, managed by Mr. Reimer, was the largest Christian booktore in Canada.

Photo: Keith McNichol.

In 1958,
a Canadian Bible
Society delegation
presented a Bible
to the Honourable
John G. Diefenbaker,
Prime Minister
of Canada.

In 1977, Dr. Kenneth G. McMillan presented a French Bible to the Honourable Pierre Elliott Trudeau, Prime Minister of Canada.

Photo: United Press International.

The Canadian Bible Society has presented special Bibles to Canadian Church leaders of all denominations. The Rev. Randolph R. Mohr, South Alberta District Secretary of the Canadian Bible Society, presents a Bible to the Right Rev. George M. Tuttle when Tuttle was elected moderator of the United Church of Canada in 1977.

Photo: Wolf Kutnahorsky, Berkeley Studio, United Church of Canada.

Pope John Paul II with Canadian Bible Society General Secretary Dr. Kenneth McMillan and his wife Isobel, at the Vatican in 1979.

Photo: Foto Felici, Rome.

The Hon. Chief Justice Frederick Johnson of Regina and Dr. Henry D. Hicks of Halifax at a meeting of the General Board. Dr. Hicks was Canadian Bible Society President from 1965 to 1968. The Hon. Chief Justice Johnson served in that position from 1977 to 1980.

Father Jean-Louis d'Aragon, SJ, current Chairman of the Conseil francophone.

Dr. Fernetta Levy of Wolfville, Nova Scotia has given leadership to the Canadian Bible Society over many years. She has been President of the Nova Scotia District, President of the National Society and a Vice-President of the United Bible Societies.

The Rev. Dr. Floyd C. Babcock, General Secretary, 1989-1997.

The Rev. Father Gregory Evan Bailey became National Director of the Canadian Bible Society June 18, 1997.

Photo: Dragon Imaging.

Walkathons have raised many thousands of dollars for the work of the Canadian Bible Society. The Rev. Stanley Snowden of the Maple, Ontario United Church registers young people for the "Walk."

Canadian Bible Society transit shelter advertising, 1990s.

Derek R. Patton served on the staff of the Canadian Bible Society from 1978 until his retirement in 1998. As manager of Scripture supply and distribution, he held one of the Society's most important offices. Maintaining adequate stocks to fill orders for thousands of Scriptures in some 100 languages is a heavy responsibility.

The Rev. Martyn C. Thomas, with 27 year of service, is the longest serving District Director. He joined the staff in 1971 as Assistant District Secretary in Montreal. In 1974 he was transferred to Ottawa, and since 1987 has been in charge of the South Alberta District.

Photo: Gordon Campbell, Brampton, Ontario.

Mr. Samuel Burke Horwood. His $50,000 legacy to the Canadian Bible Society made the publication of this history possible. Mr. Horwood was involved in the work of the Bible Society all his life.

and Mrs. Evelyn Mills of the Anglican Church agreed to chair the group planning its formation.

The first challenge was to recruit at least one woman from each congregation in the city to represent her congregation on the Auxiliary. This meant phoning all of the city's clergy and asking them for the names of women who might be suitable and willing to serve. Finally, after four months, on January 14, 1962, the first meeting was held at the Bible House in Regina. Women in attendance numbered 45, and the founders were greatly encouraged. Thirteen officers were elected. Mrs. Berta Bridle, wife of the District Secretary, was the Honorary President. Mrs. Evelyn Mills was the President and Miss Nellie Bradley, the Bookstore Manager, was first Vice-President. The officers were from five different denominations.

When the Women's Auxiliary was organized in 1962, Miss Bradley had already been on CBS staff for 20 years, and was greatly appreciated throughout all of southern Saskatchewan. Nellie was well known for the part she played in the operation of the Canadian Bible Society bookstore in Moose Jaw, Saskatchewan, as well as her management of the one in Regina. While her contribution to every aspect of Bible Society work was outstanding, the important part she played in the Women's Auxiliary deserves special recognition. Altogether she served the Society for 37 years, from February 1, 1942 until December 31, 1979.

From the beginning the Women's Auxiliary of the Saskatchewan District planned its work with great care and drew up detailed guidelines for the future. Nothing was left to chance. Meetings of the Executive Committee would be held at 2:00 p.m. the first Tuesday of each month. The Annual Meeting was to be held at the Bible House at 2:00 p.m. on the second Tuesday of January, with a meeting of the Executive immediately following. There would be four General Meetings each year in the lower hall of the Bible House. The main fundraising events would be two teas each year. These teas were to be convened in turn by the ladies of the Anglican, Baptist, Lutheran, Presbyterian, Salvation Army and United Churches. Smaller denominations were invited to share if they wished to do so.

In recent years the Annual Meeting and potluck luncheon have been held at First Presbyterian Church, Albert Street and 14th Avenue, Regina. General Meetings are now held in churches. Over the years the Saskatchewan Women's Auxiliary has raised thousands of dollars for Scripture translation. The teas and other gatherings of the Auxiliary bring together women from all the churches. They actively promote interest in all meetings of the Bible Society, and a greater understanding of the significance of the work. Women like the first President, Mrs. Evelyn Mills, Mrs. Grace Henderson of First Presbyterian Church, Miss Nellie Bradley and a host of others have, since 1962, given the leadership that has made this group a significant part of the Canadian Bible Society.

Part V

Ways and Means

Chapter 19
From Canvassing to Direct Mail:
A Paradigm Shift in Fundraising

Chapter 20
Annuities and Legacies:
Vital Elements in an
Ongoing Fundraising Program

Chapter 21
Bible Sunday and
Bible Society Sunday

Chapter 22
The Bible-a-Month Club
and the American Example

CHAPTER 19

From Canvassing to Direct Response: A Paradigm Shift in Fundraising

I am the Lord All-Powerful, and I challenge you to put me to the test. Bring the entire ten percent into the storehouse so that there will be food in my house. Then I will open the windows of heaven and flood you with blessing after blessing.

Malachi 3.1

Fundraising is one of the major responsibilities of the Canadian Bible Society. To some, this may seem a very "unspiritual" activity, but without money the Scriptures cannot be placed in people's hands. Jesus spoke a great deal about money and possessions. Our proper use of them is not a substitute for faith in Christ, but it is a very real expression of that faith. The Scriptures in English are of use to only a small fraction of the world's population, even though English is a major international language. Translators have to be supported by the gifts of interested people. Paper for printing has to be paid for. Printing presses must be operated. The Scriptures have to be transported, often under difficult conditions. Finally, when the Scriptures reach their destination, in most cases, the potential reader does not have the money to pay the full cost of a Bible, a New Testament or even a Gospel. The Scriptures must be provided below cost or free of charge. In countries where the annual income is only a dollar a day, a day's wages will not pay for a Bible. Millions of dollars are required each year for Bible Society work in countries around the world.

From the beginning, the basic organization of the Bible Society in Canada was the community Branch. The Branch's main purpose was to raise funds for the British and Foreign Bible Society's use in translating, producing and distributing Scriptures for Canada and overseas. The Parent Society held a large place in the hearts of those in the Branches. From the District Secretary the Branch received information on Bible Society work, and made this information available to the pastors and other interested people in the community.

The main way funds were raised was by a door-to-door canvass of the area's towns, villages and farms. This was done by volunteers from the community's churches, and the annual appeal became a regular community event. It was conscientiously carried out and few homes were missed. A canvasser would not hesitate to walk out to where a farmer was ploughing in a back field to ask for a donation. Often one or two people systematically covered the whole countryside, if more canvassers could not be recruited. The Bible Society canvass was a serious undertaking. In the years when 50 per cent or more of the Canadian population lived in rural areas, and when the Bible Society canvass was often the only annual canvass, it was a highly successful method of fundraising. There was no cost involved in collecting the funds, and all money received was forwarded to the District Office.

The names of all the Branches, officers and amounts collected were published in the Bible Society's Annual Reports. Branches competed with one another, and much satisfaction was derived from reading the Annual Reports and financial statements. Through the Branches, thousands of people enjoyed a direct, personal link with the Bible Society. It was a wonderful system for a largely rural population.

Canvasses in towns were as fruitful as in farming areas. As towns grew, however, it became increasingly difficult to find people to organize and carry out the street-by-street canvass. The larger the town or city, the more difficult it became. One of the last cities to discontinue the canvass was Edmonton. For over 20 years Mrs. Jean Campbell was Manager of the Bible Society bookstore in Edmonton, and she gave several weeks each year to the Bible Society canvass. Campbell was well and favourably known, and was able to recruit the large number of canvassers required. But each year, as the city grew and the character of the population changed, it became more and more difficult to find canvassers. One problem was that the work of the Bible Society was foreign to many who were approached.

Eventually the Edmonton canvass became too difficult, and it was abandoned in the 1960s.

By then nearly 70 percent of the Canadian population lived in urban areas, and the urbanization trend was continuing. As Canada changed the Branch system could not continue. The rural Branches struggled on but, as farms became larger and rural populations smaller, they too found it difficult to function.

It is no exaggeration to say that, with the failure of the Branch system as its main fundraising mechanism, the Bible Society faced a crisis. Yet there was great reluctance to change. The District Secretaries cherished the warm, personal relationship they had with faithful Branch officers and supporters, and longed for ways to restore the Branch system to its former glory. Bible Society supporters were accustomed to the local, personal appeal of the Bible Society and were suspicious of change.

Fundraising had always been strictly a District responsibility, and there was great reluctance to yield any fundraising to the National Office. However, in 1968 the National Office began to provide the Districts with material to mail to their supporters, where Branches continued to exist. There was little in the way of mailing lists and the mailings were not coordinated or unified. Preferential postal rates were not available for this type of mailing. The money was received at the District Office and each Branch was credited with all the gifts from that community. It was a labour-intensive and expensive fundraising method that proved not to be viable.

As a last attempt to rescue the Branch system, the National Office proposed establishing Congregational Branches to replace the Community Branches. It was thought that congregations might find it possible to undertake a canvass of the congregation for the work of the Bible Society. After a few years it became evident that congregations had other priorities, and this idea was abandoned.

Dr. McMillan, CBS General Secretary from 1957 to 1983, proposed Direct Mail as the only viable alternative to the Branch system. Direct Mail was opposed by the District Secretaries, the District Boards and many faithful supporters. It was a radical departure from tradition, and everyone sensed that adopting such an anti-establishment method of approaching donors was a break with the highly cherished past. On June 2, 1972, Dr. McMillan sent a letter advocating the change to the members of the Sub-Executive Committee, the District Secretaries and the Managers of the Canadian Bible Society bookstores. He wrote in part:

> **A Proposal for a Major Change in the Canadian Bible Society**
>
> For a long time the Canadian Bible Society has had the problem of finding a way to reach people in the city, to approach them with the claims of the Canadian Bible Society and to provide them with a means of making a contribution. In the country, towns, villages and small cities, there is enough community feeling to permit Canadian Bible Society Branches to function. Door-to-door canvasses, the best known method of collecting Bible Society funds, are possible in rural and smaller communities. There is reason to believe that "Donor's Choice" appeals as they are currently developing in Saskatchewan may be of real benefit to the Canadian Bible Society in towns, villages and rural areas. . . . There are still quite a few smaller communities where the church is a big community, social and religious factor and, where this is the case, the Bible Society can often find a place in the church's life and work.
>
> The larger city is quite different. A smaller and smaller percentage of the city population is connected with the church and, where there is a connection, it is increasingly tentative. If the work of the Society is presented in a city church, the . . . congregation at the services on that Sunday is usually only a small percentage of the total membership. City churches are hard pressed financially and are in constant trouble with their budgets. . . .
>
> **Direct Mail Appeal**
>
> I am proposing that the Canadian Bible Society establish a Direct Mail Appeal Program, that this be instituted in a limited number of large cities, and that it be set up on a highly specialized basis employing experts in the field. Just as an airplane is no good if it is only 50 per cent or even 90 per cent effective, so Appeal by Mail has to be based on a total, complete, professionally conducted program which utilizes the competence and highly developed skills of experienced people. This is something that can only be done nationally and carried on from one centre. . . .
>
> I do not think that fundraising by Direct Mail is a perfect method of fundraising but no one knows of a better one for urban areas. . . . To begin with I propose that the Direct Mail Appeal be limited to the

> following cities: St. John's, Halifax-Dartmouth, Montreal, Ottawa, Toronto, Hamilton, London, Sudbury, Winnipeg, Edmonton, Calgary, Vancouver, Victoria. You may wish to add cities I have not included in the above list.
>
> A new Department of the Canadian Bible Society will have to be developed which will deal exclusively with the continuous and growing program of Direct Mail Appeal. . . .
>
> I am well aware that this proposal represents a major change of direction but I believe it can be introduced without major dislocation of present staff or disruption of the present work. This new department will specialize in doing what is now being neglected – approaching in a direct way the population of our larger centres. I see the District Secretary as continuing to play a role similar to what he does now as a personal representative of the Society and as a field man. Present staff and work will give support to this new approach. I am very anxious to continue to have a CBS staff person personally involved in the District, personally visiting congregations, giving visibility to the Society and continually making the presence of the Society felt at the local level. . . .
>
> This proposal is not made as a desperate effort to rescue the Society. Actually our work is going very well. We have a warm, close and cordial relationship with all the churches, especially with the church headquarters. The image of the Bible Society among most church people, and certainly among church leaders, is good. But new plans and approaches ought to be made, not when deterioration has set in but to make sure the momentum is continuous. It is important to anticipate new needs and to introduce them before, not after, there is a crying need for them. Changes can be made too early and also too late. I believe that this is the right time to make this change. . . .

Resistance to inaugurating a full-fledged Direct Mail program continued. The Canadian Bible Society's Constitution made no provision for National Office to engage in any kind of fundraising. The Districts had the right to raise money within their own borders, to spend money within their territory as they saw fit, and then to send whatever was not spent locally to National Office. Only by ignoring the Constitution and the traditional methods of Bible Society work could Direct Mail be introduced. It was argued that donors in the West and East would not send their donations to Toronto, that Direct

Mail was too impersonal and that donors would lose contact with their District Office. While there were many objections to the proposed change, there were no proposals as to any other way to collect money.

The Canadian Bible Society owes an immense debt to the American Bible Society for the help they gave in the area of Direct Mail. At one time the ABS had had a Branch system, but changes in society had forced them to abandon it. They were leaders in the field of Direct Mail, and they had as a consultant a man who was regarded as one of the best in the world. They shared all their resources with the Canadian Bible Society. Their consultant and the Rev. Dr. John D. Erickson, head of the ABS Ways and Means Committee, came to Toronto to teach CBS the basic rules of Direct Mail. This professional help was provided at no cost. The ABS people were able to answer the questions raised by Canadian District Secretaries and others, and could speak with authority and from experience, for they were familiar with all the objections to and arguments against Direct Mail.

Gradually the Direct Mail program developed. Mr. Keith Graham of Chesterville, Ontario, in addition to mailing the CBS Quarterly Newsletter, set up a mailing system for Direct Mail. He proved to be a most faithful and diligent supplier of this service. However, as the system developed, it was necessary to utilize a computer system and this meant engaging other suppliers. In 1974 the Rev. Gunter Flemke, District Secretary in the North West District, took over the task of developing a Direct Mail program for the Canadian Bible Society. On September 6 of that same year, Dr. McMillan was able to send the following letter to the District Secretaries.

> **Direct Mail Program**
>
> We are now in the process (and have been for some time) of preparing the packet for the October 31 (last for 1974) mailing. It will go to about 275,000, (and) contain an appeal letter based on the anticipated over-expenditure of $515,000 in the United Bible Societies World Service Budget for the current year, a sheet outlining the Bible-a-Month Club, a return envelope with the District address, and the card with the name and address of the prospective donor which will have space to indicate the allocation of the gift.
>
> There is no reason to believe that a Direct Mail Program will not be a continuing element in the fundraising efforts of the Society. Coupled

with that statement I would like to reiterate that a basic and essential ingredient in the life and work of the Canadian Bible Society for the present and for the future will be the principle and policy of having District Secretaries as personal representatives of the Society in the Districts. This is basic to our operation and there should be a clear understanding that, while the role of the District Secretary may change (it is inevitable that it will change) and while we may be forced into other changes, we do not want to abandon having District Secretaries personally representing the Canadian Bible Society as we have in the past. I hope that, when this fact is firmly established, everyone will be able to approach the Direct Mail Program in a positive manner and see it as a vehicle to help them rather than as something which threatens them.

All of us are keenly aware of the difficulties in setting up a Direct Mail Program. There would appear to be two approaches to these difficulties.

i. Some recount the problems and difficulties as reasons why the DMP won't work.
ii. Some face the same problems and difficulties as obstacles which must be overcome and as challenges which must be met.

There is no question that the DMP presents problems but I hope you will endeavour to fall into "ii" and not "i" above.

Gunter Flemke has been asked to set up a "System" which will:

(1) Enable the mailing lists (Chesterville and all others) to be properly maintained.

(2) Have sufficient codes and categories to enable a central mailing service to serve the complete mailing needs of the Society both nationally and for Districts.

(3) Enable "test" mailings to be carried out.

(4) Provide a means for regular contributors to receive information through receiving the Quarterly Newsletter and appeal letters, and provide them with a way of making donations.

(5) Promote programs such as the Bible-a-Month Club.

(6) Encourage Scripture distribution.

(7) Provide us all with the information we need.

(8) Permit analysis to be carried out.

Two years later a letter Dr. McMillan wrote to the District Secretaries, in August 1976, shows that resistance to the Direct Mail Program persisted:

> It is difficult for anyone who is not familiar with all the details and intricacies of the computerization of the Canadian Bible Society mailing list to realize just how much there is to deal with and how many problems there are. I have talked to people in the computer field and I assure you they do not minimize the enormous task that we have. They all say the first months of going onto computers are horrendous.
>
> Some of the Districts were unable to get information returned to National Office on schedule, and this has resulted in it being received at the last minute. As a result a good deal of work that should have been done some weeks ago has to be handled now. The size of our list is what staggers people who deal with mailing lists. When the numbers of 'lines' and 'strokes' there are in 350,000 names and addresses are calculated, those familiar with such programs all speak of the enormity of the task we have.
>
> Literally dozens of decisions have to be made, and many are still being made, in setting up the program. If any one decision is wrong, the program will not work. When wrong decisions are made, and when these are discovered by testing the program, they have to be corrected – with all that involves. The hours of mind-wearying labour which are required has meant working 18 hours a day. While these matters are being dealt with, plans for the remainder of 1976 and also for 1977 have to be made, so this is also a current responsibility.
>
> At present we are faced with giving answers to questions which Hawker Siddeley are asking. As the program goes into operation, points have to be clarified and decisions have to be made. To give the answers which Hawker Siddeley are waiting for, we are writing a 25-page paper. If any one answer is wrong it will have serious consequences in the future. You can appreciate what a responsibility it is giving Hawker Siddeley the right answers.
>
> In all the planning, the role of the Districts and the wishes of the District Secretaries have top priority. The difficulty is that, as the program develops, no matter how much we try to do what the District Secretaries want, it is impossible to write a program to please everyone. Also, as the program develops, problems arise which were not foreseen and changes

> have to be made and decisions have to be taken. This is one of the most difficult aspects of setting up the mailing list for the Direct Mail Program. It would be a great help if you could understand that, when your wishes are not met, it is not because there is no attempt to do so, but only because there are limitations to what can be done. Also I think we have to 'come to terms' with the Direct Mailing program and use our ingenuity to 'sell' it to the District Boards, the Branches, the canvassers and all our supporters.
>
> Actually everything is going extremely well – it is just that it is such an enormous change. The helpfulness and support of some of the District Secretaries is an encouraging aspect of this major advance in our work. I am writing this letter to both thank you for your understanding and to ask for your support of the Direct Mail Program.

In spite of the many difficulties, Mr. Flemke gave able leadership to CBS's Direct Mail Program until he left to further his career in 1981. Miss Barbara A. Walkden, who had been assisting him, then became stewardship director. Over the years she developed into one of the outstanding fundraisers in the Bible Society movement.

Eventually all Districts recognized that, with all its weaknesses, Direct Mail was the way of the future and the best way to communicate with donors. It became the Society's primary method of fundraising. The computerized central mailing system under the aegis of the National Office was accepted since it was the only economical way to reach both present and potential donors. The constitutional legality of National Office taking on fundraising was never addressed. The necessity for moving most fundraising from the Districts to the National Office outweighed the letter of the law.

In 1990 the name Direct Mail was changed to Direct Response. Barbara Walkden became director of the department called Ministry Funding. Ministry Funding includes Direct Response and Planned Giving, which is the sale of Gift Annuities as well as Bequests and Wills.

Ministry Funding also became responsible for advertising and promoting the Bible Society. Its promotion activities include continuing the historic promotion of Bible reading through the publication of an annual list of Daily Bible Readings. Ministry Funding is also responsible for all news releases and for communicating with all types of media.

In 1995 a very successful "poster campaign" was undertaken. Poster displays were placed in public transit shelters in the Greater Toronto area, and the Canadian Bible Society won the "Billi Award" for outdoor advertising. The poster campaign brought the Bible Society extensive press coverage.

One of the Canadian Bible Society's promising new responsibilities is providing assistance in fundraising to many members of the United Bible Societies. In a number of developing countries, including India, Brazil, Singapore and Taiwan, there is a growing middle class. There are people who could contribute financially to Bible Society work. In recent years Walkden travelled the world conducting fundraising seminars with Bible Society staff members. The Canadian Bible Society has always helped many countries with finances; now the new resource it is providing is training of personnel. Until her recent departure from CBS, Walkden was a major participant in adapting to the transformations with which the United Bible Societies are continually involved in our rapidly changing world.

CHAPTER 20

Annuities and Legacies: Vital Elements in an Ongoing Fundraising Program

Don't store up treasures on earth! Moths and rust can destroy them, and thieves can break in and steal them. Instead, store up your treasures in heaven, where moth and rust cannot destroy them, and thieves cannot break in and steal them. Your heart will always be where your treasure is.

Matthew 6.19-21

The Canadian Bible Society always needs money to provide the Scriptures for which people are eagerly waiting. Today, however, Canadians are bombarded with appeals from hundreds of charities, and the Bible Society is in competition with a multitude of worthy causes. Fundraising has become highly sophisticated.

Also, in recent years, "ecclesiastical crime" has been growing. Dishonest appeals and highly exaggerated claims are utilized by some fraudulent charities. Programs can be designed not so much to meet a need, as to elicit a generous response from donors. The Bible Society, on the other hand, follows the practice of simply providing factual information with the conviction that, when the genuine need is known, God will put it into the hearts of Christian people to respond.

Information about the work of the Bible Society is provided through leaflets, the CBS Newsletter, Annual Reports and press releases. Sunday by Sunday the work is presented by the District Directors and volunteers in churches. Bible Society films have played an important role in making the work known. Posters, advertisements, radio spots and TV ads are in constant use. As times change, the Society is always on the alert for new and imaginative methods and appeals to motivate financial support.

One tried and true means by which people give to CBS work is through Annuities, which the Society began selling in 1926. For a gift to the Society, the donor is guaranteed an annual income for life from his or her investment. The rate of interest depends on the age of the purchaser. A husband and wife can purchase a Joint Annuity with the interest being paid until both die.

Money received from the purchase of Annuities is invested for the lifetime of the Annuitant. When the Annuitant dies, the portion of the original purchase price that has not been returned to the Annuitant in annual payments is used for the general work of the Canadian Bible Society.

People find Annuities so satisfactory that, over the years, they keep adding to their original purchase. The largest investment in the Canadian Bible Society Gift Annuity Program is by a 96-year-old man who lives in Victoria, BC. He bought his first Annuity in 1964 and, as of July 11, 1996, has a total of 73 Annuities amounting to $2,184,840. When this donor dies, many thousands of dollars will be available to the Canadian Bible Society for its work. His brother, two sons and their wives, and another daughter-in-law also have Canadian Bible Society Annuities. This is only one of many testimonies to the satisfaction people derive from an "investment" that guarantees an income for life and also serves Christ after they die. The Canadian Bible Society's income from Annuities varies from year to year, but some years it has been over $500,000.

Legacies constitute another important portion of CBS's annual financial support. When people remember the Bible Society in their wills, they have the satisfaction of knowing that their money will continue to serve the Lord on earth after they have gone to Heaven. All Christians are called to be good stewards of their material possessions. By means of their wills, they can provide for the needs of their families and also give money towards the advancement of Christ's Kingdom.

It is not generally recognized that, taking inflation into account, the Canadian nation today holds about twice as much wealth for each Canadian as it did in 1967, Canada's Centennial Year. Canadians have more wealth in their homes and more luxuries. Technical developments and possessions have risen faster than government debt. Life expectancy for women has increased by nearly six years. For men it has increased by over six years.

In the same period of years, since 1967, few would claim Canadians have become a happier and more contented people. Many of us have been living lives based on the pursuit of power, material comfort, and scientific and technological advancement. And we have discovered that these do not bring fulfilment. They do not provide any real meaning to life. Moreover, in our quiet moments, we realize that all we struggled to possess will be taken from us at death. Some try to fill the void with sports, with entertainment, with New Age religion, with constant activity. But they sense there must be something more. Christians know that "Man does not live by bread alone," and that fulfilment is found only in a personal relationship with Christ.

For Christians, the proper use of their wealth is a heavy responsibility. The purchase of a Canadian Bible Society Annuity and the leaving of a Legacy to the Society are two ways that Christian stewardship can be wisely practised.

Advertisements in the Newsletter and in the Annual Report are major ways by which people are encouraged to purchase Annuities and leave Legacies to CBS. The following, part of an ad which appeared in the Christmas 1997 Newsletter, is typical of these.

The Benefits of a CBS Gift Annuity

Income for Life – Guaranteed

Receive tax-advantaged income for life, an immediate income tax deduction, and a great rate of return (as high as 11.5% to some). You can receive these significant financial advantages while supporting the important mission of the Canadian Bible Society with a CBS Gift Annuity.

For a FREE quote (without obligation on your part), please complete and return the coupon below.

CHAPTER 21

Bible Sunday and Bible Society Sunday

The sin of this century is a loss of a sense of sin.

Pope Pius XII

A glory gilds the sacred page,
Majestic like the sun;
It gives a light to every age,
It gives, but borrows none.

William Cowper

The Second Sunday in Advent (approximately three weeks before Christmas) has long been regarded as Bible Sunday. This is the Sunday in the Christian Year when the Collect for the Day in the Anglican Book of Common Prayer is:

> Blessed Lord, who hast caused all holy Scriptures to be written for our learning: Grant that we may in such wise hear them, read, mark, learn, and inwardly digest them, that by patience and comfort of thy holy Word, we may embrace and ever hold fast the blessed hope of everlasting life, which thou hast given us in our Saviour Jesus Christ. Amen.

The Anglican Church (Church of England) can – and could – be found throughout the whole British Empire. Through its example the Second Sunday in Advent also became established as Bible Sunday in several other denominations in a number of countries including

Canada. On that Sunday the Bible's place in the life and witness of the Church is presented from many pulpits, and the importance of the Word of God is emphasized. For Bible Sunday the Bible Society provided the churches with information on its work. In some parishes and congregations, an offering for Bible Society work was received annually on that day.

Bible Sunday falls on the last Sunday in November or the first Sunday in December. It was obvious that a Sunday shortly before Christmas was not a good time for the churches to take an offering for Bible Society work. As the year draws to a close, many congregations ask their members to make additional offerings for the congregational budget and for the denomination's mission work. Special gifts are needed to balance the books for the year. Thus an offering for the Bible Society often seemed to be in competition with the local church's interests. Also, just before Christmas, most people are too busy with concerts, family celebrations, gifts, and the like to be concerned with the Bible Society.

In 1960 Dr. McMillan saw the need to establish a second Sunday when the work of the Bible Society would be presented. He proposed the first Sunday in May as Bible Society Sunday. It would be observed in addition to Bible Sunday, the Second Sunday in Advent. The advantage of instituting such a change was recognized by many, but there were diverse opinions as to which was the most suitable date. Over the next four years, a number of possible Sundays in the year were proposed as the best choice.

One problem with fixing on a day was that many Sundays already had special designations – Pentecost, Mother's Day and Thanksgiving being just a few. As well, certain times of the year, such as summer holidays, were not appropriate. There already seemed not to be enough suitable weeks in the year to allocate one to each of the many worthy Christian organizations which wanted a week to publicize their work. For several years choosing a suitable Sunday was debated at meetings of the CBS District Secretaries and in the Districts.

Since there appeared to be no way to find a date on which all could concur, Dr. McMillan arbitrarily announced that, beginning May 2, 1965, the first Sunday of May each year would be Bible Society Sunday. In May the winter weather is over, the summer holidays have not yet begun, and church activities are not being reorganized as they are in the autumn.

The General Secretary's decision was accepted. Almost immediately throughout all of Canada, the first Sunday in May was recognized as Bible Society Sunday.

The Second Sunday in Advent continued to be Bible Sunday, and some parishes and congregations promoted the work of the Bible Society on that date. Very soon, however, many people assumed that the first Sunday in May had always been Bible Society Sunday. The work of the Bible Society and the need for funds were widely publicized in the media as well as in the churches at that time of year. In the history of the Canadian Bible Society, May 2, 1965 – the first Bible Society Sunday – is a memorable date.

Bible Society Sunday continues to be featured. However, with the decline in institutional religion in Canada, only a minority of congregations now celebrate it. Similarly *Bible Fun,* a new program for boys and girls, has not been widely adopted by congregations.

Since the responses to both Bible Society Sunday and Bible Fun have been disappointing, they were combined into a new program in 1997. It is called *Celebrate the Bible.* Among promotional material provided for this program are sermon notes and ideas.

CHAPTER 22

The Bible-a-Month Club and the American Example

What is unthinkable is that our schools, which are so often and so sanctimoniously trumpeted as fitting the youth for life, should wholly reject religion, which has shaped our history since the dawn of human life and which is an inextricable element in our thought and history.

Robertson Davies

Lord, from age to age you gather a people to yourself so that, from east to west, a perfect offering may be made to your name.

Roman Catholic Sunday Liturgy

The American Bible Society has always freely shared its resources with the Canadian Bible Society and other Bible Societies around the world. Like other Bible Societies, CBS has benefited greatly from what it has received from the Americans. This has been particularly true in the area of fundraising. Dr. Robert Taylor for many years, and then Dr. John D. Erickson, gave leadership to the American Bible Society in this area.

Fundraising is not a science; it is a skill learned from working in the field. Taylor and Erickson found there was no way of determining if an appeal would meet with a response except by evaluating the results. The Canadian Bible Society has profited greatly by adopting fundraising projects already proven successful by ABS. By this means the Canadian Bible Society has often been saved the expense and time required to discover the best ways of communicating its needs to donors.

You Have to Pass the Plate

Dr. Taylor of the ABS found that, while public relations played a role in fundraising, the most important element is the means by which funds are collected. He stressed that "You have to pass the plate," illustrating this by telling of a fundraising project that failed. When Will Rogers – the popular humorist, movie star, homespun philosopher and American idol – was killed in a plane crash in 1935, a group of leading personalities in radio, motion pictures and the press decided to establish the "Will Rogers Fund." They launched a nationwide campaign to raise millions of dollars.

The sponsors were well-known and highly respected. Will Rogers was a popular American folk hero known in every household in the country. The power and prestige of the entertainment world and news media vigorously promoted the appeal. The organizers anticipated that the fund would be oversubscribed. Three months after the appeal was launched, however, the sponsors met and, to their amazement, found that only a few dollars had been received. The campaign was declared a failure and discontinued.

The reason for the failure was that the organizers had neglected to devise a way to collect the money. Without a concrete, simple, effective way to receive donations, all their prestige, propaganda, publicity, public relations and promotion amounted to nothing. The Bible Society, fortunately, has never been guilty of such a major error in judgement, but the illustration makes a good point nonetheless.

For many years an important means of financial support for the Canadian Bible Society was through donors becoming Members or Governors by making contributions ranging from a few dollars to several thousand. The Annual Report for the year 1981 lists the following Memberships and Governorships:

	$
Annual Membership	5
Life Membership in Branch	100
Life Membership in District	200
Life Membership in Canadian Bible Society	300
Life Membership in British and Foreign Bible Society	1,000
Life Governorship in CBS	1,500
Life Governorship in BFBS	2,000
Life Membership in United Bible Societies	3,000

Such Memberships and Governorships provided support for the general work of the Society. In 1985, however, the legal significance of Memberships and Governorships was called into question and they were discontinued. This was a major change in the Society for, historically, the right to vote at an Annual General Meeting of a Branch and of a District had been restricted to those who had made a contribution in the amount of at least an Annual Membership.

The American Bible Society found that supporters responded well to the Bible-a-Month-Club program. It was easy to understand, and the donors felt personally involved in placing a copy of the Scriptures in the hands of a reader every month. Each month the appeal was for a different country, and for the Scriptures in a different language. Interested people had only to join the Club to participate in Scripture distribution.

Encouraged by the American example, the Canadian Bible Society adopted the Bible-a-Month Club in 1977. The Annual Report for 1978 recorded that the membership had increased that year to 12,996. On April 1, 1979 Miss Barbara Walkden joined the CBS staff in the stewardship department. That year membership in the Bible-a-Month Club increased by 45 per cent, realizing $774,378 to place Scriptures in 12 different countries. By 1980 membership had reached 29,000, and the Club raised almost a million dollars. On December 1, 1981 Barbara Walkden became Service Manager of Information by Mail, and the Bible-a-Month Club became an even greater means for friends of the Bible Society to participate in the work.

The Bible-a-Month Club gives information about the need for Scriptures in specific areas of the world and enables people to learn about conditions in different countries. They thus become aware of the importance of the Bible Society's translation programs. Until 1988 the cost of joining was only $3 a month, and people derived great satisfaction from knowing that such a small amount of money placed a copy of the Scriptures in the hands of those eager to receive it.

Membership in the Bible-a-Month Club has declined to 18,300, but it continues to generate 30 per cent of Direct Response income. The Bible-a-Month Club continues to be one of the most cost-effective Direct Response fundraising programs, since it costs only 3 cents to raise each dollar. This allows for some 97 cents to go directly towards providing the Scriptures. One of the main reasons the Bible-a-Month Club membership has not grown may be that there is a worldwide decline in commitment. People seem to hesitate to commit themselves to making regular monthly payments.

Part VI

Past Leadership, an Inspiration for the Future

Chapter 23
Presidents

Chapter 24
General Secretaries

Chapter 25
District Secretaries

Chapter 26
The Future:
As Bright As the Promises of God

CHAPTER 23

Presidents

In the West, the primary civilizing force was Christianity. It provided a transcendent spiritual end which gave Western culture its dynamic purpose.

Historian Christopher Dawson

The Canadian Bible Society, since its inception in 1905, has been able to attract outstanding Canadians to serve as Presidents. The Presidency is an honorary position, but that does not diminish its importance. When a well-known and highly respected person serves as President, the credibility of the Society is enhanced and the confidence of the donors increased. The Society has endeavoured to recruit people from different denominations and from all the geographical regions of Canada to fill the office.

While the President presides at meetings of the General Board and Executive Committee, his or her greatest responsibility is to act as a counsellor to the General Secretary and to the Society in general. Some individuals who have served as President have also held office in the local District. For the past 50 years, however, the General Board has been free to elect any outstanding Canadian to the office.

Newman Wright Hoyles, KC, BA, LLD, President 1905-1923

The first President of the Canadian Bible Society set a standard that challenged all his successors. He was one of the principals in the formation of the Canadian Bible Society in 1905. He then served as

President from 1905 to 1923, and as Honorary President from 1922 to 1927.

He was born in St. John's, Newfoundland, on March 14, 1844. Educated in Upper Canada College, Toronto; King's College, Windsor, Nova Scotia; and Trinity College, Cambridge, England; he had a distinguished legal career. He lectured on Canadian jurisprudence at Columbia University, New York prior to becoming principal of Osgoode Hall Law Schools, Toronto in 1894. Hoyles was an active Anglican layman, and the Bible Society was one of the great interests of his life. He died November 6, 1927.

Allan McNab Denovan, BA, President 1923-1925

The second President was also a Toronto barrister. The prominence of the Upper Canada Bible Society in the Canadian Bible Society's early years meant that the first two Presidents were from Toronto. Denovan was a Baptist minister's son and a native of Glasgow, Scotland.

Sidney Thomas Smith, President 1925-1947

The third President was a prominent Winnipeg businessman. Born in London, Ontario, on November 12, 1878, he became a junior partner of G. B. Murphy & Co. and a member of the Winnipeg Grain Exchange in 1907. During the years 1932-33 he was President of the Winnipeg Grain Exchange. He acquired a national and international reputation because of his contacts with wheat markets in many lands.

Raised a Presbyterian, Smith founded Elim Chapel, an independent congregation in Winnipeg. He was a leader in the business world, but his greatest interest was in organizing Bible Conferences and addressing many types of meetings on the importance of the Bible. He said he derived more satisfaction out of Bible Conferences than out of an order for a million bushels of wheat.

The 22 years he served as CBS President spanned the Great Depression and World Wars I and II. It was a period when the Canadian Bible Society took important steps to establish itself as a significant National Society. Smith was a chief proponent of the purchase of 122 Bloor Street West, Toronto, which enabled the Canadian Bible Society to move out of the Upper Canada Bible Society building and have its own national office. Besides serving as President of CBS, he also became Vice-President of the British and Foreign Bible Society in 1928. He died January 31, 1947.

Thomas G. Rogers, President 1947-1961

An executive of the Lake Simcoe (Ontario) Ice and Fuel Company, Rogers was an officer of the Society for 30 years. He served as Honorary General Treasurer from 1931 to 1947, and as President from 1947 to 1961. Active in Eaton Memorial United Church, Toronto, and astute in business, he brought to the Society both Christian commitment and practical guidance in administration. A self-educated man, he had an interest in art and literature, and a book of his own poems was published. He died on April 8, 1974 at the age of 97.

The Honourable Dalton Courtright Wells, QC, MA, LLD, President 1961-1965

A distinguished lawyer, an active Anglican and a renowned Justice, Wells gave freely of his time and talent to serve as President. It was while he was CBS President that the Society's Constitution was changed to provide for the appointment of the General Secretary by the General Board instead of by the British and Foreign Bible Society. In 1967 Wells was appointed Chief Justice of the High Court of Ontario. When Ghana became an independent African nation, he was seconded to that country for several months to assist in organizing its justice system. He died October 4, 1982 at the age of 82.

The Honourable Henry Davis Hicks, CC, QC, BSc, MA, DCL, DEd, LLD, President 1965-1968

This distinguished Canadian was born at Bridgetown, Nova Scotia, March 5, 1915. A United Church layman, a Rhodes Scholar, and a graduate of Oxford and several other universities, he served overseas in World War II, practised law in his native province of Nova Scotia, and served as President of Dalhousie University from 1963 to 1980. In 1963 he was appointed a member of the Canada Council. In the midst of his busy career, he also found time to serve as President of the Canadian Bible Society.

In his home province of Nova Scotia, Hicks served at various times as Minister of Education, Provincial Secretary and Premier. In 1972 he became a member of the Canadian Senate – a position he held until his death. Dr. Hicks had a profound understanding of the world for which the Canadian Bible Society sought to provide the Scriptures, and of the significance of the Bible in the life of Canada and all nations.

Dr. William G. Black, MA, PhD, President 1968-1971

The seventh CBS President was from Vancouver. Born in London, England, the son of a Baptist minister, he devoted his life to the service of God and other people.

During World War II he was a Staff Officer in the Pacific Command, and after the war he taught vocational counselling at the University of British Columbia. The first Canadian Citizenship Act took effect in 1947 and Dr. Black became the first Citizenship Liaison Administrator. Deeply committed to human rights and justice, he served on the social action committee of the BC Convention of Baptist Churches, and on the Vancouver and District Council of Christian Churches. He assumed responsibility for churches being represented at each sitting of the Citizenship Court in Vancouver. There the Canadian Bible Society presented Old or New Testaments to new Canadian citizens.

As Citizenship Liaison Administrator, Dr. Black worked closely with the Multicultural Society, the Folk Festival and various ethnic groups. After he retired he continued to work with immigrants and with the Immigrant Services Society. He was one of the founders of the Inter-Faith Citizenship Association. Dr. Black saw religion as an integral part of Canada's multicultural society.

He was President of the British Columbia District of the Canadian Bible Society and a tireless worker for the Bible cause. The Bible was the basis of his involvement in promoting a sense of kinship and understanding among all Canadians, his interest in the peace movement, and his deep concern for social justice. He died in Vancouver on September 2, 1978 at age 80. In his memory his sisters installed a memorial window in Fairview Baptist Church, Vancouver. The window depicts the sower, emblem of the Canadian Bible Society.

The Rev. Dr. E. G. B. Foote, OBE, CD, BA, DD, DCL, President 1971-1974

From the days of World War I, the Bible Society has held a special place in the life of the Canadian Armed Forces, since it has supplied hundreds of thousands of Testaments to the military. Chaplains have encouraged Armed Forces chapels to provide financial support for the work of the Bible Society. Each year there has been a good response to the appeal.

Thus it was very fitting that Dr. Foote was among those who have served as CBS President. A Presbyterian minister, he was a Naval Chaplain in World War II, Chaplain of the Fleet in the Royal Canadian Navy from 1945 to 1962, and Chaplain General (P) from 1962 to 1966. From 1967 to 1975 he was a member of the War Veterans Allowances Board, and he also served as Honorary Chaplain of the Royal Canadian Legion for the Dominion Command. In addition to being an Officer of the British Empire, Foote was invested by the Governor General as an Officer of the Order of St. John.

All his life he had a profound interest in the work of the Bible Society, and in all the places he served as a Chaplain, he took part in the Society's local work. He died November 3, 1979 at the age of 70.

Dr. Frederick R. MacKinnon, OC, MA, MSW, LLD, President 1974-1977

Bible Society work is part of Nova Scotia's history, and it is not surprising that more than one of its Presidents have been from that province. A United Church layman, Dr. Frederick MacKinnon became Deputy Head of Public Welfare for the province of Nova Scotia in 1947. He taught social security and the nature of the social policy process, becoming Deputy Minister of Social Services in 1959. Serving as President of the Canadian Rehabilitation Council for the Disabled and as District Governor of Rotary International were but two of the many ways he contributed to the well-being of Canadians. In 1976 he became President of the Vanier Institute of the Family.

Besides acting as CBS President, MacKinnon also expressed his long-time interest in serving as President of the Nova Scotia District and supporting a variety of aspects of the work.

The Honourable Frederick W. Johnson, OC, SOM, QC, BA, LLB, President 1977-1980

The Honourable Frederick W. Johnson was one of Saskatchewan's most outstanding citizens. A United Church minister's son, he was active in Bible Society work in South Saskatchewan for many years. Born in Staffordshire, England and educated in Saskatchewan, he had a broad vision of the Society's responsibilities for both Canada and the world.

In 1941 Johnson joined the Canadian army and, as an Artillery Officer, served in Europe from D-Day until the war ended. When discharged in 1946, he studied law at the University of Saskatchewan, was called to the bar and practised law in Regina. His gifts were quickly recognized and in 1960 he was elected a Bencher of the Law Society of Saskatchewan. Three years later he became a member of the Council of the Canadian Bar Association. In rapid succession he was appointed Queen's Council, Chair of a Royal Commission on Administration in the province of Saskatchewan, and Chair of the planning committee for the province's centenary project. In 1965 he was appointed a Judge of the Court of Queen's Bench in Saskatchewan, and in 1977 he became Chief Justice. As Chief Justice he was a member of the Executive of the Canadian Judicial Council. The crowning achievement of his illustrious career was serving as the 16th Lieutenant Governor of Saskatchewan from July 6, 1983 to September 6, 1988.

He was named an Officer of the Order of Canada in 1990 and a member of the Saskatchewan Order of Merit in 1991.

Johnson's whole life was given to service. He served as an elder in the United Church, as a School Board trustee, on the Board of Martha House in Regina, on the Advisory Board of the Salvation Army, and with numerous other organizations. The F. W. Johnson Collegiate in Regina was named in his honour in 1986. He died suddenly June 20, 1993 at the age of 76.

The Honourable Justice E. E. Hinkson, BA, LLB, President 1980-1984

Mr. Justice Hinkson was born in Regina, Saskatchewan, where he received his early education. After graduating in History from the

University of Toronto, he studied law at the University of British Columbia, graduating in 1952. After practising law in Vancouver for 16 years, he was appointed a judge of the County Court of Vancouver. In 1970 he was appointed to the Supreme Court of British Columbia, and in 1977 to the Court of Appeal.

Hinkson was active in the British Columbia District of the Canadian Bible Society, and in 1977 became Honorary Recording Secretary of the National Society's General Board. Serving as President from 1980 to 1984, he oversaw the transition of the General Secretaryship from Dr. Kenneth McMillan to the Rev. William R. Russell. As Past President, Hinkson continued to advise the General Board until 1987. His involvement in the work of the Bible Society in British Columbia and his experiences in his profession enabled him to give wise and helpful counsel.

The Honourable Gordon L. Bennett, MSc, DCL, LLD, President 1984-1986

A native of Charlottetown, Prince Edward Island, and one of the area's most highly respected citizens, the Honourable Dr. Gordon Bennett has a distinguished record of public service.

Bennett began his career as an elementary school teacher. As a member of the Prince Edward Island Legislature from 1966 to 1974, he served as President of the Executive Committee, Minister of Education, Minister of Justice and Attorney General, and Provincial Secretary. He was Canadian Delegate to a meeting of UNESCO (United Nations Educational, Scientific and Cultural Organization) in Paris and to the Commonwealth Parliamentary Association in Sri Lanka. From 1974 to 1980 he was Lieutenant Governor of PEI.

Among the many other offices Bennett held was the presidency of the PEI British Council for Canadian Unity. For a number of years he was Chancellor of the University of Prince Edward Island. An active United Churchman, he served as Honorary Recording Secretary of the CBS General Board from 1981 until he was elected President in 1984.

Dr. Fernetta Levy, DD, President 1986-1990

No one has come to the office of President with longer or more active service than Dr. Levy. As a young girl she canvassed for the Bible Society, and as a pastor's wife she was active in local Branches. She saw Bible Society work as an integral part of the life and mission of the Christian Church as a whole, and also of the Baptist denomination in which she played such a significant role.

Dr. Levy was very much involved in the Baptist Young People's Union in the Maritime Provinces, and served as Secretary of the Convention for five years. For 10 years she was a member of the Canadian Baptist Overseas Mission Board. In 1985 she became the author of a history of the Baptist World Alliance Women's Department. She served a term as President of the North American Baptist Women, and also served on committees and boards within the Canadian Baptist Federation, both nationally and internationally.

She spent two months in Bolivia, representing the women of Canada on a Baptist Overseas Mission Board fact-finding mission. She was involved in the committees, camps and conferences of the CGIT (Canadian Girls In Training) and served on committees of the Women's Inter-Church Council of Canada, YMCA (Young Men's Christian Association) and the CNIB (Canadian National Institute for the Blind). All these, and other activities, prepared her for the service she was called upon to give the Bible Society.

In 1972 Dr. Levy was elected a Vice-President of the Canadian Bible Society. She was the first woman to hold such an office in the National Society. Four years later she became the first woman President of CBS's Nova Scotia District. From 1977 to 1984 Dr. Levy was a Vice-President of the United Bible Societies. UBS coordinates the work of some 100 national Bible Societies around the world, and it was not only a great honour for Dr. Levy to be elected to this office, but also a compliment to the Canadian Bible Society. She played an important role in Bible Society work in North, Central and South America, and attended United Bible Societies meetings in Mexico and Miami. In 1980 she was a representative of CBS at the world gathering of Bible Societies in Chiang Mai, Thailand. She was Honorary Recording Secretary of the Canadian Bible Society from 1984 to 1986.

Dr. Levy is a person of many unique honours and achievements. She was the first woman to receive the degree of Doctor of Divinity *(honoris causa)* from Acadia University, and the first lay person to deliver the baccalaureate address at the convocation. She is Honorary President of CBS's Nova Scotia District and Honorary Past President of the National Society – another first. Since 1973 she has attended every annual meeting of the National Society – still another record. She has the distinction of holding both an Honorary Life Membership and an Honorary Life Governorship in the Canadian Bible Society, as well as being a Life Member of the American Bible Society.

For many years she provided significant support to her husband, the Rev. Dr. I. Judson Levy, long-time and greatly beloved Chaplain of Acadia University. When chapel bells were dedicated as a memorial to her late husband in September 1995, she participated in the service. Dr. Levy continues to speak on behalf of the Bible Society and to provide wise counsel out of the storehouse of her wide experience.

The Right Reverend John Reginald Sperry, DD, President 1990-1997

Bishop Sperry was born in England, where he received his early education. After serving in the Royal Navy in World War II, he trained for the Anglican ministry at King's College, Halifax, and at St. Augustine's College, Canterbury, England. After ordination in 1950, he answered the Call for clergy in the Arctic and spent his entire ministry there. He served at St. Andrew's Mission, Coppermine, NWT, first as assistant missionary and then as missionary-in-charge. In 1956 he was made a canon of All Saint's Cathedral, Aklavik, and in 1961 he was appointed Archdeacon of Coppermine.

While serving in Coppermine, Sperry translated the Canadian Prayer Book into the Copper Inuktitut dialect, and completed the translation of the four Gospels and Acts of the Apostles into the same dialect. In 1969 he was made Rector of St. John's Church, Fort Smith, NWT. In 1974 he was elected the third Bishop of the Anglican Diocese of the Arctic and was consecrated on March 31 in St. Jude's Cathedral, Iqaluit.

In 1973 the College of Emmanuel and St. Chad, Saskatoon awarded Sperry the degree of Doctor of Divinity *(honoris causa)*. In 1979 Wycliffe College, Toronto, conferred the same degree on him.

As Bishop Sperry travelled over his vast diocese, he gained firsthand knowledge of the whole Arctic, and his understanding of the population became invaluable to many organizations. As a member of the Northwest Territories Boy Scouts of Canada Council and of the Northwest Territorial Historical Advisory Board, he has made significant contributions to Arctic society. Since retiring as Bishop of the Arctic in 1990, he has continued to live in Yellowknife, NWT, and to be involved in the life of the people of the North. As well he has continued to give valuable leadership to Bible Society work in all parts of Canada and overseas.

With his missionary heart and Episcopal experience, Bishop Sperry has brought to the Bible Society a deep devotion to its goals and much practical help in furthering the work. The Anglican diocese of the Arctic has a long tradition of Evangelicalism. During his years in the Arctic, Sperry promoted the development of indigenous leadership, the training of Aboriginals as clergy, and the Church's direct involvement in the life of the people. As CBS President, his experience and good judgement have been invaluable in the administration and vision of the Canadian Bible Society. He has travelled widely for the Bible Society, both in Canada and overseas. As a Vice-President of the United Bible Societies, he is involved in Bible Society work in over 100 countries.

CHAPTER 24

General Secretaries

One thing should encourage us. The graveyard of history has many stones to mark the passing of various ideologies. One marker, though, is missing. There is no gravestone for historic Biblical faith. It lives and will continue to do so for its word is eternal.

Dennis F. Kinlaw, *Christianity Today,* April 29, 1951

The Chief Executive Officer of any organization is the most important person in shaping its work. The General Secretary of the Canadian Bible Society, who is the Chief Executive Officer, occupies an office which has even greater responsibilities than are normally associated with the position. The Canadian Bible Society's Constitution provides very limited authority to the national body. Yet in practice it is the National Society which is largely responsible for the welfare of the work across Canada. This makes the office of General Secretary both demanding and frustrating. The General Secretary bears responsibilities which can only be fulfilled by diplomacy and persuasion.

Long before the business world found that an authoritarian style of leadership was ineffective, the General Secretary of the Canadian Bible Society had to display a "servant leadership" which gave him moral authority. The General Secretary could not be authoritarian, but he had to be authoritative to provide the leadership which is so essential. This required men of intellectual and moral stature who could command the respect and confidence of the Christian community in general, as well as of CBS staff, officers, Board members and donors. The General Secretary, more than any other person, gave cohesion to the organization and kept before the constituency the larger vision of

Society aims and objectives. While no human being is actually capable of filling the office adequately, the Society has been able to persuade outstanding people to accept the call of God to the position.

The Rev. Dr. R. E. Welsh, MA, General Secretary 1905-1907

In 1904, when the various Bible Societies and Auxiliaries across Canada agreed to form the Canadian Bible Society, Auxiliary to the British and Foreign Bible Society, they recognized that one specific person would be required to coordinate the work. There was no provision for Canadians to appoint such a person, as that was the prerogative of the Parent Society. (This policy continued until 1972, when the Constitution and Act of Incorporation were amended to authorize the appointment to be made by Canada.)

In April 1905 the British and Foreign Bible Society appointed the Rev. R. E. Welsh as "General Agent to supervise the work in Canada and as the representative of the British and Foreign Bible Society on the Board of the Canadian Bible Society, Auxiliary to the British and Foreign Bible Society." It appears, however, that Mr. Welsh's gifts and talents were not suitable for the duties of the office. Within two years he had left to accept a position as a professor in a Canadian university.

The Rev. W. B. Cooper, MA, DD, General Secretary 1907-1927

The 23rd Annual Report of the Canadian Bible Society, Auxiliary to the British and Foreign Bible Society, in announcing the death of Dr. Cooper, includes this tribute to him:

> Dr. Cooper brought to his office a highly trained mind, and a character that won for him the admiration and confidence of all who were brought into contact with him. He had a distinguished scholastic and ministerial career – from 1882 when he took his Master's Degree in Arts at Aberdeen, to 1907 when he accepted the General Secretaryship of the Canadian Bible Society. And he had a literary faculty of no mean order. The past 20 years have shown a very wonderful advance in Bible Society organization. Not only has it been stabilized and knit together, but public interest has been increased to a remarkable degree. The Auxiliaries have become active centres of Bible distribution and, . . . have

made a generous response to the world work of the British and Foreign Bible Society.

Dr. Cooper's term of office coincided with one of Canada's great periods of immigration, which challenged the Scripture distribution programs of the Bible Society. He travelled widely and saw Auxiliaries and Branches established from sea to sea. It is noteworthy that several Canadian Bible Society Districts give as their date of origin the period in which Dr. Cooper served: British Columbia in 1908, South Alberta in 1908, North Alberta in 1918, North Saskatchewan in 1922 and South Saskatchewan in 1922. Travels often entailed considerable hardships. The Rev. E. J. B. Salter, who served in Western Canada for 34 years, gives an entertaining account of an uncomfortably memorable expedition with Dr. Cooper. See Chapter 4, *How the West Was Won.*

Dr. Cooper did much to advance and strengthen the work of the Bible Society, leaving it much more established than when he took office.

The Rev. Dr. James Brown MacMaster Armour, MA, DD, General Secretary 1928-1947

Born in the Presbyterian manse in Ballymoney, Ireland, Dr. J. B. M. Armour studied at Belfast and at Galway, receiving his MA from Queen's College, Galway. After graduating from the Royal University of Ireland, he completed his studies for the ministry at New College, Edinburgh.

Armour began his ministry in Belfast and for nearly 15 years was minister of St. John's Presbyterian Church, South Shields, England. He served as Chaplain to the Armed Forces, 1917-1919, and was mentioned in dispatches.

The 1947 Annual Report of the North Alberta District has this tribute to Dr. Armour:

> He assumed the office of General Secretary of the British and Foreign Bible Society in Canada and Newfoundland on October 25, 1928. In this sphere of work, his many gifts and abilities found full scope for their expression. His achievements have left a deep impression both in London and in Canada. When the Rev. A. H. Wilkinson, General Secretary of the Parent Society, visited Belfast, he said that no words

> could fully express what the Bible Society owed to Dr. Armour's work in Canada. Dr. Armour, he said, had done three outstanding things for the furtherance of the cause. He had so touched the whole cultural community that there was not an educated man throughout the Dominion that had not heard of the work of the Bible Society. He had also put the claims of the Society before the common man, the man in the street, so strikingly that he had won his respect also. And then, said Mr. Wilkinson, Dr. Armour was equally at home in the company of the Governor and the backwoodsmen. All class distinction vanished in his presence and probably no man in Canada had so many friends.

It is no exaggeration to say it was under Dr. Armour's leadership that the foundation was laid for the Canadian Bible Society as it is today. He saw that the Constitution had to be changed to permit outstanding Canadians, other than those who belonged to the various Auxiliaries, to serve as President and to take other offices in the Society. This move was strenuously resisted by those who felt it would mean they would lose control of the work. It was that very control that Dr. Armour saw had to be broken and, at great cost to himself, he pursued the changes. He is the one who raised funds across Canada to buy a house at 122 Bloor Street West, Toronto, for $37,000, to serve as the National Office of the Society. This moved the office from a corner of the Upper Canada Bible Society premises to a location more worthy of a national organization.

Another change Dr. Armour initiated was to replace the name "Canadian Bible Society, Auxiliary to the British and Foreign Bible Society" with the following new name: "The British and Foreign Bible Society in Canada and Newfoundland." This might appear a backward step. Dr. Armour's motive, however, was to change the Canadian Bible Society from what he saw as a narrow, inward-looking society, without a world vision, to one which was part of a commonwealth of societies encompassing the globe. He believed the new name would link the Canadian Society with the worldwide work of the British and Foreign Bible Society and prompt it to begin sharing in the great task of providing the Scriptures for all nations. It was under Dr. Armour's leadership that Canadians became more aware of the needs of the world, as well as of Canada. In 1946, when the United Bible Societies was founded, Dr. Armour made sure that the Canadian Bible Society became a member of this world fellowship of Bible Societies.

Armour served through two difficult periods of history, the Great Depression, 1929 to 1939, and World War II, 1939-1945. His extensive travel was generally undertaken by train, but it is interesting to note that in 1944 the Parent Society's minutes reported that:

> The visit of the Canadian General Secretary to the ancient Colony of Newfoundland was made by airplane from New Brunswick, returning to Nova Scotia by the same delightful means of travel.

It was said that, in his time, Dr. Armour was the best after-dinner speaker in the nation. He used all his talents towards the one end of translating, publishing and distributing the Word of God in Canada and throughout the world. He was ably assisted by his wife, the former Norah Beryl Annesley Sankey, a daughter of Colonel Sir Stuart and Lady Sankey of London, England. Dr. and Mrs. Armour inaugurated an annual reception at the Bible Society residence, 69 St. Leonard's Ave., Toronto. This was a social event attended by churchmen and churchwomen, business leaders, the academic community and Bible Society supporters.

The reception was held at the time of the annual meeting of the General Board which each year had a distinguished Bible Society leader as its theme speaker. The speaker was the guest-of-honour at the reception. This popular yearly reception was continued by the Hudspeths, the O'Neils and the McMillans.

Dr. Armour promoted the Bible Society in Canada with great wisdom and energy until just a few weeks before his death in Northern Ireland on October 25, 1947. The popular yearly reception that he and his wife had instituted continued and grew until 1983. In that year it was discontinued to the disappointment of many, for it had become a major ecumenical event, attended by some 200 church leaders and people from many denominations, who wanted to enjoy warm Christian fellowship.

The Rev. William H. Hudspeth, MBE, MA, FRGS, General Secretary 1947-1952

The General Board of the British and Foreign Bible Society in Canada made it clear to the Parent Society that they wanted a Canadian appointed as Dr. Armour's successor. In 1947 the Rev. Arthur H.

Wilkinson, General Secretary of the Parent Society, came to Canada to discuss the appointment of a new General Secretary. He reported to the Canadian Board that he had consulted Canadian church leaders, a number of people in the Canadian academic community and also the Auxiliary Boards, and that there was no suitable candidate for the position of General Secretary. Wilkinson, however, knew of an ideal candidate. This was the Rev. W. H. Hudspeth, a 60-year-old who had been a Methodist missionary and then the Bible Society General Secretary in China, and who two years previously had been released from a Japanese prisoner of war camp.

It was agreed that the British should appoint Hudspeth General Secretary for a period of five years. Supporting this appointment, Arthur Wilkinson wrote on September 18, 1947:

> I am convinced that no better man could be found to be the leader of our fellowship here. He is a deeply spiritual man whose character stood the test of a Japanese terror camp. That he has gifts of leadership has been proved during the years he has held the post of General Secretary in China. During the 28 years he served as a pioneer missionary among the Miao tribe of South West China, he translated the Old Testament into their tongue. He is, therefore, not merely a first-class linguist but knows the problems of the translator. He has had charge of the publication of the Chinese Scriptures running to over four million copies a year, a useful experience if, as I hope, I can arrange for printing of foreign Scriptures in Canada. He has been the leader of a staff which included 400 colporteurs. He knows China, its people and language as few men do.
>
> Above all he knows the heathen world's need of the Bible. He is a good preacher and speaker. He is a man of tact and has a winsome manner. You will find in him an understanding friend and an inspiring leader. I am convinced that under his leadership the British and Foreign Bible Society in Canada will make an increasing impact on the life of this country.

Mr. Hudspeth had gone to China in 1909 with the Methodist Missionary Society. He had been attracted to West China by a famous Chinese missionary, the Rev. Sam Pollard, who had witnessed tribal movement amongst the Hwa Miao of Kweichow and Yunnan. After studying the language, Hudspeth was appointed to tribal work and in 1915 became Pollard's successor.

In 1917 Hudspeth went to France, where the British government was taking 100,000 Northern Chinese for labour purposes in connection with World War I. In France, with the rank of Staff Captain, Hudspeth served as an assistant adviser on Chinese matters. He was mentioned in dispatches and was later awarded the Order of the Wen Hu by the Chinese government.

In 1920 Hudspeth again returned to West China, where he directed educational development among the tribes and revised the New Testament in Hwa Miao. During this period he had the joy of seeing two or three of his Miao students graduating from the West China University, Chengtu. For some time Hudspeth served as Chairman of the West China English Methodist District.

In 1936 he was appointed General Secretary of the British and Foreign Bible Society for China, Mongolia and Indo-China. He moved to Shanghai. After Japan declared war on Great Britain, the Japanese began to suspect Hudspeth of being a secret agent of the British government. They based this supposition on Hudspeth's wide knowledge of Chinese matters and his many Chinese friends. For 94 days he was subjected to brutal police treatment in a Japanese prison. Later he was transferred to a political prisoner's camp, where he was behind barbed wire for nearly two and a half years.

Towards the end of the war, Hudspeth was taken to Fengtai, near Beijing, en route either to Manchuria or to Japan. Fortunately the war ended and he was in Fengtai for only five weeks. Mrs. (Mourne) Hudspeth was also interned and for many months the two had no contact with each other. There are many stories about the positive contributions Hudspeth was able to make to his fellow prisoners during his imprisonment. Prison life, however, severely affected his health and it took him several months to regain weight and return to normal.

In a letter to his mother, dated August 8, 1945, Hudspeth tells of his imprisonment, and subsequent release when the war ended. The Mourne referred to in this letter is his wife.

> As you may have heard, seven weeks ago last Sunday the camp in which I've been interned was suddenly, to our utter amazement, transferred to a centre some six or seven miles (10 or 11 km) outside of

Paiping sometimes or rather also called Peking. Three days after the cessation of hostilities, on Sunday evening August 19, we were brought into the city on lorries and, though it was midnight when we arrived, wherever we passed small and large groups of Chinese, we were very heartily clapped and welcomed. It was both thrilling and exciting, and upon our arrival we were housed in a large, clean Japanese hotel. After 93 days of close imprisonment in a prison and 930 days in an internment camp, it was lovely to be down in an hotel in which there were no bugs, and though it was 10 minutes to 3:00 before I got to bed, I was much too happy to realize the lateness of the hour.

On the Monday we were all agog to know what our status now was, and we soon learned that, though not yet free men, we were to have considerably more freedom and much better and more food than we had hitherto enjoyed. Armed guards were still stationed at the gates, but no armed guards were in the building. At about three in the afternoon a message was brought in saying there was someone at the gate waiting to speak to me. On going out I found Mr. and Mrs. Almblad. (Mr. A. has been our Secretary for Mongolia for 25 years – he is a Finn and, though confined to Paiping, he had not been interned.) [The Almblads] had come to see what clothes and food and money I needed. You will understand how deeply moving it was to speak to loving friends after so long a time of imprisonment and internment. I didn't need clothes or food, but I did want fruit and I did wish that Mourne should know as quickly as possible that I was safe and well. After a conversation therefore they went off to the telegraph office to wire to my Shanghai office saying, "Hudspeth in Paiping, looking well; inform Mrs. Hudspeth."

Soon after they had left, an American mission arrived, consisting of seven officers headed by a Major Ray A. Nicholls and, as I was one of the representatives chosen to meet the commission, I had a front seat view. It was thrilling to meet a body of . . . men who had come to arrange for our freedom and welfare.

The time has not yet come to give details of experiences, nor of what was said by a commission of seven white officers in the midst of the area throughout which there are some 750,000 Japanese troops. We were assured of food and comfort and it was arranged that each man would be allowed to send off a letter to Shanghai and to England – one to each place. Now my dear, you will have wondered often why you have heard from me so seldom – Temple and Rattenbury will have wondered, too. Well, the explanation is that we were allowed to write only one letter of 25 words once every six months and I have a suspicion that some of these didn't get through. I was also allowed to write Mourne 50 words every month. What Mourne has passed through must stagger description. I have grieved on her account, more, much more than on my own.

On the morning of October 29, I was arrested at 6:30 a.m. in my bedroom by five armed Japanese gendarmes, who took me in a car and threw me in a common jail, where I was jailed for 94 days without any means of communicating with Mourne. She has seen me three times since I came out of jail, the interviews lasting from 10 to 15 minutes in the presence of guards. She has been ill again and again; her hair, her lovely hair, has turned white, but she has been a brick and never once by word spoken or written has she grumbled. Upon my release from jail, she wrote that she had no regrets, that she was glad she was in Shanghai to be near me, and that she was quite, quite sure we had done right to stay at our post.

A braver woman has never been born and, should anything happen to me, you and Harry and Lewis will look after her, won't you? Humanly speaking things should soon run smoothly now. I'm well and fit and, though a little thin, I've come through wonderfully. Presently we are hoping that, within the next few days, we will be free men, whereupon a cable will be sent.

In May 1946 Mr. Hudspeth gave the following account in the course of an address to the Annual Meeting of the British and Foreign Bible Society.

I want to speak for a few minutes of my own experience during these harsh years. I want to say that they have been a constant testing, and an ever-deepening awareness of the truth of those closing words of St. Matthew's Gospel: "Lo, I am with you always even unto the end of the world." Christ was with your missionaries in the internment camps; Christ was with me while I was in the hands of the Japanese Gestapo.

Will you allow me to give you a very personal illustration so that I might bring out my meaning? During the early days of my detention, as I sat upon the floor of my cell (I was not allowed to have any books; I was not allowed even to have the Bible), as I sat musing on what had befallen me, I recalled the account in the Acts of the Apostles of Peter's

> imprisonment, and how the Angel of the Lord came and released him. No Angel of the Lord came and opened my prison door; but Christ was with me in the cell. I felt myself buoyed up by the prayers which I knew were being offered by friends all over the world.
>
> And one evening an angel did come. It was towards 11:00 o'clock in the night. I was led out by two guards and taken to a room, and given a curt order to enter. On crossing the threshold, and wondering what would happen to me, a Japanese dressed in European clothes jumped up and, grasping hold of my hand, said: "Mr. Hudspeth, I know you. I am a Christian. And ever since you were arrested, my wife and I have been praying for you. I cannot get you out of here; we Japanese Christians ourselves are afraid of the gendarmerie; but I can assure you that you will not be man-handled again." At that moment the interrogating officer came in, and there was no further opportunity for private conversation. But, though I was questioned until 6:00 o'clock the following morning, I was never tortured again.
>
> Now to me, that Japanese Christian was the divine hand; he was the modern angel of the Lord.

On November 29, 1947 Hudspeth, after a good crossing, arrived in Canada to take up his new appointment. He was an eloquent preacher, a powerful speaker and a great advocate of the Bible Society. He approached his work in Canada with great enthusiasm, and quickly adapted to Canadian life. One of the important moves he made was to bring onto the Bible Society staff Miss Mary Urquhart, who had been a missionary of the United Church of Canada in China. Miss Urquhart's initial position was as Secretary for audio-visual education but, over the 27 years she was on staff, she became the principal resource person for the General Secretary and one of the Society's most valuable people.

Hudspeth did not involve himself with the Constitutional controversies which had been such a burden to Dr. Armour. During Hudspeth's time there was no attempt to deal with the National Office/ Upper Canada Bible Society disputes. At age 65, at the end of the agreed-upon five years, Hudspeth reluctantly left Canada and returned to England. There he continued to be active in the Methodist Church. He preached regularly until just before his death on May 9, 1976 at age 89.

The Most Rev. Alexander Henry O'Neil, BD, MA, DCL, LLD, DD (Wycliffe), DD (King's), General Secretary 1952-1956

For some years the British and Foreign Bible Society had been under pressure to appoint a Canadian as General Secretary and, when Mr. Hudspeth retired, they realized it was imperative for them to do so. Previously when a General Secretary was needed for Canada, the Parent Society had said they could find no suitable candidate in Canada and, with the consent of the Canadian General Board, had appointed a man from Britain. When Dr. O'Neil agreed to let his name stand for consideration, it was evident that – this time – a highly qualified Canadian was indeed unarguably available. The Parent Society appointed him. He took office in June 1952 and served until Dec. 31, 1956.

Dr. O'Neil had served Anglican parishes in Atwood, Gorrie and Clinton, Ontario, and was then appointed principal and professor at Huron Theological College, London, Ontario. While serving at Huron College, he taught Hebrew at the University of Western Ontario. During the four and a half years that this outstanding Canadian churchman held the position of CBS General Secretary, he brought dynamic leadership to the Society and gave it increased visibility, prestige and credibility. In recognition of his service to the Bible Society, he was made an Honorary Life Governor of the British and Foreign Bible Society.

O'Neil's election as an Anglican bishop in 1956 cut short his time with the Bible Society. He was enthroned as Bishop of Fredericton on January 25, 1957. In 1963 he was elevated to Archbishop for the Atlantic Provinces, a position he held until his retirement in 1971.

Archbishop O'Neil's ministry was recognized in many ways including the granting of a number of honorary degrees. In 1954, when he was still General Secretary of the Bible Society, Wycliffe College in Toronto conferred on him the degree of Doctor of Divinity *(honoris causa)*. In 1958 King's College in Halifax granted him the same degree. He was a member of the Senate of the University of Western Ontario. That University, and also St. Thomas University, gave him an LLD. Bishop's University in Lennoxville, Quebec, conferred on him a DCL.

Among the services O'Neil provided to the Anglican communion was acting as Secretary of the Board of Examiners for Divinity Degrees and as Dominion Chaplain of the Anglican Young People's Association. The Bible Society is grateful that part of Archbishop O'Neil's outstanding ministry was given as its General Secretary.

The Very Reverend Dr. Kenneth G. McMillan, CM, BA, BD, MDiv, DD (Knox), DD (Wycliffe), DD (Acadia), General Secretary 1957-1983

When Dr. O'Neil was elected Bishop of Fredericton in the fall of 1956, Dr. Platt, General Secretary of the British and Foreign Bible Society, came to Canada to find someone to succeed him. Among the people considered and investigated was Kenneth G. McMillan, minister of St. Andrew's Presbyterian Church, Guelph, Ontario. At that time Dr. McMillan was also Moderator of the Presbyterian Synod of Toronto and Kingston. He was Chairman of the Overseas Section of the Presbyterian Board of Missions and active in the Canadian Council of Churches. With great reluctance, and against the strong advice of his fellow ministers, he agreed to accept the appointment, since he felt the General Secretaryship of the Bible Society was a "call" from God.

Before McMillan was able to adjust to the work of the Bible Society, he was plunged into the 50-year-old power struggle between the Upper Canada Bible Society and the National Office. The Upper Canada Bible Society felt that the appointment of an inexperienced General Secretary was a strategic time to reverse the Constitutional amendments that had been enacted under Dr. Armour (1928-1947). The Upper Canada Bible Society, with its supremacy in finances and numbers, wanted to restrict the election of officers to General Board representatives who were appointed by the Auxiliaries that comprised the national organization. Such a change would enhance the possibilities of the President and several other officers being representatives of the Upper Canada Bible Society. The policy of electing outstanding Canadian Christians who were otherwise affiliated was totally unacceptable to the leaders of the Upper Canada Bible Society. For the first years of Dr. McMillan's time with the Bible Society, the opposition of the Upper Canada Bible Society was a major concern.

In the face of strong opposition from several leaders of the Upper Canada Bible Society, Mr. Leonard Eames of Hamilton was elected President of the Upper Canada Bible Society in 1959. Mr. Eames, a highly regarded Anglican layman and the owner of Eames Department Store in Hamilton, fully supported the National Society and the policy of electing variously affiliated outstanding Canadians as officers. Mr. Kenneth Rhodes, Business Manager of the Upper Canada Bible Society, was also a strong supporter of the National Society. Under the leadership of Eames and with the support of Rhodes and others, the Upper Canada Bible Society's longstanding opposition ended.

In 1962 the Upper Canada Bible Society was reduced in size by the creation of the Hamilton District, the Northern Ontario District and the Bay of Quinte District, each with its own officers and Boards. When this change took place, some former members of the Upper Canada Bible Society's Board founded the "Canadian Colportage Society" to compete with the Canadian Bible Society. This organization, however, never gained significant support and, in a few years, disappeared. One of the significant achievements of Dr. McMillan's period of service was obtaining the full support of the Upper Canada Bible Society and ending the related tensions which had plagued the organization since 1905.

It was when Dr. McMillan was General Secretary that the name Canadian Bible Society was adopted. Also during his time, all the "Auxiliaries" agreed to be designated as "Districts" and to adopt the name Canadian Bible Society. These were significant changes and they were strongly opposed by many. However, they were adjustments that were essential in order for the Society to promote the work from sea to sea and to assume its place in the world fellowship of Bible Societies.

Significant changes in the property held by the Canadian Bible Society occurred during Dr. McMillan's tenure. Within a period of 21 years, with three real estate transactions, he moved the Society's head office from a former residence on Bloor Street, Toronto, which had been purchased for $37,000, to a prestigious property valued at over $1,200,000 – without any significant cost to the donors. (See Chapter 9 for further details regarding CBS head office location changes over the years.)

During Dr. McMillan's 26 years as General Secretary, many property changes took place in the Districts as well as in Toronto. For the first time in its long history, the National Society bought a building for Prince Edward Island. Buildings were also bought in Hamilton and North Bay when new Districts were established in those areas. After a fire, a fine new building was erected in Saskatoon. The Society took advantage of the phenomenal growth in Edmonton and acquired valuable property, which enabled the North Alberta District to operate the largest Christian bookstore in Canada. These transactions, and similar ones in Vancouver and other Canadian cities, proved to be highly advantageous to the Society. They served the immediate needs of the Society and, when sold, provided thousands of dollars for the work. In 1964 another significant property decision was made. To mark the 60th anniversary of the decision to establish the Canadian Bible Society, Canada paid $60,000 for a new Bible Society office and warehouse in Jamaica.

Among other important advances that occurred between 1957 and 1983 were:

- Introducing the Direct Mail Program.
- Adding *La Société biblique canadienne* to the Bible Society's name.
- Amending the Act of Incorporation and the Constitution.
- Assuming a significant role in the United Bible Societies. (Dr. McMillan was active in the work of the United Bible Societies and served as chairman of its General Committee for four years.)
- Initiating the Central Stock Depot.
- Developing Scripture production in Canada for Canadian needs as well as for some other countries.
- Enlarging the Scripture translation program.

Dr. McMillan played an important role in Canadian church life and became recognized as a missionary statesman. He was called upon to give lectures at many conferences. He delivered the MacKay Memorial Lectures entitled "The Church Encounters the New Age" at the eight United Church of Canada Theological Colleges. In Canada's Centennial Year, 1967, he was a speaker at the famous Chautauqua Conference in New York State.

In 1974, when the Bible Society in Australia inaugurated the Olivier Béguin Lectures, he was selected to be the first lecturer. This annual lectureship on "The Authority and Relevance of the Bible in the Modern World" has since 1974 been given by such distinguished people as Malcolm Muggeridge, Dr. John R. Stott, Dr. Donald Coggan and Dr. Oswald C. J. Hoffmann. Dr. McMillan was the theme speaker at several conferences under the auspices of the Department of Overseas Missions of the Canadian Council of Churches. In Salem, Oregon he was the Conference Speaker at a USA/Canada missionary assembly. The book *Against the Tide,* of which he was the author, was published in 1984 and went into a second printing in 1985.

Among biographical publications noting people of distinction in which Dr. McMillan is included are: *Who's Who in the World, Canadian Who's Who, Who's Who in Toronto, The Canadian Encyclopedia, Personalities of the Americas, International Directory of Distinguished Leaders, Men of Achievement, Five Thousand Personalities of the World, The International Yearbook and Statesman's Who's Who,* and *Dictionary of International Biography.*

Dr. McMillan's wife, the former Isobel McCannel of Burgoyne, Ontario was not only his supporter and helper but she also played an active role in Bible Society work. She visited overseas at her own expense, spoke at church services and Bible Society gatherings, provided hospitality to hundreds of international visitors and, for all practical purposes, was a full-time unpaid worker. She had the distinction of being the first woman in 160 years to address the annual meeting of the Nova Scotia District of the Canadian Bible Society. Without her help the General Secretary could not have achieved what he did.

The work of Dr. McMillan has been recognized in many ways. In 1984 the Governor General of Canada appointed him a Member of the Order of Canada, the country's highest distinction. He is the only Presbyterian minister to have received this honour. In 1992 the Governor General awarded him the Commemorative Medal. He is a Patron of "Global Cooperation for a Better World," a non-political and non-fundraising organization which assembles creative ideas and actions for the building of a better world. He was awarded the degree of Doctor of Divinity *(honoris causa)* by Knox College (Presbyterian), Wycliffe College (Anglican) and Acadia University (Baptist).

When Dr. McMillan left the Society in 1983, he asked that, instead of a farewell gift, an appeal should be made for the United Bible

Societies' Scripture Production Fund. In recognition of his 26 years as General Secretary, an appeal for $260,000 was made, $10,000 for each year of his service. The appeal was oversubscribed and some $600,000 was received.

After leaving the Canadian Bible Society, Dr. McMillan was interim minister at St. Andrew's Presbyterian Church in Hamilton, Bermuda for five months. Then, on October 1, 1983, he joined the staff of the Christian humanitarian organization World Vision Canada. He served first as Secretary for Church Relations and then as Minister-at-Large, an office he continues to hold. Dr. McMillan is a valued member of the senior management team of World Vision Canada. He also keeps some 150 Canadian church leaders informed about the work of World Vision.

The Rev. William R. Russell, BA, BD, General Secretary 1983-1988

The Rev. William R. Russell served as General Secretary from 1983 until his resignation on September 1, 1988. Before joining the Bible Society, he had been pastor of one of the largest congregations of the Presbyterian Church in Canada, the prestigious St. Andrew and St. Paul Church in Montreal. A graduate of the world-renowned Princeton Seminary, New Jersey, and fluent in both French and English, he was highly qualified for the position.

Under Russell's leadership the property at 10 Carnforth Road was renovated, and the space that had been rented to tenants was incorporated into the Bible Society offices. The house at 69 St. Leonard's Avenue, Lawrence Park, Toronto, which had been the official residence of General Secretaries since it was built in 1928, was sold and an apartment was acquired for the General Secretary. During Mr. Russell's tenure, translation work on several languages spoken by Native Canadians was considerably increased and Scripture production became a large feature of the work of the Society.

Mr. Russell guided the Society through significant amendments to the Constitution and Bylaws. The Sub-Executive Committee, which had consisted of the members of the Finance Committee and five Board members, was discontinued. It was replaced with an Executive Committee comprised of people from all regions of Canada. Membership on the General Board was reduced from two representatives from each District to one, and meetings of the Board were held annually. The fiscal year, which had previously been the same as the calendar year, was changed to March 1 – February 28.

Neither Mr. Russell nor his wife enjoyed good health and, after more than five years of service, he resigned to return to the pastorate.

Following Russell's resignation, Mr. Robert D. Busby, Associate Secretary, became responsible for the day-to-day activities of the Society. Mr. Busby oversaw changes in the Society's computer systems and in District staff. At meetings of the United Bible Societies, he represented Canada. He ably filled the vacant position until June 2, 1989, when the Rev. Dr. Floyd C. Babcock assumed the office of General Secretary.

The Rev. Dr. Floyd Calvin Babcock, BA, MDiv, DMin, General Secretary 1989-1997

Dr. Babcock became General Secretary on June 2, 1989 and was inducted into the office on November 5 that year. The Rev. Dr. Ciril A. Rigos, General Secretary of the United Bible Societies, was present for the induction service and gave the address. The service was held in Toronto, Wesley Chapel Free Methodist Church, where Dr. Babcock had been Associate Pastor and then Senior Pastor from 1983 to 1985.

Although only 40 years of age, Dr. Babcock came to the office with a wealth of experience. He had served pastorates in Western Canada and Ontario, one of them as student minister at Smithfield, Carmen United Church. From 1985 to 1989 he was District Secretary in the Central Ontario District of CBS. This meant he was well acquainted with the work of the Society.

In 1973 he received a BA with a double major in religious studies and English from the University of Winnipeg, Manitoba. He then continued his studies at Queen's University, Kingston, Ontario for the Master of Divinity degree, which he received in 1977. The degree of Doctor of Ministry was conferred on him by Asbury Theological Seminary, Wilmore, Kentucky in 1991. The title of his thesis for this degree was "Christian Charities and Cultural Changes: A Descriptive Study." His research focused on leadership and organizational theory. Culturally diverse Metropolitan Toronto was a major field of his studies and this provided him with valuable insights into Canadian culture in general.

In addition to his extensive responsibilities for the leadership of the Canadian Bible Society, Dr. Babcock also made a major contribution to the United Bible Societies. From 1993 to 1997 he was a member of the Americas Regional Committee of UBS, which oversees the work of 27 Bible Societies in the Americas. He served as Chairman of the Americas Region Sub-Committee on Translation, as a member of the Publishing Sub-Committee and as Chairman of the Structure and Administration Committee. He contributed to UBS by serving with *Francosec,* which oversees the translation, publication and distribution of all the French language Scripture projects in the world.

As General Secretary Dr. Babcock was in demand to give leadership in workshops and to promote CBS work in Canada and in some thirty countries throughout the world.

In 1996 Dr. Babcock received the distinct honour of being elected Chair and President of the Americas Regional Committee of the United Bible Societies. That year he was also Chair of *Anglosec,* which represents the English-Speaking Bible Societies. Dr. Babcock was a member of the Structure and Administration Sub-Committee of the UBS Executive Committee until it was discontinued. Then he was elected to the United Bible Societies Executive Committee and also to the six-member Sub-Committee which makes major decisions between meetings of the Executive Committee. Election to these offices was a recognition of the respect in which both Dr. Babcock and the Canadian Bible Society were held by other Bible Societies.

Dr. Babcock is married to the former Janice Greenshields. They have two daughters and one son.

The Rev. Father Gregory Evan Bailey, BMin, National Director 1997-

On June 18, 1997, when the title General Secretary was officially changed to National Director, the Rev. Gregory Evan Bailey assumed the office.

An Anglican clergyman, Bailey was born in Cleethorpes, England and came to Canada as a child. Following a career in electronic engineering technology in the field of biomedical engineering, he studied for the ministry at St. John's College, Winnipeg. After his ordination as an Anglican priest in 1982, he pastored several churches in the Anglican dioceses of Brandon and Montreal, and also served as a hospital Chaplain in the diocese of Quebec. He holds a certificate in clinical pastoral education from the Health Sciences Centre in Winnipeg.

A person of many abilities, Bailey edited *The Manitoba Technologist* during the course of his engineering career. He was also radio host of *Candlelight Classics* on CJUM-FM radio in Winnipeg. He speaks French as well as English, and his interests include reading, herb gardening, bird watching, airplane flying, astronomy and computer science. He and his wife, Rosemary, have one daughter, Elizabeth.

CHAPTER 25

District Secretaries

Regardless of what anyone may personally think or believe about Him, Jesus of Nazareth has been the dominant figure in the history of the Western culture for almost twenty centuries.

Jaroslav Pelikan

In the life and work of the Canadian Bible Society, the second most important person is the District Secretary. (The most important is the donor.) Since 1905 a great number have served in this important office. Some have found the work too strenuous; some found it involved being away from home too much; others found it too different from parish ministry and did not continue in it. Yet many others have found it rewarding and fulfilling, and have continued in the position until retirement.

The District Secretary is the person who puts a human face on the Bible Society. Direct Mail, literature and the media can reach many more people than the District Secretaries, but there is no substitute for a personal relationship. The Canadian Bible Society has a multitude of concerned donors who express their interest by sacrificial and generous giving. One day a humble and poorly dressed man came into the Canadian Bible bookstore in Ottawa and asked to see the District Secretary, the Rev. Martyn C. Thomas. He gave the District Secretary a Weetabix box with some money in it. When Mr. Thomas opened the box, he found $2,000 in cash. That same man came in regularly with very generous gifts for the work of the Bible Society. The Bible Society is not so much an organization as a multitude of people committed to helping others receive a copy of the Word of

God in their own language. To hundreds of these "friends of the Bible Society," the District Secretary is a personal friend and valued mentor.

The District Secretary establishes a relationship not only with a wide variety of lay people, but also with clergy of all denominations and Christian traditions. In traditions that baptize babies, it is not at all unusual for the District Secretary to be asked to administer the Sacrament of Baptism to a pastor's child. Many District Secretaries become the persons with whom both ministers and lay people share the deepest concerns of their lives. They are neutral figures and are non-threatening. Having constant contact with Christians of all theological persuasions, District Secretaries soon come to recognize the distinctive contributions of different communions and to realize that God works through all churches. Their acquaintance with all kinds of Christians enriches their Christian lives and gives them a greater appreciation and understanding of their own faith communities.

A District Secretary's parish is not only the large District of the Canadian Bible Society that he/she serves. It is also the world at large, for the Bible Society works in nearly 200 countries, and he/she is continually hearing what the Word of God is accomplishing near and far. The District Secretary brings a larger, more global perspective to those who daily deal with pastoral problems and parish concerns. One problem a District Secretary faces is the physical strain of late-night conversations with those who are anxious to gaze through an open window on the world by means of the District Secretary's annual visit.

District Secretaries have several responsibilities. They present the work of the Bible Society in one or more churches each Sunday. They disseminate CBS information, and are fundraisers for the work. They are distributors of Scriptures and sources of information as to where Scriptures in a specific language or format can be obtained. They are goodwill ambassadors for the Bible Society. The response to appeals and the general success of the work depend to a large extent on the relationship they have with hundreds of people in the Districts they serve.

Though the laity are the backbone of Bible Society work, the Canadian Bible Society has almost exclusively called ordained ministers to be District Secretaries. Congregations are more willing to have an ordained person than a lay person in their pulpits. Community support for the Bible Society is greatly determined by the local clergy's attitude to the work, and usually an ordained individual can relate better to pastors than a lay Christian can. There is no policy of having only ordained ministers as District Secretaries, but it is the practice that has been followed.

Traditionally, when an appointment was made, careful consideration was given to the candidate's denomination, so that as many denominations as possible would be represented on the team of District Secretaries across the nation. At times, in the group of 18 or 20 District Secretaries, ministers of at least a dozen different denominations could be found. For many years all District Secretaries were from mainline churches but, with the growth of the evangelical churches, this has changed. In March 1977, the Rev. Sandra Tilley became the first female District Director – for Newfoundland and Labrador District.

The wives of the District Secretaries all deserve honourable mention. They have made significant sacrifices, as their husbands have been away from home for long periods and they have had to assume family responsibilities. Several wives have become the District Secretary's administrative assistant and secretary, and their office and Bible depot work has been of great value.

District Secretaries are appointed by, and remunerated by, the National Office of the Canadian Bible Society. They are required to work in harmony with and in the closest cooperation with the District Boards. Their ultimate accountability, however, is to the National Office. The polity of the Canadian Bible Society is more akin to the Episcopal or Presbyterian form of government than to the Congregational. The District Secretary is not an employee of the District. This has been important for the Society, since it means all District Secretaries are responsible to the same National Society and are all on the same team. The District Board issues the "call," but it is the National Office that approves or disapproves the District Board's request. This means District Secretaries are responsible for carrying out national policy in the Districts where they have their responsibilities.

Until recently, when a vacancy in the ranks of District Secretaries occurred, the position was not advertised. Dr. J. B. M. Armour, General Secretary from 1928 to 1947, strongly opposed advertising for District Secretaries because he knew that the qualifications for the position were not generally understood.

Over the years, District Secretaries, in their close contact with the clergy of their Districts, discovered those few individuals who were committed to the work of the Bible Society and who appeared to have the energy, interest and flexibility that the job called for. When a vacancy arose, the District Secretaries could always suggest to the General Secretary individuals who might be considered for the opening. In this way, the people who knew best what the job called for played a large part in finding their potential colleagues. It was a system that worked well, and most District Secretaries were discovered this way.

"Who supervises the District Secretaries?" was a frequently asked question when Dr. McMillan was General Secretary (1957-1983). His reply was, "They supervise themselves." When men and women were being interviewed for the position, Dr. McMillan emphasized that one major difference between parish ministry and that of District Secretary was that District Secretaries were all members of a team. The individualism prevalent in the ministry would not be possible if they became District Secretaries. The District Secretaries were a team with the General Secretary as the captain. A District Secretary could not just "do his or her own thing," but instead had to focus on the Society's goals and carry out the agreed-upon policies.

This came as a shock to many applicants. They lost interest in joining the staff when they realized that the Bible Society was not a field for the style of ministry they preferred. At the annual District Secretaries' conference, held for a few days immediately prior to the General Board meeting, the District Secretaries, under the leadership of the General Secretary, agreed upon ways they would work to achieve certain objectives in the next 12 months. All District Secretaries shared in the decision-making. While there was always considerable disagreement, once a consensus was reached, all put aside their own personal feelings and worked as a team. On the other hand, District Secretaries had considerable freedom to carry out the agreed-upon policies in ways that suited their own personalities and areas of work. This proved to be a satisfactory arrangement and, over the 26 years Dr. McMillan was General Secretary, it resulted in the resignation of only one District Secretary. Also, only one District Secretary was dismissed, and that was when the District Board unanimously requested it.

When District Secretaries joined the staff, they were provided with an expense account and told they were trusted to keep honest and accurate records of their expenses. This "honour system" meant their expenses were not reviewed by National Office. District Secretaries knew that every dollar spent on salaries and expenses meant one less dollar for the translation, production and distribution of the Scriptures. Each year at the District Secretaries' Conference, all District Secretaries' expenses for the previous year were circulated for everyone to see. This enabled District Secretaries to compare their expenses with those of others. There was always some rivalry in achieving the lowest expenses – an honour that, for many years, was won by the Rev. Andrew Brndjar.

Another policy followed until recently was that all District Secretaries were paid the same salary no matter what part of the country they served. This created a feeling of equality, and helped bind the men into a team. The housing allowance paid was, however, determined by the cost of housing in the particular District. This practice reflected the major differences in the cost of accommodation across the country. There are arguments in favour of paying some District Secretaries more than others. Some have rugged territory to serve; others are in urban areas. But which is the more difficult? Each has its advantages and each its liabilities. Having all District Secretaries receive the same salary was an important factor in building a strong, united team. When the District Secretaries are a close-knit fellowship, the unity of the Society is strengthened.

The large degree of autonomy enjoyed by the Districts is a continual threat to the unity of the Canadian Bible Society. There is a constant need for forces to draw the Districts together so they have a common goal. The sole purpose of the Society is the translation, publication and distribution of the Word of God, but this can be implemented in widely different ways by the Districts. Theoretically a District can spend all the money it raises within its own District on the translation, production and distribution of the word of God in that District. The attitude of the District is all-important and the persons who, most of all, determine that attitude are the District Secretaries. They are known and trusted and, when they see themselves not as isolated servants of the District, but as members of a team, all appointed by the National Office and all with the same vision, they provide that cohesion which is not found in the Constitution. The importance of the District

Secretary's role cannot be exaggerated. It is crucial to the well-being of the Society and the whole work.

One of the ways District Secretaries have been recognized is by the conferring of the degree of Doctor of Divinity, *honoris causa.* Dr. Leonard W. Schnell and Dr. George E. Ward received Doctor of Divinity degrees from St. Andrew's College, Saskatoon, and Dr. J. A. R. Tingley received a doctorate from Acadia University, Wolfville, NS. Trinity College in Florida granted a Doctor of Divinity degree to Dr. Gerald E. Benson. On September 16, 1954, Wycliffe College in Toronto held a "Missionary Convocation" to mark the 150th anniversary of BFBS. At that convocation the DD degree was conferred on the General Secretary, Dr. A. H. O'Neil, and on three District Secretaries who were Anglicans: the Rev. Dennis Bright of London, the Rev. Canon J. A. Harrington of Toronto and the Rev. R. T. McKim of Halifax. That same year, on September 22, 1954, Knox College in Toronto held a special convocation to confer Doctor of Divinity degrees on the Bishop of Lund and on the Rev. William J. Platt, General Secretary of BFBS.

How Long Did They Serve?

The Rev. Ernest Joseph Bold Salter, pioneer District Secretary in Western Canada, has the distinction of having served longer than any other District Secretary. On January 19, 1943 a plaque honouring his 38 years of service, from 1904 to 1942, was placed in the boardroom of the Winnipeg Bible House. It would seem that the Rev. E. M. B. Wheelock, with 29 years of service, is the District Secretary with the second longest period of service. After serving as District Secretary in New Brunswick and Prince Edward Island for 17 years, he was transferred to North Alberta, where he served for 12 years, retiring on June 30, 1976.

Three served for 28 years: the Rev. Andrew S. Wood was District Secretary in South Alberta from July 1, 1944 to June 30, 1972. Dr. Leonard W. Schnell's service continued from 1937 to 1965 and Dr. J. A. Raymond Tingley's from 1946 to 1974.

The Rev. Dr. R. Stuart Johnston became District Secretary in the Montreal and Quebec Districts on February 1, 1959 and served for 26 years. The Rev. Martyn C. Thomas, a District Secretary whose office is in Calgary, has served for over 25 years. He became Assistant Secretary in Montreal on January 1, 1971. He was transferred to Ottawa on January 1, 1974, and to South Alberta on August 1, 1987. For 24 years, from April 15, 1952 to June 30, 1976, the Rev. M. C. P. Macintosh was District Secretary in Nova Scotia. The Rev. Donald S. Collins was District Secretary in the Manitoba District for 21 years.

All of the following served for 20 years: the Rev. J. C. Thompson in the Western Ontario District, the Rev. D. Blain Thierry in the Hamilton District, and the Rev. Robert H. Grey in the North Alberta and British Columbia Districts. Many others ought to be recognized for, even though they served fewer than 20 years, their contributions were also highly significant.

Each of the many District Secretaries who have served since 1905 merits generous space in the annals of history. When the history of the Districts is written, the District Secretaries will be given the recognition that is their due. However, because it is not possible to write about all their service in this book, the work of only three is related below. One served in British Columbia, one in the North Saskatchewan District and one in Newfoundland.

The Rev. Dr. J. A. Raymond Tingley, BTh, BD, DD, District Secretary 1946-1974

The Rev. Dr. J. A. Raymond Tingley was the energetic and dedicated District Secretary in the British Columbia District for 28 years. A native of New Brunswick, he studied at Mount Alison University, Sackville, New Brunswick and at Acadia University, Wolfville, Nova Scotia, where he received the degree of Bachelor of Theology. He took post-graduate studies for the degree of Bachelor of Divinity at Andover-Newton Theological College in Newton,

Massachusetts. Prior to being called to the Bible Society, Tingley was minister of Edith Avenue Baptist Church, Saint John, NB, where he was ordained in 1930, and of Chipman Baptist Church, Dartmouth, NS. In 1982 Acadia University recognized his outstanding ministry by awarding him the degree of Doctor of Divinity *(honoris causa).*

Like all District Secretaries, Dr. Tingley was a loyal church member and worker. His devotion to the church began early in his life; when the Baptist Young People's Union was formed in 1930, he was elected its first President. Later he was one of the founders of the Baptist Federation of Canada. He reached out beyond his own denomination by giving leadership in the Maritime Religious Education Council, the Boys Work Board in Saint John and Halifax, the Social Service Council of NS, and in camp ministry. These experiences stood him in good stead when he joined the staff of the Bible Society, which serves all Christian churches. As a District Secretary he worked with the Vancouver Council of Churches and, on two occasions, served as its President. The YMCA and Ecumenical Action were among other organizations that profited from his interest. His marriage to Margaret E. Whitman in 1930 provided him with a wife whose sacrifices and support helped make his many achievements possible.

Beginning his work in British Columbia was a major adjustment. Picturesque Nova Scotia was enormously different from the rugged grandeur of the Rockies, Cascades and other BC mountain ranges. Tingley's journey by car on gravel roads to northern British Columbia tested his nerve. The drive through the Fraser Canyon on a narrow gravel road with hairpin curves, and no protection from the deep canyon below, was never forgotten. Visiting the communities of his vast territory required him to be away from home for a month at a time. Most communities had a Branch of the Canadian Bible Society and the Branch Officers, the local Clergy and the Bible Society supporters all looked forward to his annual visit. He drew up an itinerary covering the weeks of his travel and, well in advance of his visits, notified the Branches of the dates he would be with them. This gave them time to plan the most effective use of his time in each community.

When Tingley was not on a lengthy itinerary, he visited Branches adjacent to Vancouver, which meant he was away for only a few days at a time. Every Sunday he presented the Bible Society's work at church services, and sometimes was able to speak at as many as five churches on a Sunday. He soon learned to adapt so well to the liturgies and forms of worship of the different communions that the various congregations did not realize he was not a clergyman of their own denomination. Branch meetings were held during the week; this meant he was busy almost every evening. Though he had administrative responsibilities, the work of a District Secretary was not an "office job," and he could spare little time to spend in the office. This required him to recruit responsible help in both the District Office and the Canadian Bible Society bookstore, so he could be free to pursue his field work.

Dr. Tingley not only did his work well, but he was extremely conscious of the administration costs of the Society. The Vancouver Canadian Bible Society bookstore generated enough profit each year to cover all the District's overhead costs. Thus he was able to assure donors that their contributions went only for the translation, production and distribution of the Scriptures – the real work of the Society. On his field trips he was afforded a good deal of hospitality, which made his travel comparatively inexpensive.

Every two years Dr. Tingley was able to trade in his well-used Bible Society car for a new one, and pay a difference of only $1,000, by dealing with an automobile company located on Vancouver Island and taking delivery of the new car where it was manufactured in Ontario. Getting a new car by trading in a used one and paying only $1,000 was a remarkable business achievement. Every second year, after the annual meeting of the District Secretaries in Toronto, Tingley drove a new car across the country back to Vancouver. This was only one of the many ways he saved the Society thousands of dollars.

Realizing the importance of the District Secretaries all being members of a "team," Dr. Tingley was a strong force in promoting unity among the District Secretaries and in the work of the Society. He was widely known, loved and respected by the clergy and people of all churches in British Columbia, but he never lost sight of the Canadian Bible Society's needs as a national organization.

After leaving the Canadian Bible Society staff in 1974, he was minister of visitation at First United Church in downtown Vancouver for 10 years. His 28 years with the Bible Society had made it easy for him to serve the needs of a denomination other than his own. He was active in interdenominational work and in Fairview Baptist Church, Vancouver until shortly before his death. He died October 23, 1994 at the age of 85. His widow installed a memorial window in Fairview Baptist Church in his memory.

The Rev. Dr. Leonard W. Schnell, BA, BD, DD, District Secretary 1937-1965

After graduating from the University of Saskatchewan and St. Andrew's College, Saskatoon, Dr. Leonard Schnell served in Saskatchewan pastorates in Saskatoon, St. Walburg and Maymont. Dr. J. B. M. Armour, General Secretary of the Bible Society, was adept at finding the right people to fill positions. On July 1, 1937, when the West was still staggering through the Depression, he persuaded Leonard and Nellie Schnell to leave pastoral work so Len could become District Secretary for the North Saskatchewan District. The West had been blessed with outstanding District Secretaries, and Dr. Schnell not only continued the high level of service of those who had gone before, he was one of the best.

As Dr. Schnell moved rapidly through his heavy workload and extensive travel schedule, he often reminded people that his name in German means "swift." He lived up to his name. Schnell possessed remarkable energy, and his accomplishments were much above average because he moved with lightning speed every working hour. For 28 years through the blizzards of winter, the mud of spring, the heat and drought of summer, and the golden season of harvest, he visited individuals, schools, churches, Bible Society Branches and community gatherings. His enthusiasm and dedication were contagious, and the work of the Bible Society came to be well known and supported throughout the North Saskatchewan District.

Electrical power was not generally available in rural Saskatchewan when Dr. Schnell began his work, so lantern slides and movies were a novelty in many communities. He carried with him a projector and boxes of four-inch by four-inch (10-cm by 10-cm) glass slides to give illustrated lectures or lantern slide presentations on the work of the Bible Society. He also carried a box of black curtains to cover the windows of the rural schools and church halls he visited during the daylight hours. To make sure of giving high quality presentations, he had a screen five feet by five feet (1.5 m by 1.5 m), which was safely carried in a box. In place of a stand, the screen was set on chairs or on a table. That his presentations were considered ingenious and the lantern slides significant is testified by the fact that some of the things he used are now a major attraction in the Western Development Museum in Saskatoon. To provide electricity for the projector, Schnell carried a small portable generator operated by a gasoline engine. This had a long extension cord so the generator could be installed at a distance and its noise did not interfere with the presentations. When 8-mm movie projectors came on the market, Schnell was able to show movies. It is easy to imagine the impact these presentations had in the years before electricity came to rural Saskatchewan.

Important as public meetings are, personal contacts are also a major part of fostering interest in the work of the Bible Society. Dr. Schnell was good company and an interesting conversationalist. His sense of humour was known and appreciated, and he always had a fund of good stories which he told with obvious personal delight. In addition he was an accomplished violinist. If there was no organ or piano in a place where he was giving a presentation, Dr. Schnell accompanied the hymns on his violin. His visits to the schools often included musical selections on the violin. He was extended hospitality in private homes, and the evenings were especially rewarding for the host and hostess since Dr. Schnell played for singsongs and square dances, and for the general entertainment of all present.

Today older people still remember Dr. Schnell's visits to the rural schools they attended long ago. He projected a happy and joyful image of the Bible Society with his music, displays of "tricks," and humorously illustrated talks. He always had "dime cards" for the children to fill out and, after his visits, the money collected by means of these dime cards provided Scriptures for the world. Bible Society Branches were established in nearly every community in Schnell's large District. In addition he organized Bible Society committees in many congregations. It took him two years to cover the District and his bi-annual visits were highlights for many communities.

In 1966 the small Bible Society building on Second Avenue South, Saskatoon was destroyed by fire. The Canadian Bible Society bookstore and District Office were lost in the blaze. Such a catastrophe might have crushed some people, but Dr. Schnell saw it as an opportunity to advance. The building adjacent to the Bible Society was also destroyed in the fire. The National Office of the Bible Society bought the entire burnt-out area and built a two-storey building on the two lots, with the result that the Canadian Bible Society now has a fine building in a good location to serve Saskatchewan.

One secret of Dr. Schnell's success was the meticulous way he kept records. When he visited a community, he knew exactly what had transpired there on his last visit. He kept a record of the number and names of many who attended meetings, the amount of the offering, and other details of his previous visit. When the meeting was over – with the excitement of a child at a birthday party – he counted the offering and enthusiastically assessed the meeting.

Without the support and sacrifices of Dr. Schnell's wife and children, he would not have been able to serve the Bible Society as he did. He was away from home a great deal and, when he was home, the Bible Society demanded much of his time and energy. His family, however, did not appear to suffer from Len's dedication to his work. Len's wife Nellie had a busy and fruitful church life and the children's achievements were a joy to their parents. It is gratifying that Dr. Schnell's work and the support of his family were widely appreciated. One indication of this was that St. Andrew's College awarded him, in 1953, and Nellie Schnell, in 1992, the degree of Doctor of Divinity. Dr. Leonard Schnell died May 22, 1985 at the age of 87.

The Rev. Dr. Allan James Barrett, CD, BA, BD, DD, District Secretary 1966-1973

The Newfoundland District of the Canadian Bible Society, founded in 1812, has the distinction of being the oldest in Canada. For much of its history, it had no resident District Secretary, being served from the mainland of Canada. In 1923 it was decided to change the boundaries of the Maritime Auxiliaries. Nova Scotia and Newfoundland were constituted as one District, with the Rev. Canon G. M. Ambrose, who lived in Halifax, as District Secretary. This arrangement continued until 1950, when Cape Breton was separated from Nova Scotia (for the purposes of CBS administration) and the Rev. S. J. Davies, BA was appointed as District Secretary for Cape

Breton and Newfoundland. The District Secretary lived in Sydney, NS and travelled to Newfoundland to visit the Branches.

When Mr. Davies resigned on July 1st, 1955, he was succeeded by the Rev. Bernard P. Mohan, MA, who had been a District Secretary in England. Like Davies, Mohan also lived in Sydney, NS. Faithful volunteers, both clergy and lay, were largely responsible for continued interest in the work of the Bible Society in Newfoundland and Labrador.

With Mohan's retirement June 30, 1966 and the appointment of his successor, the Bible Society in Newfoundland entered a new era. From that date the Cape Breton District was served by the Rev. M. C. P. Macintosh, District Secretary of the Nova Scotia District. Newfoundland and Labrador, for the first time, were to have their own District Secretary. The National Office purchased 190 University Avenue in St. John's, to serve as a residence for the new District Secretary and also as an office for the Newfoundland District. With this purchase the Bible Society, for the first time in 154 years, had a visible presence in the province.

Mohan's successor, the first native Newfoundlander to serve as the province's CBS District Secretary, was the Rev. Dr. Allan James Barrett, CD, BA, BD, DD, a distinguished minister of the United Church of Canada. His appointment, on July 1, 1966, marked the beginning of unprecedented growth and greatly increased interest in Bible Society work in Newfoundland. Allan Barrett was a true son of Newfoundland. In him, for the first time, the Bible Society had a staff person who understood the culture, the history and the soul of the people.

Barrett, one of four boys in a fishing family, was born February 20, 1907 at Old Perlican, Newfoundland. One of the Barrett boys became a Methodist minister, one was a banker, and one was employed in Old Perlican. Allan was slated to follow in his father's footsteps and make his living fishing. However, he suffered from seasickness, and this disqualified him for that work. He had to move in a different direction.

After studying at St. John's Normal School, Prince of Wales College, and Memorial University, he taught school in Old Perlican, Tilt Cove and Bishop's Falls. His home life had instilled in him a true understanding of the Gospel and a love for the Church. His father could not read or write, but he had Allan read the Bible to him. This gave the young Barrett the Scriptural grounding he needed to start preaching; he was already serving as a part-time lay preacher during his school-teaching years.

In 1936 he began his official training for the ministry. He graduated from Dalhousie University in 1939 and from Pine Hill Divinity College in 1941, with honours in Church History and the highest award in Oratory. In addition to the BA he earned from Dalhousie, he received, from Pine Hill, a BD in 1951 and a Doctor of Divinity in 1970.

From his ordination in 1941, Barrett was recognized as an outstanding preacher. He served in Musgravetown and then in Cochrane Street Centennial and Wesley United in St. John's before serving in Grand Falls for 11 years. He acted as Secretary and then as President of the Newfoundland Conference of the United Church of Canada. An army Chaplain with the rank of Major, he received the Canadian Decoration in 1963. When Allan accepted the call to the Canadian Bible Society in 1966, his denomination felt they were losing one of their most outstanding ministers and were reluctant to let him leave.

Allan Barrett is an example of how significant one man's work can be. Immediately upon his joining CBS, the Canadian Bible Society became known across the province. For a number of years, Allan had been a Gospel singer over the Wesley Church's radio station and his was a household name, even in remote outports. The credibility of the Bible Society went to the top of the charts. This was reflected in greatly increased Scripture distribution and a ten-fold increase in financial support. Newfoundlanders are noted for the highest per capita charitable donations, and the Bible Society now benefited from their generosity. In the seven years Dr. Barrett was with the Bible Society, it was literally transformed. Much of the credit for the success of his ministry must be given to his wife. She was a gracious Nova Scotia lady who was not only a charming hostess but also an able assistant. When Allan joined the Bible Society, his wife Verda became responsible for the District Office and proved to be a most competent secretary. Allan's death December 1, 1974 at age 67 was mourned by the whole province.

The Rev. Mark Genge, another Newfoundlander, was Dr. Barrett's able successor until he was elected a Bishop in 1976. Then his brother, the Rev. David Genge, provided inspiring leadership until the Rev.

Dr. Gerald E. Benson was appointed in 1979. Dr. Benson, with his wife Ruth as his assistant, built on the foundations of his predecessors, moulding the District into a truly ecumenical missionary enterprise which has the support and confidence of the whole population. The Rev. Sandra Tilley began to follow in their footsteps in 1997. The work Dr. Barrett began has been enlarged and enhanced by those who followed him.

CHAPTER 26

The Future: As Bright As the Promises of God

There are few organizations, societies or fraternities that have any secure future in the years ahead despite all the third-millennium optimism. But in our uncertain and unpredictable age, and aside from the Christian Church (which is built on an indestructible foundation), the Canadian Bible Society is in a category all by itself. It has been entrusted by Almighty God to translate, produce and distribute the eternal and sacred Word of God.

Inspired by the unfolding traditions of historic writing by prophets, apostles and saints, CBS stands in direct succession as a sharer of the Good News. Encouraged and supported by enthusiastic, prayerful and committed Christians from a variety of denominations, the Society faces the third millennium reassured about its mandate, committed to its ministry and expectant in the sure promise of the Lord who declared, "Heaven and earth will pass away, but my words will never pass away" (Matthew 24.35). Could any future have any surer guarantee than that? Thanks be to God.

The Right Reverend John Reginald Sperry, DD,
Canadian Bible Society President 1990-1997

A humorist has said, "It is hard to prophesy, especially regarding the future." When one looks at the lack of accuracy in past predictions, there is great hesitancy to say what the future holds for the Canadian Bible Society. However, with the conviction that God is alive and active and that His Word is true, we can look to tomorrow with a great deal of confidence.

It is a truism to say we are living in an age of unprecedented change. There has always been change, but change today is more rapid and universal than at any previous period of history. This presents the Canadian Bible Society with both a challenge and an opportunity. The writer of the Book of Hebrews lived in a time of turmoil, when the true and the tried were being swept away. As he saw the foundations being shaken, he spoke of the things which cannot be shaken. When kingdoms were tottering, he spoke of a "kingdom that cannot be shaken" (Hebrews 12.28). He described his faith as "an anchor sure and steadfast" (6.19) and his Lord as "the same yesterday, today and forever" (13.8).

In the past, great civilizations have declined and passed away, and there are some grounds for believing that our civilization is also in the process of disintegration. Edward Gibbon, in his 1776 history of the Roman Empire, said that the rapid increase in divorce, the craze for pleasure, higher and higher taxes, expenditures on armaments, and the decay of religion were the chief causes of the decline of that great empire. Those same trends characterize our present age. Some 57 per cent of Canadians believe that values and ethics are not determined by the Bible, but are purely a matter of personal opinion, and 72 per cent say that all religions are equally valid.

Non-Christian religions are flourishing in our world today. In France there are 50,000 full-time witches. Some 25 wars are raging, and recent conflicts around the world have put 42 million people at risk of starvation or life-threatening diseases. The Canadian Bible Society believes there is a special place for the Enduring Word in a world that is perishing. World conditions make its work more necessary and more urgent than ever before.

There is much to be learned from looking at how Christians responded to similar conditions in the past. The year 410 AD saw the sack of Rome by Alaric the Goth. In 476 Romulus Augustulus, the last Roman emperor of the West (until Charlemagne), was captured in the battle of Ravenna. Over the next 66 years, Rome's ancient civilization came visibly and rapidly to its violent end. As the lights went out, there were a few who, though they understood exactly what was happening, refused to abandon themselves to despair. They preferred to devote themselves to building a new and different culture that expressed the spirit of their Christian faith.

When St. Jerome, in his monk's abode in distant Bethlehem, received the news of the sack of Rome, he beat his head against the stone walls of his cell in despair. Nevertheless he continued with his life's work – editing existing Latin Scripture translations and translating further portions into that language. Seemingly an esoteric occupation undertaken to sustain Christian belief, it had the side-effect of helping to transfer rudiments of Greek culture to the barbarians, who at that time ruled the Western provinces of the old empire.

The slightly younger St. Augustine, after having tasted the fleshpots, was converted to Christianity in 387 AD. His book *City of God,* written between 418 and 427, laid the philosophical foundations of the immense achievements of medieval civilization.

A lowly monk, St. Benedict, in a day like our own – when carnality was glorified – also exercised a tremendous influence. Born about 480, he was neither a politician nor an economist, nor yet a philosopher. He did not belong to any of the professions to which, today, so many look for salvation. He was just a practical man of ascetic bent. Apparently able to look beyond the hopelessness of the situation around him, he devoted himself to work and prayer. The result was the founding of an Abbey that became the centre of European religious life, and the writing of the Rule of St. Benedict, which became a foundation of Christian faith and practice for all Western religious orders and congregations.

These Christians from the past are an example and inspiration to everyone today who discerns the times in which we live. The hope found in the Word of God is not based on anything in this world, but on the central figure of the Scriptures, Jesus Christ. Today the need for the salvation He offers is more apparent than ever. In times like these, the way God's Word pierces the hearts of human beings is seen in dramatic relief.

The past provides us with some remarkable stories of how the Scriptures have brought people to Christ. Feodor Mikhailovich Dostoyevsky (1821-1881) is regarded as one of the greatest writers of all time. As a young man he was an atheist, but the gift of a New Testament at a critical point in his life resulted in his becoming a devout Christian whose faith shone through the great novels that he wrote.

It was in Siberia that Dostoyevsky became a Christian. When, in chains, he was on his way to a penal settlement near Omsk, a woman visiting the convicts gave him a New Testament, the only book allowed by prison authorities. Dostoyevsky read his New Testament diligently. It assuaged the bitterness of prison and brought him to a personal faith in Christ, "Who alone was perfect and could raise up the sinner and give new life to the humble." From then on, for Dostoyevsky, God was "not somewhere, but everywhere," the centre of his life and of the novels he wrote. The name of the woman who gave him the New Testament which so changed his life and thinking, is now known only to God. Dostoyevsky's works, with their profoundly Christian message, will probably be read until Christ returns. During the 70 years of Communism in the former Soviet Union, the authorities failed to ban the writings of Dostoyevsky, and the Christian witness of these writings profoundly affected thousands of Russian intellectuals.

The transformation brought about by a single copy of the Bible is also an inspiring part of the story of the *Mutiny on the Bounty.* This famous story has often been retold – in novels, biographies and motion pictures. It was on April 28, 1789 that the British naval ship *Bounty* became the scene of a mutiny. Captain William Bligh and 18 others were set adrift and the mutineers, under Fletcher Christian, eventually reached Pitcairn Island (in the South Pacific). The crew of 34, along with six Tahitian men and 19 Tahitian women, settled on the island. They were violent, drunken people and as a result many were murdered.

Eventually only two of the original *Bounty* crew, Edward Young and John Adams, were left. They found a Bible in a sea chest and Young taught Adams to read, using the Bible as a textbook. Young died, but Adams found new life in Christ and became a leader to the Tahitian children and adults. The community was totally transformed. When Captain Folger arrived at Pitcairn Island 20 years later, he found a whole community seeking to live according to the Bible.

Across the centuries Christians have become an ever larger proportion of the world's population. Today about 30 per cent of the world's approximately six billion people are Christians. Though the faith of some, admittedly, is only nominal, the body of believers is growing. Nepal, for example, had practically no Christians 50 years ago and now there are more than 100,000 in that country. In Korea, the first Christian missionary arrived in the 1880s, and now Korea is one-third Christian. One of the largest churches in the world, a Gospel

Church, is in Korea. The world's largest Presbyterian church is in Seoul. South Korea has sent out more than 1,500 missionaries.

RELIGIOUS ADHERENTS AROUND THE WORLD

Christian	
Roman Catholic	952 million
Protestant	337 million
Orthodox	162 million
Anglican/Church of England	70 million
Other Christian	148 million
Total	*1,667 million*
Muslim	
Sunni	841 million
Shi'a	40 million
Total	*881 million*
Hindu	663 million
Buddhist	312 million
Chinese Folk	172 million
Tribal	92 million
Jewish	18 million
Sikh	17 million

Source: Oxford Atlas of the World, fourth edition. *London: Reed International Books, 1996, page 27.*

The growth of Christianity is not keeping up with global population growth, but it is actually exceeding population growth in some parts of the world. In Asia, for example, population growth is 1.92 per cent and Christian growth is 4.62 per cent. In Africa population growth is 2.81 per cent and Christian growth is 3.64 per cent.

The increase in the number of Christians continues even though there is intense persecution. More Christians have been killed for their faith during the 20th century than in all other centuries combined. Today two-thirds of the world's population lives under regimes that persecute Christians. But this does not prevent the Church from growing.

Though the Church is growing in the developing world, it is declining in the developed world. In countries such as Canada, unfortunately, Church attendance is going down. Surveys indicate, however, that the majority of people in Canada and many other developed countries still claim to believe basic Christian doctrines. They call themselves Christians, but do not choose to be part of organized religion.

Surveys show that people working in the media in developed countries seldom or never attend church or synagogue. In fact, about 85 per cent do not participate in religion at all. The media in general have decided that religion is not news, and have screened out most positive aspects relating to it. The media give the impression that the Church is dying out. In some places it is, but the truth is that the Church is alive and well in the world. Moreover the influence of its founder, Jesus Christ, is growing and today He is still the central figure of history.

In the future the Canadian Bible Society will continue to do what it has done in the past. It will work in cooperation with other Bible Societies around the world who are part of the United Bible Societies. Long before the word "ecumenical" became popular, the Bible Society was working with all Christian churches in thousands of Canadian communities, as well as with the churches of many other lands. This will continue. The Society will pursue the single task of translating, publishing and distributing the Word of God and making the Scriptures available to as many people as possible.

The challenges before the Canadian Bible Society are greater than ever. Society today is faced with three major challenges: a crisis of justice, a crisis of the environment and a crisis of spirituality. The Bible speaks to all three. World population is growing rapidly. People are learning to read as never before. But what will they read?

Over the years there has been enormous progress in Scripture translation. The complete Bible is now available in 363 languages. The New Testament is available in 905 languages, and at least one book of the Bible is available in another 929 languages. This means the Scriptures are available to most of the world's largest language groups. However, there are 6,528 languages (not dialects) spoken in the world altogether. This means 4,500 languages still have no part of the Bible. CBS will continue to address this need.

Here at home it is apparent that Canadian society is being severed from its Christian roots, and Canada has become a mission field. The Canadian Bible Society will continue to provide the Scriptures in our own country in some 100 languages each year.

The golden cord that has run through the life of the Canadian Bible Society has been the commitment of thousands of people to the Bible cause. Dedicated and competent staff, hundreds of volunteers and thousands of donors make the work possible. How bright is the future? The Right Reverend and Right Honourable Lord Coggan, former Archbishop of Canterbury and Honorary President of the United Bible Societies, answered that question when he said, "The future is as bright as the promises of God."

Dr. Fernetta Levy, Past-President of the Canadian Bible Society and former Vice-President of the United Bible Societies, expressed her vision for CBS's future in the following words.

> We must continually stress how absolutely essential it is to have all the churches involved and to keep before them the fact that the Bible Society is a servant of the Church.
>
> If we in the Bible Society are to claim the future, we must take more seriously our responsibility to assist the churches to grow in an understanding of what the Society is and what it does. In 1 Cor. 3.6 we read, "You plant and dream but God makes it grow." We must keep on planting and dreaming . . . sowing the seed. Unless we do, there will be no harvest. Sometimes our dreams send us to our knees. . . . CBS has a long and distinguished history, and all through that history prayer has played an important role. We must emphasize how vital it is that we continue to be a praying fellowship. This is something in which everyone can share.
>
> We give glory to God for all that has been accomplished over these many years. But we must move forward so that we can be used of God to bring men and women, boys and girls, in our own country and around the world, to come to know and serve the One who is the centre of the Bible. We must be deeply aware of the task before us as we enter a new century.